The Sources of Military Doctrine

CORNELL STUDIES IN SECURITY AFFAIRS

edited by Robert J. Art and Robert Jervis

The Sources
of Military Doctrine

FRANCE, BRITAIN, AND GERMANY
BETWEEN THE WORLD WARS

BARRY R. POSEN

Cornell University Press

ITHACA AND LONDON

*This book was written under the auspices of the
Center for International Affairs, Harvard University.*

First published 1984 by Cornell University Press.
First printing, Cornell Paperbacks, 1986.
Second printing, 1988.

International Standard Book Number 0–8014–1633–7 (cloth)
International Standard Book Number 0–8014–9427–3 (paper)
Library of Congress Catalog Card Number 84–7610
Printed in the United States of America
*Librarians: Library of Congress cataloging information
appears on the last page of the book.*

*The paper in this book is acid-free and meets the guidelines for permanence
and durability of the Committee on Production Guidelines for
Book Longevity of the Council on Library Resources.*

Contents

[5]

Preface

This book explains how military doctrine takes shape and how it figures in grand strategy—that collection of military, economic, and political means and ends with which a state attempts to achieve security. I weigh the bureaucratic, "power political," technological, and geographic influences that shape the grand strategies and military doctrines of states. A comparative investigation of French, British, and German military doctrine between the World Wars is the substantive core of the study. Particularly, I focus on explaining the two great military successes of the period, the German Blitzkrieg and the British air defense system, and the one great failure, the French Army's defensive doctrine, often associated with the Maginot Line.

Within grand strategy, military doctrine sets priorities among various military forces and prescribes how those forces should be structured and employed to achieve the ends in view. I have selected three important aspects of military doctrine for close scrutiny: its offensive, defensive, or deterrent character; its coordination with foreign policy (political-military integration); and the degree of innovation it contains. These aspects are explained in chapter 1.

I use organization theory and balance of power theory to analyze interwar French, British, and German military doctrine. Both types of explanation have achieved widespread currency in the study of international relations and foreign policy. Advocates of each have at various times criticized the perspective of the other. In the realm of *theory* these explanations are competitive, not complementary. The debate is best framed by Graham Allison in *Essence of Decision* and Kenneth Waltz in *Man, the State, and War* and *Theory of International Politics*. Allison explains a state's actions in international politics as the outcome of pulling and hauling among various self-interested, semi-autonomous military and civilian bureaucracies. He contrasts this approach with explanations consistent with Waltz's statement of balance of power theory, which view such actions as reasonable responses to the real security threats thrown up by the lawless environment outside the state's borders.

I test these two theories by deducing specific propositions from them about the three aspects of military doctrine selected for study, then applying the propositions to French, British, and German interwar military doctrine to see which theory better explains/predicts what happened. The two theories and their implications for military doctrine are discussed in chapter 2. Chapter 2 also contains an examination of some popular propositions about the impact of technology and geography on military doctrine. Chapter 3 summarizes the Battle of France and the Battle of Britain, the two great military confrontations of 1940 that throw into vivid relief the real-world consequences of each nation's doctrine. Chapters 4, 5, and 6 are case studies of French, British, and German doctrine respectively.

The comparative case method allows the scholar to sample a range of causes identified as important by each theory, and to see if variations in those causes do indeed produce variations in outcomes. When they do, the theory gains in credibility. Organization theory and balance of power theory frequently predict very different outcomes, so the tests are quite suggestive of the power of each theory. When the predictions conflict, we can examine the real outcomes to see which theory predicts more reliably. Of course, no test can be definitive, and the presence of perturbing variables (such as domestic politics) unaccounted for by either theory makes this test less than perfect. That caution duly acknowledged, the test shows that both theories have great utility in the study of military doctrine; both are more powerful than simple propositions that stress the direct causal impact of technology or geography; and finally, of the two, balance of power theory is the more powerful.

This "theory testing" exercise produces an important dividend for our substantive understanding of interwar military developments. The competitive application of the two theories is analogous to the use of different lenses, tools for the apprehension of reality. By using two explicit theories, each of which highlights the influence of different causes, we can gain a more focused understanding of military developments between the wars than by a conventional historical treatment. Each theory allows us to view some aspects of the same phenomenon more clearly (albeit at the cost of reducing the visibility of other aspects). Each theory tells us something useful and important about the military doctrines in question. Although the explicit

[8]

purpose of the theoretical exercise is to come to some conclusion about which theory is more powerful, it is clear that substantively the two theories provide complementary explanations of a complicated and important aspect of state behavior.

This book fills three gaps in the literature on international politics and strategy. First, for nearly twenty years a debate has been sustained among international relations theorists between those who would locate the causes of state behavior at the level of the state and those who would explain it in terms of the constraints and incentives that all states face in their attempt to survive in the unregulated "anarchical" environment of international politics. This book *explicitly* tests theories of both types against each other, a task rarely undertaken.

Second, with the exception of D. C. Watt's rather impressionistic *Too Serious a Business*, no single work has systematically examined and explained in comparative perspective the grand strategies and military doctrines of the major western European actors in the interwar period—France, Britain, and Germany. I hope that by doing so here I have sharpened our understanding of the origins of World War II.

Finally, there are few general guides to the study of national strategy. This book not only offers such a guide, but illustrates in three cases how to employ it. It offers a set of categories, questions, and explanations useful for studying the grand strategy and military doctrine of any state.

Many individuals and organizations contributed to the completion of this book. The Institute for the Study of World Politics, the Regents of the University of California, and, at Harvard University, the Center for Science and International Affairs and the National Security Studies Program of the Center for International Affairs all gave financial support. The Brookings Institution, the International Institute for Strategic Studies, the Center for Science and International Affairs, and the Center for International Affairs provided office space and research support.

I thank Professors Walter McDougall, Todd LaPorte, and especially Kenneth Waltz of the University of California at Berkeley for their assistance during the initial work on this book. My friends and colleagues Michael Mandelbaum, John Mearsheimer, Steven Miller, and Jack Snyder offered invaluable advice on the development and presentation of the book's central themes; I particularly thank Stephen Van Evera. The editors of this series, Robert Jervis and, especially,

Robert Art provided detailed guidance for improving the manuscript. My old friend Andrew Willard made useful comments on early drafts of several chapters. My parents gave great emotional support over the last several years. I thank Rebecca Lee Grindheim for her friendship and understanding during the crucial two years in which the manuscript was written. Joshua Epstein, who was completing his own book while I was writing this one, was a source of much encouragement.

BARRY R. POSEN

Washington, D.C.

The Sources of Military Doctrine

[1]

The Importance of Military Doctrine

GRAND STRATEGY AND MILITARY DOCTRINE

Military doctrines are critical components of national security policy or grand strategy. A grand strategy is a political-military, means-ends chain, a state's theory about how it can best "cause" security for itself.[1] Ideally, it includes an explanation of why the theory is expected to work. A grand strategy must identify likely threats to the state's security and it must devise political, economic, military, and other remedies for those threats. Priorities must be established among both threats and remedies because given an anarchical international environment, the number of possible threats is great, and given the inescapable limits of a national economy, resources are scarce.[2] Because resources are scarce, the most appropriate military means should be selected to achieve the political ends in view. Of course, grand strategies are almost never stated in such rigorous form, but the analyst may be guided by this conceptualization in his attempt to ferret out the grand strategy of a state, and to compare the strategies of states.

I use the term "military doctrine" for the subcomponent of grand strategy that deals explicitly with military means. Two questions are important: *What* means shall be employed? and *How* shall they be employed? Priorities must be set among the various types of military forces available to the modern state. A set of prescriptions must be generated specifying how military forces should be structured and employed to respond to recognized threats and opportunities. Ideally, modes of cooperation between different types of forces should be specified.

Since the close of World War I, modern states have had land, sea,

[13]

and air forces with which to achieve their goals. Since the close of World War II, some have had nuclear forces. States stress one type of force over another for geographical, technological, economic, or political reasons. Within forces, different sorts of weaponry could be stressed. Navies might stress submarines or aircraft carriers. Armies might stress armor or infantry. Air forces might stress long-range bombing of industry or short-range support of army formations. These latter choices shade off into the realm known as tactics.[3]

Military doctrine includes the preferred mode of a group of services, a single service, or a subservice for fighting wars. It reflects the judgments of professional military officers, and to a lesser but important extent civilian leaders, about what is and is not militarily possible and necessary. Such judgments are based on appraisals of military technology, national geography, adversary capabilities, and the skills of one's own military organization. Military doctrine, particularly the aspects that relate directly to combat, is strongly reflected in the forces that are acquired by the military organization. Force posture, the inventory of weapons any military organization controls, can be used as evidence to discover military doctrine.

For what *military* ends shall *military* means be employed? Military operations can be broken into three different categories: offensive, defensive, and deterrent. *Offensive* doctrines aim to *disarm* an adversary—to destroy his armed forces. *Defensive* doctrines aim to *deny* an adversary the objective that he seeks. *Deterrent* doctrines aim to *punish* an aggressor—to raise his costs without reference to reducing one's own.

Examples of Military Doctrine

An example of an offensive military doctrine is the method of combining tanks, motorized infantry, and combat aircraft to achieve rapid victory invented by the Germans in the 1930s, and called Blitzkrieg ever since. Modern Israel, since 1956, has to some extent imitated the operational aspects of the Blitzkrieg military format, with outstanding success in 1956 and 1967 and more limited success in 1973. The equipment has changed, but the method of combining the different types of forces for high-speed warfare has remained the same.

All of the land powers on the eve of World War I held offensive doctrines. The French are perhaps best known for their commitment to "l'offense à l'outrance"—offense to the limit. After the fact, this same commitment has come to be known as the "cult of the offensive." All of these offensive doctrines call for early and intense attack. All include important preemptive strains.

A well-known example of a defensive doctrine is the complex of French policies, much misunderstood, that are symbolized in current discourse by the Maginot Line. The apparent ease with which the line was flanked by the Germans in 1940 has given defense a bad name ever since. Plans to protect part of the U.S. strategic bomber deterrent in the 1950s with concrete blast shelters were derided by the U.S. Air Force as Maginot-Line-thinking. In 1973 such shelters stood Egypt in good stead against Israel, discouraging a 1967 style aerial preemption. Like the Maginot Line, the Great Wall of China played an important role in a defensive doctrine. For the British Empire the English Channel, a large fleet, and a small army provided the elements of what was essentially a defensive doctrine.

An example of a deterrent doctrine, and as pure a one as is likely to be found, is that associated with present-day France and its Force de Frappe. France has managed to build enough atomic-powered, nuclear-armed submarines to keep at least one at sea at any given time. Eventually this number will rise to two. France also maintains some thirty-three strategic bombers and eighteen intermediate-range ballistic missiles. While the small size of this force makes it more vulnerable to surprise attack than that of the United States, the French believe that the threat to eliminate even a small number of the most important Soviet cities is menacing enough to discourage aggression by her most probable adversary.

An example of a deterrent doctrine achieved with conventional military technology is that of modern Switzerland. The Swiss Army has little hope of denying much of the country to a large and determined adversary. Rather, the army and air force are deliberately and carefully structured so as to make the price of action against Switzerland very high. It is of critical importance not only that the initial defense be stalwart but also that painful and determined resistance continue over an extended period. The Swiss cannot deny their country to an adversary, but they can make him pay for the privilege of entry, and punish him for staying around.

THE IMPORTANCE OF MILITARY DOCTRINE

Military doctrine is important for two reasons. First, the doctrines held by the states within a system affect the quality of international political life. By their *offensive, defensive, or deterrent* character, doctrines affect the probability and intensity of arms races and of wars. Second, by both the political and military appropriateness of the means employed, a military doctrine affects the security of the state that holds it. A military doctrine may harm the security interests of the state if it is not *integrated* with the political objectives of the state's grand strategy—if it fails to provide the statesman with the tools suitable for the pursuit of those objectives. A military doctrine may also harm the security interests of the state if it fails to respond to changes in political circumstances, adversary capabilities, or available military technology—if it is insufficiently *innovative* for the competitive and dynamic environment of international politics. If war comes, such a doctrine may lead to defeat.

Offense, Defense, and Deterrence: Military Doctrine and International Conflict

The offensive, defensive, or deterrent quality of a military doctrine is important because it affects states' perceptions of and reactions to one another. International politics is a competitive arena. Because offensive doctrines appear to make some states more competitive, they encourage the rest to compete even harder. Defensive and deterrent doctrines should tend to produce more benign effects.

Offensive doctrines increase the probability and intensity of arms races and of wars. To argue this is to argue that the international system is more than a mere group of dissimilar states coexisting in a particular historical period. Much of the unsavory behavior of states is best explained by similarities among them and the identical condition that they face. States are alike insofar as they are autonomous social organisms that wish to remain so. They may wish to grow larger, but they do not wish either to be subsumed in some larger organism or to be made smaller. They also share at least one important condition—anarchy, the absence of a world sovereign. So long as technology, geography, and economy make it possible for states to aggress against one another, and so long as there is no international authority to protect those satisfied with the status quo and to punish those who violate it, states will be strongly encouraged to take steps to protect themselves from one another. These steps are all part of a state's grand strategy.

Because behavior is unregulated, because states must look to their own defenses, they watch their neighbors carefully. Military doctrines and capabilities are hard to hide, but the political intentions that lie behind the military preparations are obscure. This being the

[16]

case, in watching one another, states tend to focus on military doctrines and military capabilities. They take these capabilities at face value. Arabs infer malign intent from the offensive military doctrine of the Israel Defense Forces. Both the United States and the Soviet Union infer malign intent from each other's offensive, counterforce capability. Israel, the United States, and the Soviet Union all maintain offensive military capabilities; their opponents infer aggressive motives. As Robert Jervis has observed: "Arms procured to defend can usually be used to attack. Economic and military preparedness designed to hold what one has is apt to create the potential for taking territory from others. What one state regards as insurance, the adversary will see as encirclement."[4] In short, "many of the means by which a state tries to increase its security decrease the security of others."[5] International relations theorists call this the security dilemma. The security dilemma arises "not because of misperception or imagined hostility, but because of the anarchic context of international relations."[6] States seek to preserve their autonomy in an environment where perhaps any other state can become a threat, and where "self-help" is the fundamental prerequisite for security. The more offensive are the military doctrines of one or more states, the more nervous everyone else in the system is likely to become.

A foregone conclusion, given these considerations, is that offensive doctrines tend to promote arms races and war. Because states take measures to ensure their security in the context of anarchy, and because they carefully watch the measures that other states take to improve their security, it follows that they also *respond* to the measures that others take with additional measures of their own, if others' measures appear to make them less secure. In short, states engage in what balance of power theorists call "balancing behavior." This is perfectly reasonable behavior for states that enjoy being autonomous and notice that others are doing things that might threaten their autonomy.[7]

Traditionally, balance of power theorists focused on coalition formation as the principal type of balancing behavior. The concept of balancing behavior should logically be expanded, however, to include internally generated military or economic preparations for possible wars.[8] If another power is increasing its capabilities by coalition building, arms buildup, or any other measure that can be construed as threatening the security of a given state, a reaction in the form of coalition building and/or arms-racing is probable. A good deal of diplomatic history is loosely informed by this view of how international politics works.[9] The important thing to bear in mind is that the history of relations among states is rife with all sorts of action-reaction phenomena, political and military.[10]

Arms Races

Offensive military doctrines promote arms races in two ways. First, a tenet of offensive doctrines is that an effective first strike can quickly, cheaply, and successfully end a war; so the state will support that first strike with large resources. Second, since offensive doctrines imply a belief in the superiority of offensive action over defensive action, states feel greatly threatened by increases in one another's military capabilities and react quite strongly to those increases.[11]

The Soviet-American nuclear arms race illustrates how the offensive doctrines of two great powers affect their views of each other and their military preparations. Each interprets the other's military doctrine as offensive. In some measure, each imitates the other.[12] Both states have tended to expand their ability to attack each other. Both have allocated very substantial resources to the military competition.

Current Western views of the offensive character of Soviet military doctrine are well known.[13] The doctrine of the Soviet Strategic Rocket Forces does appear to aim at disarming the United States. We assume that our own doctrine, one of deterrence, could not have anything to do with Soviet doctrine. Yet, careful observers of U.S. military forces agree that the Strategic Air Command has always targeted enemy nuclear forces and targeted them massively.[14] Moreover, the United States has usually tried to deploy sufficient forces to allow counterforce missions to be completed after a Soviet first strike. Of course, this much insurance may appear to the Russians as an attempt to achieve a high-confidence, disarming, first-strike capability against them. Indeed, while it is difficult to separate genuine fear from propaganda, passages in Soviet Marshall V. D. Sokolovsky's *Military Strategy* impute to the United States offensive inclinations that we have come to identify with Soviet doctrine.[15]

Fortunately, although the two superpowers have both maintained an offensive doctrine, each has also prudently guarded its second-strike retaliatory forces, thwarting the best efforts of the other to achive a war-winning capability. The hypothesized consequences of mutually offensive doctrines have emerged, however. Soviet and U.S. strategic nuclear arsenals have grown substantially, measured in numbers of nuclear warheads. In the last ten years the number of U.S. warheads has doubled, reaching eight to ten thousand. The Soviets have reached a similar level.[16]

In gauging the relative threat of each other's military spending,

[18]

each seems to have overensured in response. Soviet and U.S. military spending, measured in terms of percentage of GNP, has been very high for a long time. For the last fifteen years the Soviets have spent 11-14 percent of their GNP on defense.[17] During the peak Korean War period, U.S. spending rose to nearly 15 percent of GNP, but averaged around 10 percent during the 1950s. American GNP has of course been much larger than the Soviets' during the entire Cold War period. Recently, U.S. spending has fallen to 6-7 percent of GNP, but that GNP is double the size of the Soviets'.

Still, even a 6-7 percent share is fairly high when compared to the previous "golden age" of offensive doctrines—the pre–World War I period. Of the six major powers in 1914 only two, Austria-Hungary with 6.1 percent of national income and Russia with 6.3 percent, spent as great a share of national wealth on defense as does the United States today; the figures for Germany, France, Great Britain, and Italy were all between 3 and 5 percent.[18] Whatever the figures, military spending at that time was perceived as very high, and certainly represented a great increase over the rate of military spending in 1870–an increase owing in part to the pernicious effects of offensive doctrines.[19]

Do defensive doctrines affect arms race behavior differently? The effects of defensive and deterrent doctrines should be opposite from those of offensive ones.[20] Defensive and deterrent doctrines allow status quo states and aggressor states to be clearly identified. They tend to assume longer wars, with more time for mobilization, and thus require smaller forces in being. Large forces are not believed to substantially raise the probability of rapid and cheap victory. Finally, since an integral assumption of defensive doctrines is that defense or punishment is cheaper than offense, status quo states may counter aggressor military build-ups with smaller incremental increases of their own.[21] If all states adopted defensive or deterrent doctrines, the result should be a downward trend in military spending. While there are few examples of arms competitions strictly among powers with defensive doctrines, data from the interwar period lend support to the general proposition that states with offensive and those with defensive doctrines tend to compete at different levels of intensity (table 1).

It is no surprise that Germany, with an offensive doctrine and a revisionist grand strategy, spent the most. Nor is it surprising that German and Japanese armament expenditures show the largest percentage increases. However, because these two states were not arms racing against other states with offensive doctrines, these data offer

Table 1. Pre–World War II Military Spending of Major Powers

Country	Spending in Millions of Pounds Sterling, 1933–1938	Percentage Increase in Real Value of Military Spending, 1934–1938
Germany	2,868	470
Russia	2,808	370
Japan	1,266	455
U.K.	1,200	250
U.S.A.	1,175	no data
France	1,088	41
Italy	930	56

SOURCES: H. C. Hillman, "Comparative Strength of the Great Powers," in *Survey of International Affairs, 1939–1946*, vol. 1, *The World in March 1939*, ed. Arnold Toynbee and Frank T. Ashton-Gwatkin (London: Royal Institute of International Affairs and Oxford University Press, 1952), p. 454; and Alan S. Milward, *War, Economy, and Society, 1939–45* (Berkeley: University of California Press, 1977), pp. 25–41.

only partial support for the arms race effects of offensive doctrines. The purpose of conquest provides sufficient explanation for the high spending in these cases.

The United Kingdom, the United States, and France all had broadly defensive military doctrines during this period. Their spending was low, and its rate of increase was also fairly low compared to that of the more offensive-minded powers. These states believed, consistent with their choice of doctrines, that the defense held the advantage and that less than a pound sterling spent on defense could offset a pound spent on offense. These data lend some support to the proposition that defensive doctrines tend to dampen arms race behavior.

The Probability and Intensity of War

When a number of states in a system hold offensive doctrines, wars may be easy to start and they may be very intense. If a state has arrived at an offensive doctrine, it has concluded, rightly or wrongly, that there is a substantial advantage to be derived by attacking. Defending is assumed to carry a corresponding disadvantage. War may be cheap or short if only the state can take the offensive. Such calculations strongly discourage conceding the initiative in war to any adversary—regardless of the adversary's doctrine. If the adversary's doctrine is known to be offensive, then conceding the initiative is doubly discouraged. To put it more directly, even if only one side holds an offensive doctrine, preemption is encouraged—for that side. If all sides hold offensive doctrines, and all know that the others do, then when war appears possible, all will begin contemplating a first strike, and all will know that everyone else is doing so. This situation is not favorable for continued peace, as events in Europe in 1914 demonstrate.

Wars are likely to be intense under such circumstances for some of the same reasons that offensive doctrines promote arms races. When states hold offensive doctrines, and know that their adversaries do as well, there is good reason for them to fear that a decision will be reached early in a war. Industrial mobilization is not likely to be possible. This encourages large peacetime military inventories.

When the decision for war is made, the state is encouraged to use as much of its resources as it can. If an advantage is imputed to the offense, and the adversary is believed to have an offensive doctrine, then it is important to ensure the decisiveness of one's first strike. Otherwise the enemy may be left with forces useful and dangerous in a possibly simultaneous counterattack. Figuratively, each side may race past the other into the guts of enemy territory, in the hope that its offensive will cause the other to surrender and end the other's offensive. The most powerful offensive should have the greatest chance of early success. Therefore, such offensives are likely to be supported with maximum resources. These calculations are exemplified by the simultaneous German and French offensives of 1914.[22]

In the decade prior to World War I, the soldiers of Europe had come to believe that the offense had the advantage. In the succinct words of the American Civil War general Nathan Bedford Forrest, victory would go to the side that "got there first, with the most." Defense budgets, mobilization plans, and war plans of the land powers were influenced by this simple notion. As Alfred Vagts has observed, little thought was given to whether the terrain or the military technology of the European environment actually made getting there first with the most very decisive.[23] It simply became an article of faith that this was so.

As noted earlier, offensive doctrines contribute to arms racing. They provide an incentive for making a large and decisive first strike. The rise in European defense budgets during the tenure of these offensive doctrines certainly bears this out. The extra money was spent to create larger and more effective combat organizations. Weaponry not only became more lethal, it appeared in greater quantity, and was organized into increasing numbers of combat formations.[24]

However, the desired punch could be achieved only by mobilizing millions of men out of their civilian occupations or their peacetime barracks, organizing them into military formations, packing them into trains, and delivering them to the front. The state that achieved this task first could initiate its offensive first, deriving the supposed advantages of being on the attack. This calculation drove two mobilization races.

First, in peacetime the general staffs continuously honed their plans to increase the speed of mobilization once it was declared.[25] Second, if there were a crisis soldiers could be relied on to explain to their civilian "masters" that the side initiating its mobilization first would gain a significant advantage. The French military estimated the cost of each twenty-four-hour delay in mobilization at 15–20 km of German advance.[26] The important thing about these beliefs is, as Jervis has observed, "Each side knew that the other saw the situation the same way, thus increasing the perceived danger that the other would attack and giving each added reasons to precipitate a war if conditions seemed favorable."[27] One might add the clause, "or if war seemed probable." If for any reason a state drew the conclusion that its adversaries were getting closer to war, there was a powerful incentive to start its own great machine into motion.

The closely linked system of offensive doctrines comprised four powers—Germany, France, Russia, and Austria-Hungary. All held offensive doctrines. Germany's Schlieffen Plan had become more or less common knowledge to her potential adversaries.[28] Its purpose was to defeat her enemies sequentially, first France, then Russia, because the Germans perceived that the combination of fully mobilized French and Russian military power would provide the Entente with decisive superiority. France's mobilization rate and the proximity of her railroads made her the greater threat. Russia's slower mobilization and the sparseness of her rail net near the German frontier would give Germany time. Russia faced two enemies on her borders, Germany and Austria-Hungary. Her fundamental political conflict was with the latter, but given the Triple Alliance she could not be sure that a conflict with Austria-Hungary would not bring in the Germans. Moreover, to frustrate the German plan of defeating France and Russia sequentially, Russia wanted to find a way to ready herself for an offensive against Germany that would take place early enough to take some heat off the French. This encouraged Russia to try to beat the speed of Germany's mobilization by developing ways to get an undetected head start. Finally, Count Helmuth von Moltke, the German chief of staff, had endeavored to wean Austria-Hungary from a partial mobilization plan that had been directed mainly against Serbia. Moltke, aware that the Russians would strive for an early strike against Germany's eastern borders, which were weakened by virtue of the heavy troop commitment of the Schlieffen plan, pressed Austria for an early offensive against Russia.

[22]

These events illustrate how everyone's behavior was conditioned by their worst fears of what everyone else was likely to do, if a war came. To prepare for that war within a crisis context was to make oneself more capable of committing a dangerous offensive act against one's neighbors. Seeing such preparations, neighboring states were obliged to respond in the only way that was believed efficacious—by preparing to execute their own offensive doctrines. Such preparations in their turn frightened the others; and so the spiral went. With each round of preparations, the requirement to execute the next set, and to execute them quickly, grew more pressing. Time was a commodity in short supply. Misunderstandings, delays, and lost tempers could easily start the spiral. Once started, it was hard to stop. The currency of diplomacy is talk, and at distances of hundreds of miles, talk takes time. The military had cornered the market on time.

The effects of defensive doctrines on the probability and intensity of war are best illustrated by the opening days of World War II in Europe. The so-called Sitzkrieg or Phoney War is explained by French and British defensive doctrines, and the notion inherent in those doctrines that the defender had the advantage. Both France and Britain had extended security guarantees to Poland. These two states held remarkably defensive military doctrines (see chapters 4 and 5). Germany held an offensive doctrine, and was known to do so. Poland's doctrine is unclear. Holding defensive doctrines, the French and the British were confident of their own ability to stop a German offensive. They also were sure that an offensive early in the war against Germany would be costly. This was of more concern to France than to England, since only France had the forces on hand for an offensive against the German western defenses. The French guarantee to Poland, however, promised immediate offensives if required to deflect military pressure from Poland. In no case were such offensives to be delayed past the sixteenth day of the war.

What happened is revealing. Germany began her attack on September 1. France and Britain formally entered the war on the third. On September 8 the French Fourth Army made a small advance in the Saar. Upon coming into contact with the German defenses, the Siegfried Line, they engaged them with artillery fire but made no attempt at an assault.[29] In mid-October mild German counterattacks drove the French back across the border. The memory of 1914 was strong, and the French were not willing to risk a repetition of their costly offensives.

The doctrines of the French in 1939 and 1914 were remarkably different—defensive and offensive caricatures, respectively. In 1914 the French rushed into Germany, believing that the war could be

[23]

ended quickly and cheaply if she did so, and that it would be lost quickly if she did not. In 1939 the French ran for their trenches and fortifications, certain that offense was costly, and defense cheap. Whatever additions Germany might make to her long-war capabilities by a successful conquest of Poland were not seen as a sufficient threat to the advantages of France's defensive doctrine to merit counter-measures in the form of an offensive to relieve Poland. French and British belief in the dominance of the defensive survived the conquest of Poland, and determined their lack of direct action against Germany until Hitler chose to attack them in May 1940. Not only had it taken years of provocation to get Britain and France to oppose Hitler, but once that decision was made it was hard to get an actual fight going. Closely held defensive doctrines contributed to cautious and limited action on the part of the democracies.

Deterrent doctrines should produce many of the same effects as defensive doctrines. Logically they should be among the most difficult doctrines to misperceive. Military forces that are designed to punish aggressors, whether conventionally, such as those of Switzerland or Yugoslavia, or with nuclear weapons, such as those of France, Britain, or the People's Republic of China, partially derive their effectiveness through extreme specialization. Their lack of offensive, disarming capability is plain. Moreover, again as a consequence of extreme specialization, such forces generally lack defensive, denial capability as well. This leaves states that hold deterrent doctrines vulnerable to enemy attack. These states have thrown their political willingness to suffer into the military balance—a remarkable commitment, the meaning of which should not easily be misunderstood. While it is not difficult to believe that a state would accept great pain to preserve or regain its sovereignty, it is more difficult to suppose that it would willingly leave itself open to such suffering as the price for a chancy attempt at expansion.

Thus, true deterrent doctrines, when backed up by an appropriate force posture, should limit the possibilities of misperception and overreaction. As noted earlier, many of the problems of the superpower nuclear relationship arise from the fact that neither side has ever embraced a purely deterrent doctrine. Rather, each has at various times talked deterrence while seeking military advantages that might produce "victory" in a nuclear war. This remains a fundamental cause of the arms race.

Political-Military Integration and the Security of States

In the most general terms, the ultimate purpose of a military doctrine is the continued survival of the state that holds it. Disintegrated grand strategies, in which political objectives and military doctrine are poorly reconciled, can lead to both war and defeat—jeopardizing the state's survival. In time of peace, a military doctrine should allow the state to ensure its security at economic, political, and human costs that it can afford. A successful grand strategy for a status quo state will so knit together ends and means that aggressors will be dissuaded from attack. Ideally, the military means chosen by states seeking to change the status quo will appear so effective that those states threatened would rather accommodate than fight. In time of crisis or war, military doctrine will be tested against the qualitative and quantitative adequacy of the forces provided in time of peace. Finally, and again ideally, the grand strategy of a state should account for its effects on other states. It should try to minimize any negative consequences that accompany a military doctrine, such as the tendency of defensive military doctrines to create opportunities for piecemeal aggression, or of offensive doctrines to create impressions of malign intent.

I have conceived of grand strategy as a chain of political ends and military means. Its effectiveness is highly dependent on the extent to which the ends and means are related to one another. The "knitting-together" of political ends and military means I call political-military integration.[30] In peace or war, the fundamental question of political-military integration is whether the statesman has at hand the military instruments required to achieve those political goals deemed essential to the security of the state. It is also fair to ask whether the political goals in view fall within the state's military means, and whether the military means selected unnecessarily inhibit the discretion of political authorities.

Political-military integration is a good thing. The use of force and the threat of force are necessary expedients in the context of international anarchy. Yet they are never without danger or cost, either for individual states or for the international political system. Wars seem to take on a life of their own. If these dangerous means are to be controlled, every effort must be made to subject them to the minimal discipline of political goals.[31]

Many states have failed to achieve an adequate degree of political-military integration. Two examples illustrate the problem: France on the eve of the Franco-Prussian War, and Israel at the outbreak of the 1973 October War.

During the early years of his reign Napoleon III had encouraged the "national principle" as a guide for organizing changes in the boundaries of the major and minor states of Europe. He apparently believed that the spread of nationalism would be a disintegrative force in European politics, producing many weak states that would be subject to superior French power. As part of this policy Napoleon III had tolerated and indeed supported the expansion of Prussia.[32] He hoped for the emergence of "three Germanys"—Prussia, the south German states, and Austria.[33] Unfortunately for France, Napoleon III overestimated his capacity to control the forces of nationalism. After the Prussian victory over Austria-Hungary in 1866, France faced the prospect of the unification of all the smaller German states under Prussia. This greater Germany could only be damaging to French ambitions and security. By the summer of 1867 Napoleon opted for a more conservative policy of resistance to further Prussian expansion.

Such a shift in foreign policy would seem to demand some changes in military policy. Prussia had just badly beaten Austria-Hungary, one of the great powers of Europe, and one that had given the French a good fight in 1859. The Prussian Army, combined with the rest of the North German Confederation, revealed considerable strengths in 1866. The most obvious of its strengths was the ability of its conscript/reserve system to muster nearly a million men at mobilization—the largest armed force Europe had ever seen. The Prussians had proven themselves adept not only at mobilizing this large force quickly and efficiently and at moving it by rail to the vicinity of the enemy, but also at commanding it in battle. Additionally, Prussia's army was the first to deploy repeating rifles in large numbers. The Prussians had been less successful at supplying this large force, and their artillery had proven inferior to the Austrian guns. The Prussian General Staff was known to be hard at work rectifying these problems, however.[34]

Several French military figures, and Napoleon III, took a closer look at the French Army and did not like what they found. Most French soldiers were less worried, and served to obstruct needed reforms. The French Army was a small corps of long-service professionals that had gained most of its experience in small-unit police actions in the Empire. It would have been hard put to mobilize 300,000 men in Europe. Although it had won its most recent European war against Austria-Hungary in 1859, and had successfully exploited the railroad to do so, the French logistics effort had been badly bungled. The French General Staff was a far less professional body than that of Prussia; its members were almost completely divorced from the fighting units. The French professional military school system was very poor; some officers were practically illiterate. Finally, as of 1866 the French had yet to adopt a repeating rifle.

The French were quickest to fix the last problem. Napoleon III began to equip his troops with the excellent Chassepot repeater in 1866; a million were on hand by 1870. On the other hand, although France had evidence that Prussia was effectively modernizing and improving its artillery, it failed to respond to that recognition, ostensibly because of financial constraints. Funds were available for the mitrailleuse, a primitive but murderous forerunner of the machine gun; but in an attempt to keep the weapon secret, no plans were worked out for its effective employment.

The French did make efforts to offset their numerical inferiority, but those efforts in the end did not produce much of a dividend. A military reform law passed in 1868 placed greater reliance on a shorter term of military service and greater numbers of reserves. The system would have yielded 800,000 men by 1875, but no more than half a million by 1870. In the actual event, by the seventeenth day of mobilization in 1870, the French only managed to concentrate 240,000 men on the Rhine, by which time German strength was already over 300,000.

Other reforms, which might have been speedily completed, were not. The French failed to increase the efficiency of their system of mobilization and concentration. They did not improve their ability to exploit the railroad for this purpose, or to provide logistics support to the army. Only the most rudimentary war plans were drawn up. Efforts to turn the French General Staff into professional military managers, capable of deploying and controlling large forces, were opposed by the army and dropped.

In sum, while French foreign policy changed in the direction of firmer opposition to Prussia, French military doctrine and organization failed to adapt itself to the revolutionary methods of its new principal adversary. Some efforts were made, but these failed to cope with the major problem—the *combined size and speed* of the German Army.

Another example of political-military disintegration is found in Israeli grand strategy between the 1967 and 1973 wars. Israeli military doctrine has for the most part been closely integrated with the political elements of the state's grand strategy, but in 1973 that integration was dangerously loose.

Before 1970 Israel and the Arab states were arms-racing with a mixture of new and obsolescent equipment, obtained mainly by using or *exchanging* resources that they could extract from their own economies. Roughly speaking, Israel was arms-racing with the Arab states, and vice versa. After the War of Attrition, this was no longer the case. (The "War of Attrition" is the name given to the fighting between

Israel and Egypt along the Suez Canal from March 1969 through August 1970.)[35] The Soviets pulled out the stops in their aid to Egypt and Syria, going so far as to set up and operate an air defense system for Egypt. Israel was now engaged in an arms competition with the Soviet Union. To run this race, it was necessary to acquire a superpower patron of her own, the United States. For the first three years after the Six Day War (June 1967), U.S. military assistance to Israel ran to forty million dollars a year. In the next three years it ran to four hundred million dollars a year, or 28 percent of Israel's total annual defense spending.[36]

One of the fundamental political objects of Israel's doctrine was to gain the support or at least the sympathy of one large or middle power. At the same time, a fundamental military principle was that the IDF (Israel Defense Forces) would "undertake a preemptive attack if the security of the state is endangered."[37] With the new dependence upon the United States for armaments, brought on by the closer relationship between the Arab states and the Soviet Union, "sympathy" was no longer sufficient; it would have to be support.

Would support be forthcoming if Israel launched a preemptive attack? This is the question that should have been asked and *fully* answered sometime between 1970 and 1973. It apparently was not addressed until the morning of the Yom Kippur War. On the morning of October 6, at approximately 4:30 A.M., Israel received warning from at least one and perhaps two reliable sources that the Arabs would definitely attack that evening at 6:00 P.M. (The attack came at 2:00 P.M.) The air force, based on its own intelligence, had begun readying itself for a preemption the previous day. Chief of Staff General Elazar recommended an aerial preemption to begin at noon on the sixth.[38] The government could have ordered it at almost any time that day. No preemption order was issued. Full mobilization was not ordered until 9:30 A.M., after a discussion between Prime Minister Golda Meir and U.S. ambassador Keating. According to several accounts of this meeting, the U.S. ambassador made it clear that immediate and timely resupply of equipment, sure to be lost in the war, might not be forthcoming if Israel struck first. Even before this discussion, both Meir and Defense Minister Moshe Dayan agreed that no preemption could take place for diplomatic-political reasons. Dayan even argued for a partial rather than a total mobilization.[39]

Israel's dependence on the United States had been growing for three years. The relationship had been sufficiently troubled for both Dayan and Meir to realize, in the moment of crisis, that the tie might not stand the strain of an Israeli preemption. Evidence to support this conclusion existed long before the crisis. Fundamental changes in the military aspects of Israeli doctrine were in order.

Admittedly, Israeli doctrine did not stress preemption in the years prior to the Yom Kippur War. Instead, it had come to depend on the forty-eight hours of forewarning promised by Israeli Military Intelligence for mobilizing sufficient ground forces to wage an initially defensive battle. It is not clear that the IDF made any special plans to cope with less than forty-eight hours' warning. The behavior of the Israeli Air Force on the eve of the war suggests that Israeli planners felt they could fall back on some sort of disruptive aerial preemption in the event of insufficient warning. Or perhaps Israeli self-confidence was so high that the possibility of an Arab surprise was simply not entertained. In either case, the absence of the expected warning was a major source of Israeli troubles on October 6.

Just as important as the absence of warning was the inability to use the air force effectively once it was known that war was imminent. The air force, as a capital- rather than labor-intensive fighting force, was Israel's ever-ready ace-in-the-hole. It was the insurance policy against the possibility of surprise, the cutting edge of any preemptive strike. Yet at this moment of crisis, a hidden obstacle suddenly emerged. There was apparently no way to use the air force that was consistent with the major political change in Israel's grand strategy, the increased dependence on the United States. Thus, on the morning of October 6, Israeli military doctrine could not provide an answer to the state's predicament.

In 1870 and in 1973, the disintegration of grand strategy, the disconnection between military means and political ends, severely damaged the states in which it obtained. In 1870 a disastrous defeat was precipitated. In 1973, a perhaps inevitable war was rendered more dangerous and costly for Israel than it needed to be.

Innovation

Innovation in military doctrine and its converse, stagnation, can affect national security in two ways. First, they can affect integration; second, they can affect the likelihood of victory or defeat.

Neither innovation nor stagnation (*stability* might be a better choice of terms, as it is less loaded) should be valued a priori. The benefits of innovation can be judged, in part, in terms of its effect on integration. Do means and ends retain a working relationship to each other? In part, innovation must be judged in terms of the general military and technological environment. Do the military forces of the state stand a good chance of doing their job successfully, whether that job is offense, defense, or deterrence? On balance, given the large number of possible changes in a state's environment and technological changes in military hardware, absence of innovation should always attract the strategist's attention. Close inspection may show that no innovation is required, but this should never be assumed.

Although innovation can and does occur at the political level of a state's grand strategy, I will be more concerned with explaining innovation and stagnation at the military level. Many of the political aspects of grand strategy are determined by factors in the international environment that the state cannot control. Military aspects are within the purview of the state and are more controllable. The task of political-military integration begins at home, with military doctrine. If political-military integration is important to the security of the state, then we should be interested in how to promote it. Innovation and stagnation at the military level are not only important determinants of integration, they are manipulable ones.

Innovation and stagnation do not merely affect whether or not the means are at hand for the policies of statesmen. Should war come, they affect the probability of victory or defeat. Soldiers must plan to operate their forces with a great many considerations in mind—most of which can change. Soldiers must identify an enemy, if only for planning purposes. If statesmen change the enemy's identity, the soldiers must change their plans. The same is true if the identity of allies changes. Changing enemies or allies may take less time than changing plans or procedures. Soldiers must also identify the military capabilities of any particular enemy. These may change quickly, and demand changes of one's own. Finally, technological opportunities, both for the adversary and for oneself, may change. Soldiers must identify which ones are worth exploring, and at what rate. Is a response in order, and how soon? Should the response imitate, or should a different technological counter be employed? Soldiering is a complicated business.

Both soldiers and civilians have frequently guessed wrong on the many aspects of military doctrine. In some cases soldiers have innovated in ways that were inconsistent with the political goals of their states. In others, they have failed to innovate at all. Some innovations are successful, such as the German Blitzkrieg and the RAF Fighter Command. Others, such as the Maginot Line, appear to be unsuccessful. Under certain conditions, especially when war appears imminent, it may be more dangerous to change an obsolescent military doctrine than to keep it. Changing doctrines takes time; it disorients a military organization. A war during such a period of transition can be

[30]

very dangerous. Hitler caught the Soviet Army during such a change in 1941. At Jena, Napoleon caught the Prussians in the midst of such a reorganization.

Israel has already been advanced as a case of failure to achieve military innovation consistent with the state's political goals. Analysts have discussed the various military failures of the Israel Defense Forces at great length. A number of them were tactical and technical failures that were remedied in the first few days of the war itself. For instance, prior to the war the IDF failed to adjust tactically to the increasing density of anti-tank weapons of all kinds—guns, recoilless rifles, shoulder-fired rockets, and most notably anti-tank guided missiles—known to be in the hands of their adversaries. During World War II, close coordination of the action of tanks, infantry, artillery, and mortars had been necessary to thwart high densities of anti-tank weapons. Israel had not faced this problem in 1956 and 1967, and had become overly daring in the independent employment of tanks. This cost Israel dearly in the changed circumstances of the first few days of the 1973 war. By the middle of the war, however, the always flexible IDF had successfully resurrected "combined arms" tactics.

The IDF was, however, constrained throughout the war by previous high-level decisions about the character of military operations, embodied in the forces in such a way that little could be done about them. Once war came, one problem was materiel. The Israeli air arm, and to a lesser extent the tank arm, had been endowed with excessive resources, while the infantry and artillery arms had been neglected. Although the IDF quickly resurrected combined arms tactics, it continued to suffer from insufficient numbers of well-trained infantry, of armored personnel carriers to move the infantry, of mortars at the lower tactical echelons, and of self-propelled artillery to support the tanks and infantry in fast-moving operations. Initial battles of a war are fought with the equipment on hand. Decisions made long before the war will determine some operational possibilities during the war.

In the last defense budget before the 1973 war, 50 percent of all spending reportedly went to the air force, 30 percent to the armored corps.[40] Given the difficulties provided by the Egyptian air defense during the War of Attrition, using only half of the air defense capabilities that Israel was to face in 1973, was it intelligent to place this much reliance on the air force? Might not the money have been better spent on increased artillery to substitute for some of the support tasks that the IAF had previously performed? While the question is seldom put in this way, some commentators have noted the weakness of Israeli artillery during the war.[41]

When the test came, the Israeli Air Force was not in a position to perform all of the missions expected of it. Quite the reverse. As noted above, an Israeli Air Force preemption was opposed by the prime minister on political grounds. Dayan opposed it on political *and* military grounds. He questioned how great the military gains of an aerial preemption could be, balanced against the political consequences. The Egyptian Air Force was based in underground hangars or concrete shelters, so hitting it on the ground would be impossible. A preemption seems to have been deemed unnecessary for knocking out the Syrian Air Force. Dayan argued that an air strike against Arab ground forces "could only hope to disrupt the Arab preparations for a few hours." Moreover, the IAF would be hitting "an alert enemy protected by a lethal missile screen."[42] Potential losses might cripple the air force for the rest of the war.

These arguments would all hold true during a war as well. Dayan's admission is quite remarkable. As Defense Minister, he had just spent 50 percent of his country's scarce defense resources on forces that he suddenly deemed both politically and militarily useless. His air force seems to have presented him with preemptive strike plans that acknowledged little change since 1967, when clearly a great deal had changed. Preemption was politically unacceptable and, even if ordered, apparently militarily ineffective. A military doctrine suitable for 1967 was forced to confront 1973 and was found wanting.

We may return to World War I for a case of mixed doctrinal innovation and stagnation. The major armies of Europe had drawn their lessons for the future from wars that occurred in 1866 and 1870. The successes of Prussian arms were attributed in both cases to the numbers of reservists that Prussia had been able to call out of civilian life, and the orderliness and speed with which these troops were moved to the battle area by train. Conversely, the chaos and ineptitude of the French mobilization in 1870 was taken as a lesson on how not to proceed. The soldiers spent the next four decades looking for improved "mass times velocity." These preparations were a major innovation, but they failed to produce the quick and decisive victories that military leaders had predicted.

Where had military planners gone wrong? How did their forces end up in the trenches for four years? The minds of the soldiers had fixated only on those lessons of 1866 and 1870 that favored offensives. Evidence from those and subsequent wars suggesting that modern weaponry could *decisively* affect the course of engagements was *systematically* misinterpreted. Soldiers grasped at any straw to avoid reckoning with the obvious defensive potential of new weapons technology.[43]

As late as 1917 the lessons had still not been learned. Perhaps the most grisly statistic from that grisly war is that at Ypres 56,000 British soldiers simply disappeared, their bodies obliterated by a mixture of high explosives and mud. The cult of the offensive died hard, and many men died with it. The longevity of the offensive doctrine is troubling not merely because there were objective pre–World War I lessons on the effects of the new technology, but because in France, Germany, and Britain, young military officer-scholars correctly interpreted these lessons.[44]

SUMMARY

A grand strategy is a chain of political and military ends and means. Military doctrine is a key component of grand strategy. Military doctrines are important because they affect the quality of life in the international political system and the security of the states that hold them. Military doctrines may stress different military operations—offensive, defensive, or deterrent. Military doctrines may or may not be integrated with the political objectives of a grand strategy. They may be innovative or stagnant. In the next chapter, two theories will be introduced that help explain why military doctrines vary along the three dimensions discussed in this chapter.

[2]

Explaining Military Doctrine

THEORY AND EXPLANATION

In this chapter a number of hypotheses about what causes military doctrines to vary along the dimensions of offense-defense-deterrence, integration-disintegration, and innovation-stagnation will be introduced. These hypotheses are grouped into two families, representing two distinct perspectives on state behavior: that of "organization theory" and that of "balance of power theory." Both are summarized in this chapter. These two theoretical perspectives have achieved widespread currency in the study of national security policy. Both encompass a substantial literature. Thus, they seem a sensible place to start in an attempt to explain military doctrine. They have rarely been employed in this fashion.

The term "perspective" is perhaps more appropriate than the term "theory" as a description of the two families of hypotheses. Organization theory is a much larger and more diverse body of thought than that outlined below. I only summarize the fundamentals of the organization theory literature from which students of international politics have borrowed. Similarly, balance of power theory consists of a large and diverse literature, prescriptive and descriptive, which includes many disputes among its proponents. My summary of the theory borrows largely from Kenneth Waltz, but his work is perhaps the most abstract in the field, and his views are by no means universally shared.

Waltz and other balance of power theorists might quarrel with my use of the theory, since I have pulled it in the direction of "political realism" or "Realpolitik," with which it is closely identified, but not synonymous.[1] Waltz stresses the influence of general systemic constraints and incentives on the behavior of all states, and on the behav-

[34]

ior of the system as a whole. Students of "Realpolitik" focus on how these general constraints and incentives combine with the unique situations of individual states to lead them to specific foreign or military policies. Thus, the use of the terms "organization theory" and "balance of power theory" may be somewhat misleading. For the sake of brevity, however, and to indicate clearly the general origins of the hypotheses introduced, these shall be the labels for the two "perspectives" on the causes of military doctrine examined in this book.

I will introduce a few hypotheses regarding the influence of technology and geography on military doctrine that are consistent with one or the other of the two perspectives discussed above. One finds in the study of national security matters today a widespread belief that technology influences doctrine in decisive ways. In the past, as in the present, similar influence has sometimes been attributed to geography. I am unaware of any general theoretical statement that explains how and why either technology or geography affects military doctrine. Hence, these propositions will be integrated with the discussions of organization theory and balance of power theory.

Both organization theory and balance of power theory should be useful for explaining a good deal of state behavior during the last two or three hundred years. Balance of power theory should be able to explain the behavior of sovereign political units in any unregulated environment. Organization theory can be used to explain organizational behavior wherever we find large, functionally specialized bureaucracies. This latter condition has partially characterized European states since the end of the seventeenth century, and fully characterized them since the second half of the nineteenth century. Additionally, the two theories can be used to generate new hypotheses which can be tested against state behavior during this period. Because of the nature of the theories, valid comparisons can be made of different states across time and space. Lessons derived from such comparisons should be valid for many years to come, and should allow some rough predictions about the future.

Both of the theories under consideration are of the same type—structural theories. Such theories attempt to abstract from a particular political system the unique characteristics of its constituent parts and the interactions among those parts. As Kenneth Waltz puts it, the object is to discover the "arrangement" of a system's parts and the "principle of that arrangement."[2] To put it another way, such theories are inspired by the desire to discover what makes a system a system, what holds it together and causes it to behave in characteristic ways. Students of international politics have observed that certain outcomes tend to recur, often contrary to the intentions of the actors. Organization theorists have noted the same phenomenon in their field of inquiry. In spite of real differences of substance, the behaviors of a great diversity of states in a wide range of historical circumstances seem to exhibit important underlying similarities. Thucydides' account of the rivalry between Athens and Sparta and his explanation for that rivalry are uncannily reminiscent of the Soviet-American Cold War. At the organizational level, students of large businesses, large bureaucracies, and large military organizations have found striking behavioral similarities.

Waltz argues that the concept of "structure" can be used to understand what holds an international system together and what produces certain characteristic outcomes. Implicitly, this view is shared by organization theorists, who frequently use the term "structure," albeit with little rigor. A common thread runs through Waltz's use of the term and that of many organization theorists.[3] The distribution of capabilities—of *power* within a system—is considered to be of critical long-term importance.

Why is the distribution of capabilities important? Because it is fair to assume that individual political actors are constrained by both the limits of their own power and the extent of others' power. Another fair assumption is that individual political actors are sufficiently rational to have some sense of what both they and their fellows can do. Beyond determining the mere distribution of power, it is important to know if that power is distributed according to any fixed principle. Does the distribution of power, intendedly or unintendedly, protect any particular value?

Within organizations (and states, for that matter) power is distributed to achieve functional specialization—an intense division of labor. The coordination of functionally specialized sub-units demands a hierarchical distribution of power. Power is distributed functionally and hierarchically to protect the purposes of the organization—be it a corporation, bureaucracy, or state.

The same is obviously not true of international politics. There, power is distributed more equally than in organizations. Moreover, it is distributed to protect no group purpose. There is no functional specialization among states. We can, however, conceptualize the value protected. States "read" the distribution of international political power rather easily to learn that it does not protect them and may endanger them. Sovereign units, mindful that no outside party will help them, help themselves. They nurture the power that they have, and they often seek to gain more. Power protects itself in international politics. Such behavior tends to preserve individual sovereignty. Anarchy, the absence of an overarching sovereign, remains. The distribution of power in international politics thus *unintendedly* protects anarchy—the "value" in this case.

Both balance of power theory and organization theory assume that actors do what they can with their own power and what they must with reference to the power of others. This being the case, each theory predicts similar behavior of units in the context of similar structures. Anarchical environments should produce some similar behavior among the states that inhabit them. Purposeful, functionally specialized organizations should produce some similarity of behavior among sub-components.

The structural emphasis of both of these theories gives them their special utility in undertaking the task of comparing and explaining variations in military doctrine among different states, states all defended by professional military organizations but differently positioned in the international political system. A more thorough understanding of the origins of military doctrine can be achieved by employing the two theories in combination than by employing either separately or by proceeding empirically, with no theory at all. Both theories abstract the constraints that affect the behavior of national security decision-makers in the modern state. In some cases the external and internal constraints work at cross-purposes, in others they reinforce each other; in no case are they unimportant.

Theory Testing

A theory can be tested by logically deducing from it a series of "empirical statements." If it turns out that the empirical statements are true, the theory appears "more credible." The more times one can accomplish this, the more credible a given theory becomes. The hypotheses introduced in this chapter are empirical statements of this kind. To the extent that they are confirmed by the cases examined later in this book, the theories from which they are deduced gain more credibility.[4]

A second powerful type of test pits theories against each other. Arthur Stinchcombe makes use of the notion of the crucial experiment. "By eliminating the most likely alternative theory, we increase the credibility of our theory much more than we do by eliminating alternatives at random by checking consequences of our theory without thinking."[5] This test is difficult to perform in the present case. Inasmuch as there has been little attempt to develop theoretical explanations of military doctrine, it is hard to say what are the most likely alternative theories. My goal is, perforce, more modest—to take two of the most widely employed theories of state behavior in international politics and compare their explanatory power. As far as explaining military doctrine is concerned, the theories introduced here are among the "most likely alternative" theories to each other. Stinchcombe suggests that we "look for those consequences of our theory whose negation is implied by the alternatives."[6] It will not escape the student of international politics that the balance of power family of hypotheses introduced in this chapter is closely akin to Graham Allison's "Model I" or rational actor model, Hans Morgenthau's "realist" theory of international politics, and Kenneth Waltz's "third image." The organization theory family of hypotheses is closely akin to Allison's "Models II and III," and falls within Waltz's "second image" of political theorizing.[7] In explaining international outcomes, balance of power theorists have stressed the influence of the *system*; organization theorists the state and its constituent parts. The reader will realize that some of the hypotheses advanced in this chapter conflict. Thus, the battle is joined. To the extent that hypotheses deduced from one or the other school seem to better explain the character of military doctrine, the theory from which those hypotheses are deduced achieves greater credibility.

Military doctrine, as discussed here, is a response to both national and international influences. It represents the state's response to the constraints and incentives of the external world, yet it encompasses means that are in the custody of military organizations. These are perhaps the most "organized" of organizations. It is from their basic structure that most subsequent organizations take their inspiration. Thus, military doctrine provides an excellent ground upon which the two theories can do battle.

One goal of theory testing should be the construction of particularly difficult tests—tests that one intuitively expects the theory to pass only with difficulty. Military doctrine offers a hard test for both balance of power theory and organization theory. In matters directly relating to the security of the state, it is reasonable to expect the maximum influence of environmental constraints and incentives and a high level of civilian political control over military organizations, outcomes consistent with balance of power theory. Organization theory gains in credibility if hypotheses derived from it provide the best explanation for the character of a particular military doctrine. Its defeat in such a competition for explanatory value must be judged a weakness in an area in which it claims to be strong.

Military doctrine also provides a difficult test for balance of power theory, since military organizations should, based on organization theory predictions, be among the hardest to control. They are parochial, closed, large, endowed with all sorts of resources, and masters of a particularly arcane technology. They should be out of control much of the time, as they were prior to World War I. If it turns out that balance of power theory has a lot to say about military doctrine, this should give us more confidence in the theory.

Neither the notion that technology exerts a decisive influence on military doctrine, nor that geography does so, is specifically addressed by any general theory. Nevertheless, it would be useful to test each notion for its validity. In our own time, technological developments such as multiple independently targeted re-entry vehicles and guidance improvements are often blamed for the emergence of nuclear warfighting doctrines.[8] Britain's geographical separation from the European continent has long been cited as an explanation for her unique mode of participation in continental politics and wars.[9] After the fact, military historians are often willing to conclude that a particular technology had objective implications which either did find or should have found their way into military doctrine. Theorists such as Robert Jervis and George Quester use military technology and geography to explain international political events, frequently treating them as objective factors.[10]

States and military organizations are responsible for interpreting new military technologies and responding to geographic constraints and opportunities. Theories about states and military organizations can help us understand how new military technologies are assimilated and how geography is understood. To the extent that objective implications of technology or geography can be identified, balance of power theory would seem to predict some appreciation of these factors by the actors on the scene. Organization theory, on the other hand, predicts rather selective and idiosyncratic understanding of technology and geography.

While limited evidence and the quirks of history make most "tests" of international political theories less than decisive, I will argue that balance of power theory emerges from this exercise with a good deal more credit than it has enjoyed in recent years. Organization theory, on the other hand, emerges with somewhat less credit. The analysis does not show that organizational factors are unimportant, but rather that they are more often than not overridden by constraints and incentives that lie at the level of the international political system. Finally, crude notions of technological or geographical determinism find little vindication, although these factors do influence military doctrine in important ways.

Predictions about the behavior of civilians and soldiers derived from the organization theory and civil-military relations literature broadly suggest a tendency toward offensive, stagnant military doctrine—doctrine poorly integrated with the political objectives of a state's grand strategy. The cases will illustrate that these tendencies do exist; organization theory does successfully predict a fair amount of military behavior and does explain much about civil-military relations. Yet, by 1940, outcomes different from those predicted by the theory emerged. Why?

Balance of power theory suggests that states respond to potentially dangerous increases in the power of their putative adversaries. Contrary to what is often supposed, balancing behavior was widely in evidence in the 1930s. For instance, by the time of the Battle of France, total British and French military assets probably exceeded those of Germany. Balancing behavior is both qualitative and quantitative. States not only seek allies and build up their military power, they audit their military doctrines. Such audits mitigate the tendency toward stagnation predicted by organization theory.

Balance of power theory predicts heterogeneity along the dimension of offense-defense-deterrence, depending on the political objectives of a state's grand strategy and on the geographical, technological, and political constraints and opportunities it faces. Balance of power theory can predict some details of military doctrine on the basis of the state's political "position" in the international system. It also predicts closer integration of a state's military doctrine with the political aspects of its grand strategy than does organization theory. Finally, as a function of the competition among states, it predicts a tendency toward innovation in military doctrine. These tendencies are not manifest all the time. In times of relative international calm, organizational dynamics are allowed to flourish. But in times of threat, the actions of both statesmen and, to a lesser extent, soldiers will tend to override these dynamics.

Thus, although my analysis affirms the utility of organization theory to the study of military doctrine, it also challenges the widespread popularity that the theory has enjoyed over the last decade in the study of national security matters; conversely, it enhances the credibility, and expands the explanatory power, of balance of power theory.

[40]

Choice of Cases

The preceding remarks directly raise the questions of the choice of cases and the method by which the cases have been researched. The prewar doctrines of Britain, France, and Germany were chosen as cases for five reasons. First, this period is one in which widespread conclusions were drawn about the implications of military technology based upon experiences with the technology. Second, this is a period that saw major innovations in doctrine—Blitzkrieg and Fighter Command (the first integrated air defense in history)—and one minor innovation—the Maginot Line. Third, the political relationship between Britain and France, and between them and their various smaller client states, contrasts sharply with the relative political isolation of Germany during most of the interwar period. This offers an opportunity to test hypotheses that I have derived from balance of power theory concerning the influence of political isolation on the doctrines of states. Fourth, the states in this period were defended by large, modern, professional military organizations. These three cases thus provide three major military organizations to examine. Indeed, since separate services will be examined in each case, more than three military organizations will be examined. Thus, an excellent opportunity to test organization theory hypotheses is provided. Finally, two of these states, Britain and France, were status quo powers initially confident of their security but gradually being confronted by more and more evidence to the contrary. Thus, "balancing" propositions can be tested.

In examining prewar doctrines, I have placed primary reliance on the large body of secondary literature concerning the period. Currently, the archives of Britain and France are releasing material from this period, and authors of recently published histories have had access to large quantities of primary source material. In some cases, I have supplemented secondary sources with primary source material when such material was useful to elaborate certain points or fill in gaps.

MILITARY ORGANIZATIONS AND MILITARY DOCTRINE

The national security functions of the modern state are divided among specialists. These specialists, particularly professional soldiers, live out their lives and accomplish their tasks in highly structured, complex organizations. These two characteristics of the modern state, functional specialization and bureaucratization, exert an important influence on those aspects of military doctrine singled out for study in this work.

Military doctrines are in the day-to-day custody of military organizations. Such organizations have a large part of the responsibility both for the construction of military doctrine and for its execution in wartime. Intuitively, one would be surprised if such organizations did not exert a powerful and distinctive influence on military doctrine, and through it on grand strategy as a whole. Reliance on intuition alone is unnecessary, however. A rich, interrelated (if not entirely coherent) body of propositions about organizations, militaries, and states provides a useful starting point for generating new hypotheses about the influence of military organizations on military doctrine. These propositions are propounded in the literature of organization theory, civil-military relations, and state-building and state structure. Two fundamental points stand out. First, certain attributes of modern military organizations affect their attitudes to offense, defense, and deterrence; to political-military integration; and to innovation. Second, some aspects of the structure of modern states make it difficult, though not impossible, for civilians to exercise their authority along the dimensions of military doctrine selected for study.

Numerous propositions relevant to the study of military organizations are scattered through the organization theory literature. Regrettably, organization theory itself is a rather incoherent field. While propositions proliferate wildly, connections among them are vague. Although these propositions are by no means always clear about what causes what, and why, a number of propositions do bear on the central questions of this study. The literature on civil-military relations, though it has tended to focus on the question of military intervention into politics, also includes propositions relevant to the study of military doctrine. What follows is not a review of the literature from those two fields, but a discussion solely of those insights that may help yield answers to the central questions of this study.

Organization theory tries to explain organizational behavior and structure—what organizations do and how they look. In military affairs, the offensive proclivity of military organizations is an example of the kind of behavior we would wish to explain. Organization theorists explain things by reference to three important causal forces: *purpose, people,* and *environment.*

[42]

Purpose

Organizations come into existence for the pursuit of specific purposes. Purpose demands coordination, planning, and supervision. It requires the systematic introduction of rationality criteria, of cause and effect, cost and benefit. The pursuit of purpose encourages behavior and structure aimed at reducing uncertainty. All of this gives rise to that characteristic organizational form, bureaucracy. The specificity of functions in a bureaucracy mirrors the specificity of its purposes. Research and development requires a different bureaucratic structure than does the manufacture of steel.[11]

People

Organizations must pursue their purposes with people. People are a great source of uncertainty. While purpose demands rationality, people may not be able to provide it. People seldom approach the perfect rationality assumed in classical economics.[12] Capabilities are limited and unevenly distributed. Moreover, people are not tools; their inputs and outputs are not calculable in the same way as are inputs and outputs of raw materials or machinery. People seek more than simply wages from the organizations that they join. Power, authority, prestige, deference, good fellowship, and so on all condition the behavior of people in organizations. Thus, achieving the rationality required to pursue a purpose is problematical.

Environment

In the most basic sense, the environment spawns the organization; it produces the purpose that calls the organization into being. From the environment, contributions of people and materiel must be obtained. The organization's output is sold or traded to the environment in return for more contributions. The environment is, however, a source of great uncertainty. Will the organization's output satisfy those in the environment on whom the organization depends? Will essential contributions turn up at the time and place required for the organization to accomplish its purpose? The environment, like the organization's people, is often an obstacle to the coordination, control, and rationality that are required for the pursuit of purpose.[13]

Most of the propositions in organization theory stress one or more of these causal forces, and their relationship to one another. From these forces, a picture of organizational behavior and structure can be built. To pursue their purposes, organizations must coordinate and control the contributions of large numbers of variable human beings

[43]

in the context of an uncertain environment. Purpose demands rationality. Uncertainty is the enemy of rationality. Organizations attempt to reduce both internal and external sources of uncertainty.

Managing Uncertainty—Internal Mechanisms

Organizations develop routines for dealing with particular tasks, problems, and events standard in the everyday life of the organization. These are the now well-known "standard operating procedures" (SOPs) and programs combining such procedures popularized in the work of Graham Allison.[14] SOPs are the simplest rules of thumb for accomplishing basic tasks. In most Western armies it is SOP for tanks to fire from a "hull-down" or "hull-defilade" position. Positioning the tank on the reverse slope of a small hill and depressing the muzzle of the gun exposes very little of the tank's body to enemy fire, but allows it to fire. It is also SOP, on the offensive, to make the maximum possible use of irregularities in the terrain to mask the advancing tank.

SOPs are combined in standard ways to produce programs. It might take a large number of SOPs to produce a program.[15] The two SOPs above can be combined into an effective offensive program: some tanks in a unit may stand in a hull-down, overwatch position, covering the advance of other tanks that are exploiting the terrain. Organizations customarily have few programs, and making new ones is not easy. The package of programs held by an organization is called its repertoire, and is roughly analogous to a military doctrine.

Organizations develop preferred ways of doing things in order to control and coordinate the contributions of large numbers of sub-units. Individuals and sub-organizations that specialize in one particular SOP or program develop a personal and professional stake in it. Organizations ensure that tasks are carried out by endowing sub-organizations with the capability and authority to do so.

Individuals in sub-organizations are trained, rewarded, and promoted according to a particular way of doing business. Those socialized and promoted by the organization to do things in a particular way will, in their turn, apply the same criteria to their subordinates. Thus, SOPs, programs, and the organizations that are responsible for them become institutionalized.[16] They may hang on long after they have outlived their usefulness. The remarkable longevity of the horse cavalry in Western armies is a good example. Allison has observed that primary responsibility for any set of problems gives rise to "paro-

[44]

chial priorities and perceptions."[17] This phenomenon is particularly acute in military organizations.[18]

Environmental Uncertainty

The environment can be a source of much interference and uncertainty. Organizations do what they can to minimize environmental interference that might disrupt their normal routines.[19] Broadly, there are two sorts of strategies used by organizations to reduce their dependence on the environment—material and political. Material strategies aim to bring uncertainties under the direct control of the organization. Organizations stockpile or warehouse, make a fetish of scheduling, and industriously gather all the information they can on possible changes in the supply of what they need or the demand for what they do.[20] In some cases organizations engage in imperial policies that take some of these contingencies into their own domain. The determination of the United States Marine Corps to retain its own private air force is a good example. Bad experience with navy carrier-based aviation in World War II convinced the Corps that the Marine rifleman could only depend on a brother Marine for reliable close air support.

Organizations resort to political strategies when material ones are too expensive or are proscribed. For instance, military organizations might like to determine the size of their own budgets. One cannot, however, be at the same time a specialist in organized violence and a specialist in the collection of taxes. Hence, militaries are dependent on legitimate political authorities for critical contributions.

Those with formal authority over the organization are a cause of uncertainty. Organizations struggle for *independence* from legitimate authority, fearful that capricious, uninformed exercise of that authority will upset the delicate balance of internal structure and routine. To preserve their autonomy, organizations use political strategies such as the maintenance of alternative suppliers, the pursuit of prestige, or the pursuit of power over those on whom they are dependent. Militarism is one prestige strategy practiced by military organizations.[21] Military organizations have a certain inherent power within states that stems from the function that they serve, and they try to increase this power by mystifying their art, and concealing that art from civilian authorities. As Max Weber observed of all bureaucracies, militaries seem to know that knowledge is power, and take steps to keep their knowledge secret.[22]

Students of civil-military relations have noted the tendency of military organizations to seek autonomy. Samuel Finer argues that militaries may intervene in politics precisely because of their professionalism. "As specialists in their field, the military leaders may feel that they alone are competent to judge on such matters as size, organization, recruitment, and equipment of the forces."[23]

Richard Betts, in his thorough investigation of postwar civil-military relations during crises, concludes that not much has changed. More often than not the Joint Chiefs of Staff have, since World War II, sought to maintain a distinction between "policy" decisions, in which they advise civilian leadership, and military decisions, over which they claim authority. In many cases, they have preferred organizational autonomy and poverty to political control and wealth.[24]

Other contingencies in the environment include attempts by rivals to take over an organization's primary task. This sometimes elicits violent reactions from threatened organizations. The Navy bitterly opposed Air Force attempts to establish preeminence in the immediate postwar period. These dangers can be alleviated by arranging a "negotiated environment." "The primary environment (relations with other organizations comprising the government) is stabilized by such arrangements as agreed budgetary splits, accepted areas of responsibility, and established practices."[25] In short, organizations seek alliances and make treaties.

Allison's comments on the international environment are of special utility. "Where the international environment cannot be negotiated, organizations deal with remaining uncertainty by establishing a set of *standard scenarios* that constitute the contingencies for which they prepare."[26] This has a special bearing on military organizations. Once military organizations have prepared such standard scenarios, they have an interest in finding ways to impose the scenarios on their adversaries through offensive action.

Uncertainty and Innovation

Very little of the preceding summary of organization theory suggests that organizational innovation is either probable or simple. As "rational," purposeful instruments, organizations place a premium on predictability, stability, and certainty. These values are inimical to innovation. Individuals within organizations develop personal stakes in particular elements of their organizations. They have little interest in change. For these reasons, students of organizational behavior have more frequently addressed incremental change than innovation.[27]

However, innovation—large change—is not unknown in organizations. What are it causes?

First, organizations innovate when they fail. This hypothesis recurs in the literature. Events understood to be serious failures challenge the organization's basic existence. It owes its existence to achievement of a certain purpose. The organization must innovate in a way that achieves the purpose, or it will suffer.[28]

Second, organizations innovate when they are pressured from without. Unsatisfied clients tell the organization what is wrong. If they have formal authority over the organization, they will change it to set things right. Pressure may be indirect. The organization may face diminishing contributions of resources because its customers or clients are doing business with someone else. The organization must innovate or face grievous losses.[29]

Third, organizations innovate because they wish to expand. Organizations often wish to expand in order to control environmental uncertainty and to seize new resources that can be used to reward their members. Of course, innovation is just one strategy for expansion, and not necessarily a preferred one.[30]

In the preceding pages, I have summarized the major hypotheses of organization theory useful to this inquiry. It is now possible, drawing on those major hypotheses, to infer more specific hypotheses concerning the three dimensions of military doctrine particularly focused on in this book: offense-defense-deterrence, integration-disintegration, and innovation-stagnation.

Hypotheses—Offense, Defense, and Deterrence

Most soldiers and many civilians are intuitively attracted to the offense as somehow the stronger form of war. Clausewitz, often misconstrued as the apostle of the offensive, was very mindful of the advantages of a defensive strategy. He called defense "the stronger form of war." However, every aspect of his work that *could be taken* as offensive advocacy has been so taken. What accounts for such systematic misinterpretation?

Uncertainty Reduction
Military organizations will generally prefer offensive doctrines because they *reduce uncertainty* in important ways.

1. The need for standard scenarios encourages military organizations to prefer offensive doctrines. In order to have a set of SOPs and programs, they must plan for a "standard scenario." Once SOPs and

The Sources of Military Doctrine

programs have been tailored to such a scenario, the organization, in order to be "fought"—used in combat—must be used with those SOPs and programs. If the organization is to be "fought" successfully, it must respond to command in predictable ways. Commanders must have orders to give that generate predictable responses. Thus, it is strongly in the interests of a military organization to impose its "standard scenario" on the adversary through offensive action before the adversary does the same to it.

2. Warfare is an extremely competitive endeavor. Its most successful practitioners strive for even the smallest advantages. Thus, military organizations seem to prefer offensive doctrines not only because they appear to guarantee the side on the offense its standard scenario, but because they also *deny* the enemy his standard scenario. A military organization prefers to fight its own war and *prevent* its adversary from doing so. Taking the offensive, exercising the initiative, is a way of structuring the battle. The advantages seen to lie with surprise are more than psychological. An organization fighting the war that it planned is likely to do better than one that is not. For example, in the Arab attack on Israel in 1973, Egyptian and Syrian preparations were aimed at imposing an uncongenial style of warfare on Israel.

Defensive warfare might also seem to allow an organization to structure the battle. However, the defending organization is often in a reactive position, improvising new programs to cope with the adversary's initiative. If the defending organization is, for whatever reasons, a fast learner, it may rapidly improvise countermeasures that destroy the offender's programs. (The Israel Defense Forces achieved this with their Suez Canal crossing in 1973.) This leaves both organizations fighting a battle of improvisation which both would probably prefer to avoid. Victory goes to the most flexible command structure. Generally, however, professional soldiers appear to believe that striking the first blow is beneficial because, at least initially, it reduces the attacker's necessity to improvise and the defender's ability to improvise. This military judgment may reflect an implicit understanding that military organizations are not fast learners, precisely because they are the structured systems portrayed earlier. The perceived advantage of taking the offensive is thus magnified.

3. Because predicting whose national will can be broken first is a political task, not susceptible to the analytical skills of a military organization, military organizations dislike deterrent doctrines. Punishment warfare, conventional or nuclear, tends not to address an adversary's capabilities, but his will. Calculating in advance of a war whose

will is likely to break first is inherently somewhat more difficult for a military organization than devising plausible scenarios for destroying enemy capabilities. Calculations of enemy determination demand an entirely different set of skills than those commanded by a military organization. Calculations about military outcomes are at least somewhat susceptible to "engineering" criteria; calculations of relative will are not. However, this argument may be a weak one. There are more powerful reasons why military organizations do not favor deterrent doctrines.

4. Military organizations will prefer offensive doctrines because they help increase organizational size and wealth. Size and wealth help reduce internal uncertainty by increasing the rewards that the organization can distribute to its members. Size and wealth help reduce external uncertainty by providing a buffer against unforeseen events such as huge losses or partial defeats.

While the offensive allows the attacking force to be more certain of how its organization will perform, and to deny that certainty to an adversary, the offensive is likely to be technically more complex, quantitatively more demanding. There are many extra contingencies for which an offensive military instrument must be prepared. An attacking army encounters natural obstacles that must be crossed, creating a demand for engineers. Fortifications encountered may demand more and heavier artillery for their reduction. The offensive army may have to go anywhere, requiring special technical capabilities in its equipment. Nothing can be specialized for the environment of the home country. Aircraft need greater range and payload. All of these factors require an extensive logistics capability to uncoil behind the advancing military force. Troops will be required to guard and defend this line of communication. Operations at range will impose greater wear and tear on the equipment—demanding large numbers in reserve, and still more support capability. While various characteristics of geography, politics, and technology might place these same demands on a defensive force, as a general rule offensive doctrines impose them to a greater extent. Deterrent doctrines offer the most minimal material opportunities for military organizations. This is partly because they are more dependent on political will than on military capabilities. Partly it is a result of the clarity of the punishment mission, which allows rather extreme specialization.

5. Military organizations will prefer offensive doctrines because they enhance military autonomy. As noted earlier, civilian intervention in operational matters can be a key source of uncertainty for military organizations. Offensive doctrines tend to be more compli-

cated than defensive or deterrent doctrines, and thus increase the difficulties for civilians who wish to understand military matters. Defense and deterrence are relatively easy for civilians to master. Deterrent warfare with nuclear weapons has consistently proved to be the easiest form of warfare for civilian analysts to understand in the postwar period. Deterrent warfare by means of popular resistance—extended guerrilla action, for example—depends so heavily on the legitimacy of the government and its authority over its people that it may be the highest form of political-military warfare. Defense or denial does not present the complications of the offensive, and again includes such strong cooperation with civilian authorities as to restrict the operational autonomy of the army. The offensive, however, can be waged off national soil, and therefore immediately involves less civilian interference. Offensive operations are elaborate combinations of forces and stratagems—more art than science. Denial is more straightforward, and punishment is simplest of all. From specialists in victory, defense turns soldiers into specialists in attrition, and deterrence makes them specialists in slaughter.

There is little in organization theory or the civil-military relations literature to suggest that modern militaries will prefer anything but offensive doctrines, if such doctrines are in any way feasible.

Geography

6. Organization theory suggests a somewhat muted geographical influence on military doctrine. (The influence of technology will be discussed below.) Where geography can plausibly be argued to favor an offensive doctrine, it reinforces the organizational tendencies outlined above. For instance, it has become commonplace to explain the affinity of Prussia-Germany (in the past) and Israel (in the present) for offensive doctrines by their a) being surrounded and outnumbered by powerful enemies and b) enjoying the advantage of interior lines (with the ability to shift forces quickly from one front to another). Thus, the sequential defeat of the members of an enemy coalition with a series of rapid offensives, before they can pull their forces together and coordinate an attack, is deemed to be very attractive. Presumably, any state finding itself in a similar position would agree.

One less often finds the reverse argued—that some particular geographic configuration generally and sensibly leads to a defensive military doctrine. At the level of grand strategy, of course, both Britain and the United States have exploited the defensive advantage bestowed by ocean barriers. Yet, the navies of both powers have periodically argued for offensive military strategies to achieve "command of the sea."[31] They usually have been constrained to operate in a more limited fashion, but the preference for the offensive, even in situations where it seems unreasonable, is striking.

Numerous examples of military organizations that undervalue the defensive utility of geography can be found. British colonial soldiers in India viewed Afghanistan as a potential Russian invasion route, and sought to control it. Yet, one British military expedition after another met with disaster brought on by wild Afghan raiders, treacherous terrain and weather, and long distances.[32] This stark evidence of the area's unsuitability as an invasion route was ignored, as subsequent expeditions were deemed necessary. In World War I the Russians underrated the defensive value of the Masurian Lakes to the Germans. The lakes ultimately split the large Russian force, allowing a smaller German army to defeat it piecemeal.[33] At the outset of World War I the British dispatched a small force to Persia, to guard the Abadan oil facilities. Its commanders opted for an attack on Baghdad, a distant objective for which the force was woefully inadequate.[36] Currently, the U.S. Navy advocates an offensive strategy against Soviet Naval forces based in the Barents Sea and Murmansk— a tough and distant target.[35] NATO has geographic choke points off the Norwegian North Cape, and in the Greenland-Iceland–United Kingdom Gap, that provide a powerful defensive advantage against any Soviet naval offensive, and all but obviate the need for an offensive against the north. In short, organization theory suggests that geographic factors that support offensive doctrines will more often be correctly assessed than those that support a defensive doctrine. History seems to confirm this observation.

Hypotheses—Integration

It was over a century and a half ago that Clausewitz made his now famous remarks on the relationship of war to policy. Most simply, "war is not a mere act of policy but a true political instrument, a continuation of political activity by other means."[36] Political considerations reach into the military means, to influence *"the planning of war, of the campaign, and often even of the battle"* (my emphasis).[37] Clausewitz clearly believed that statesmen could and should ensure that policy infuse military operations. Those in charge of policy require "a certain grasp of military affairs."[38] They need not be soldiers, however. "What is needed in the post is distinguished intellect and character. He [the statesman] can always get the necessary military information somehow or other."[39] Clausewitz was over-optimistic on this score. Few have challenged his judgment that policy must infuse acts of war, but the achievement of this goal has proven more difficult than he imagined. Social developments under way in his own time were to make political-military integration highly problematical.

Russell Weigley, the American military historian, has observed that political-military integration remains an "intractable problem," endemic to "the whole history of the modern state."[40] Moreover, the problem does not seem to be affected by whether the form of government is democratic or totalitarian. It arises in all types of political systems. In singling out the "modern state" Weigley is on the track of an explanation; for the distinctive structure of the modern state creates the problem.

The modern state emerged in its present form during the seventeenth and eighteenth centuries. Its most outstanding characteristic in terms of military doctrine is functional specialization. The separate responsibilities for diplomacy and war of organizations and individuals commanding different skills, information, and materiel generates a structural barrier to political-military integration. Ironically, such functional specialization was caused by the power struggle among the monarchies of Europe. Specialization and professionalization of foreign policy and national security functions spread because they improved the war-making capability of individual states.[41] "War made the state, and the state made war."[42]

The division of functions, and of expertise, is not an insurmountable obstacle to political-military integration. It is a real one, however. Even if soldiers could be relied upon to carry out the wishes of their civilian masters without resistance—even if they were the neutral tools that public administration theorists once assumed all bureaucracies to be—the problem of reconciling policy with administration, political objectives with military doctrine, still would exist. Ignorance of each other's problems, and barriers to coordination, would create difficulties. Grand strategies would tend toward disintegration.

The problem is rendered more serious, however, by those internal characteristics of the military as *combat organizations* discussed earlier. These affect not only the extent to which a doctrine will be offensive, but the degree of integration and the chances of innovation as well. Moreover, the division of functions within the modern state tends to magnify the impact of these internal characteristics on overall grand strategy.

Functional specialization between soldiers and statesmen, and the tendency of soldiers to seek as much independence from civilian interference as possible, combine to make political-military integration an uncertain prospect. These two fundamental aspects of state structure and organization lead to the following deductions:

1. As a rule, soldiers are not going to go out of their way to reconcile the means they employ with the ends of state policy. This is not necessarily to argue that they deliberately try to disconnect their means from political ends. Often, however, soldiers will elevate the narrow technical requirements of preferred operations above the needs of civilian policy. In the case of the European militaries prior to World War I, the single-minded pursuit of battlefield advantage closed off diplomatic options for statesmen.

2. This cause of disintegration is exacerbated because military organizations are unwilling to provide civilian authorities with information that relates to doctrinal questions, especially those having the most to do with the actual conduct of operations. Thus, civilians are simply unaware of the ways military doctrine may conflict with the ends of state policy. Policy-makers may simply not know enough about the operational practices of their military organizations to either alter their political strategy or force changes in military doctrine that would bring it in line with the existing political strategy. Nevertheless, in spite of the limits of information, organization theory would seem to suggest that if political-military integration is to be achieved, civilian intervention into doctrinal matters is essential. The question is, given the obstacles, what is sufficient to cause civilian intervention? This is a question better answered by balance of power theory.

3. The setting of priorities among military forces and missions is a key aspect of political-military integration. In multiservice military organizations, civilian intervention is critical to the setting of priorities. This is another way civilian intervention causes integration. In chapter 1 it was argued that one of the tasks of grand strategy is to set priorities among threats and opportunities in the environment, and to set priorities among forces to match these threats and opportunities. Interpreting the external environment is the specialty of civilians. Building and operating military forces is the task of services. Setting priorities among the services, and among forces or branches within services, is a central task of grand strategy. Yet, the tendency of individuals within organizations to preserve the task and power of their organization or sub-organization suggests that *among* or *within* services the goal of autonomy should be just as strong as it is for the military as a whole. Thus, it is very difficult for a group of services to accomplish the task of setting priorities. The inclination of a group of

services or sub-services to set priorities among themselves is going to be low.

In the absence of civilian intervention, and the exercise of the legitimate authority that only the civilians possess, militaries will arrange a "negotiated environment." This is likely to take the form of either preserving a customary budgetary split or dividing shares equally. Each service will prepare for its own war. Forces will not cooperate effectively. Neither will they be well balanced. A tendency will emerge for each service to set requirements as if it were fighting the war alone. This can easily result in misallocation of the scarce security resources of the state.

Left to themselves, a group of services cannot make a military doctrine that will be well integrated with the political aspects of the state's grand strategy. They can simply assemble a batch of service doctrines. This is less true within services, where higher authority can make allocation decisions. Even within services, priorities may not be set according to strategic criteria. A service doctrine may be as difficult to produce as an overall grand strategy.

Different branches within a service may have different goals and interests. For example, within the interwar German Army the artillerymen who dominated the upper ranks tended to oppose armor developments, perhaps fearing that direct-fire, armored tank guns might actually eclipse the former preeminence of the artillery and the artillerymen. Within services, and among services, priorities must be set according to grand strategic as well as strictly military criteria. There is no guarantee that the priorities set will reflect policy judgments and policy needs unless civilians intervene to assure this.

Hypotheses—Innovation in Military Doctrine

Obstacles

1. Because of the process of institutionalization, innovation in military doctrine should be rare. It will only occasionally be sponsored by the military organization itself. As already remarked, according to organization theory organizations try to control the behavior of their members in order to achieve purposes. One way of doing this is by distributing power through the organization so as to ensure that certain tasks will be accomplished. Individuals develop a vested interest in the distribution of power and in the purposes it protects. Generally, it is not in the interests of most of an organization's members to promote or succumb to radical change.

2. Innovations in military doctrine will be rare because they in-

crease operational uncertainty. While innovation is in process, the organization's SOPs and programs will be in turmoil. The ability of commanders to "fight" the organization with confidence will decline. Should a war come during the transition, the organization will find itself between doctrines. Under combat conditions, even a bad doctrine may be better than no doctrine. It is possible to argue that the Prussians at Jena, the French in 1940, and the Russians in 1941 were taken in the midst of doctrinal transition.

3. Because of the obstacles to innovation discussed above, a technology that has not been tested in war can seldom function by itself as the catalyst for doctrinal innovation. Military organizations often graft new pieces of technology on to old doctrines. As Bernard Brodie has noted, "Conservatism of the military, about which we hear so much, seems always to have been confined to their adaptation to new weaponry rather than their acceptance of it."[43] Several subsidiary propositions are in order.

A new technology will normally be assimilated to an old doctrine rather than stimulate change to a new one. This proposition is entirely consistent with organization theory, but it is derived empirically by both Bernard Brodie and Edward L. Katzenbach.[44] In his tightly written study of the longevity of the horse cavalry, the latter observes that ". . . in the military it is quite impossible to prove that minor adjustments in a traditional pattern of organization and doctrine will not suffice to absorb technological innovation of genuine magnitude."[45] This problem stems from the difficulty of proving anything about a new military technology without using it in a major war. We see the problem replicated today, with the apparently endless debate on the implications of precision-guided munitions.

Military organizations have a hard time learning about the operational implications of new technology from the wars of other military organizations. This proposition is derived empirically, although it is entirely consistent with the parochialism expected from large organizations. The failure of most European armies prior to World War I to adapt to the emerging defensive power of new military technology demonstrated in the American Civil War, the Russo-Japanese War of 1905, the Russo-Turkish War of 1877, and the Boer War of 1899–1902, supports the proposition.[46]

Causes of Innovation

In the military sphere, there are two exceptions to the preceding proposition that military organizations generally fail to innovate in response to new technology:

[55]

4. Military organizations do seem willing to learn from wars fought by their client states—with the weapons and perhaps the doctrine of the patron. Both the U.S. and Soviet militaries are willing to draw lessons from the 1973 Arab-Israeli war, although many of the "lessons" are not entirely clear.

5. Military organizations are even better able to learn about technology by using it in their own wars. Perhaps the best example of direct experience leading to correct appraisal of technology is found in the evolution of Prussian doctrine from 1850 to 1870. Prussia's attempted railroad mobilization against Austria in 1850 was a fiasco. Learning from the experience, the Prussians turned the railroad into an efficient war instrument by 1866.[47]

There are limits to the power of this proposition. In the American Civil War, frontline soldiers adjusted rapidly to the technological facts of modern firepower. They "dug in" whenever they had the chance. The generals understood the least, ordering frontal assaults against prepared positions throughout the war.[48] The same occurred in World War I, with generals ordering repeated costly offensives. Bernard Brodie notes that the generals "seemed incapable of learning from experience, largely because of the unprecedented separation of the high command from the front lines."[49] This seems a plausible explanation, and again is entirely consistent with organization theory.

Even in its own war, a military organization can misperceive the implications of a new technology unless the lessons are very stark. Katzenbach shows that both the Prussian Army in the Franco-Prussian War and the British Army in the Boer War managed to evade the lessons taught by those engagements about the effects of modern firepower on the cavalry charge.[50] The French Army at first correctly drew from the Franco-Prussian War the lesson that technology favored the defensive, but subsequently concluded that their defeat had resulted from an insufficiently offensive strategy. This ultimately allowed the Army to justify the offensive Plan XVII at the outset of World War I. Even the notion that direct experience with a new technology will lead to its correct integration into doctrine should be accepted cautiously.

The preceding examples also offer insights into the relationship between technology and the offensive, defensive, or deterrent character of military doctrine. Most simply, if a military organization has adopted an offensive doctrine, or is bent on adopting one, technological lessons on the advantage of defense are likely to be ignored, corrupted, or suppressed. This is consistent with the argument advanced earlier concerning the probable offensive preferences of most military organizations.

Organization theory predicts at least two causes of innovation that are much stronger and more reliable in their operation than experience with new technology: (6) military organizations innovate when they have failed—suffered a defeat—and (7) they innovate when civilians intervene from without. These hypotheses can be deduced from the basic survival motive of large organizations. Failure to achieve their organizational purpose, the successful defense of the state, can cause military organizations to reexamine their basic doctrinal preferences. Similarly, soldiers may respond to the civilian intervention that defeat often precipitates in order to defend the organization's autonomy, which is under attack.

Failure and civilian intervention often go hand in hand. Soldiers fail; civilians get angry and scared; pressure is put on the military. Sometimes the pressure is indirect. Civilian leaders become disenchanted with the performance of one service and shift resources to another. These resources may provide the "slack" for the newly favored service to attempt some innovations. The loser strives to win back his lost position. Interservice rivalry in postwar America may have produced some benefits—a menu of innovations for policymakers. Arguably, interservice rivalry has been a major factor in the growth of the "Triad," which has on the whole increased U.S. security. Similarly, aggrandizement at the expense of another service may be a motive for innovation.

Although civilian intervention into military doctrine would seem to be a key determinant of innovation, it involves special problems. The division of labor between civilians and soldiers is intense. Civilians are not likely to have the capability to dream up whole new doctrines. Thus, civil intervention is dependent on finding sources of military knowledge. Civil intervention should take the form of choosing from the thin innovation menu thrown up by the services. In multiservice defense establishments, civilians have the possibility, depending on the strategic position of the state, of choosing among competing services. Within services, hierarchy and the chain of command should tend to suppress the emergence of new doctrinal alternatives at levels where the civilians cannot find them.

None of this is to say that innovation in military doctrine is impossible. These are merely tendencies. Innovation is possible. Major innovations in doctrine occurred in two of the cases discussed in this book—Britain and Germany.

Summary: Organization Theory Hypotheses

Offense, Defense, and Deterrence

1. The need for standard scenarios to reduce operational uncertainty encourages military organizations to prefer offensive doctrines.

2. The incentive, arising from the highly competitive nature of warfare, to deny an adversary his "standard scenario" encourages offensive doctrines.

3. The inability of military organizations to calculate comparative national will causes them to dislike deterrent doctrines.

4. Offensive doctrines will be preferred by military organizations because they increase organizational size and wealth.

5. Offensive doctrines will be preferred by military organizations because they enhance organizational independence from civilian authority.

6. Because the organizational incentives to pursue offensive doctrines are strong, military organizations will generally fix on geographic and technological factors that favor the offensive, but underrate or overlook such factors that favor defense or deterrence.

Integration

1. Because military organizations seek independence from civilian authority in order to reduce the uncertainties of combat, military doctrines tend to be poorly integrated with the political aspects of grand strategy. Soldiers will avoid including political criteria in their military doctrine if such criteria interfere with strictly instrumental military logic.

2. Because of functional specialization, civilians and soldiers tend to know too little about each other's affairs. Soldiers, again in the quest for autonomy, will exacerbate this problem by withholding important military information from civilians. Inadequate civilian understanding of military matters creates obstacles to political-military integration.

3. Technical specialization within military organizations works against a strategically rational setting of priorities among different services, further contributing to disintegration.

In spite of the obstacles, civilian intervention into military doctrine is likely to be the primary cause of political-military integration of grand strategy, simply because civilians alone have the interest and the authority to reconcile political ends with military means and set priorities among military services according to some rational calculus.

[58]

Innovation

Most propositions about military innovation are negative.

1. Because of the process of institutionalization, which gives most members of an organization a stake in the way things are, doctrinal innovation will only rarely be sponsored by the organization itself.

2. Because doctrinal innovation increases operational uncertainty, it will rarely be sponsored by the organization itself.

3. New technology, when it has not been tried in combat, is seldom by itself a catalyst of doctrinal innovation.

4. A client state's combat experience with a new technology may spur innovation.

5. Direct combat experience with a new technology can cause innovation.

6. Failure on the battlefield can cause doctrinal innovation.

7. Civilian intervention can cause military innovation.

BALANCE OF POWER THEORY AND MILITARY DOCTRINE

Organization theory suggests a tendency toward offensive, stagnant military doctrines, poorly integrated with the political elements of a state's grand strategy. Balance of power theory predicts greater heterogeneity in military doctrine, dependent on reasonable appraisals by each state of its political, technological, economic, and geographical problems and possibilities in the international political system. The three case studies will show that although organization theory does accurately predict certain tendencies in military doctrine, overall outcomes are more consistent with balance of power theory predictions.

From balance of power theory specific propositions about the variables offense-defense-deterrence, innovation-stagnation, and integration-disintegration can be deduced. Balance of power theory also describes the circumstances under which these propositions are most likely to hold true. In times of relative international calm, when statesmen and soldiers perceive the probability of war as remote, the organizational dynamics outlined above tend to operate. When threats appear greater, or war appears more probable, balancing behavior occurs. A key element of that behavior is greater civilian attention to matters military.

Such attention puts the more ossified, organizationally self-serving, and politically unacceptable aspects of military doctrine under a harsher light. Fear of disaster or defeat prompts statesmen to question long-standing beliefs, to challenge service preferences, to alter budget shares, and to find new sources of military advice and leadership. Civilians intervene to change details, including posture and doctrine, not merely general principles. Organization theory would view civilian influence at such a level as unlikely. Moreover, soldiers, fearful that policies long preferred for their peacetime utility may be found wanting in war, are (according to balance of power theory) somewhat more amenable to outside criticism than in times of international calm. Soldiers themselves are more likely to examine their traditional premises. They will not abandon them, but they may hedge against their failure. These military tendencies are insufficiently strong in their own right to produce military doctrines consistent with balance of power theory predictions. It is the combination of civilian intervention and increased military open-mindedness that produces the results predicted.

In chapter 1, the concept of the "security dilemma" was employed to explain the pernicious effects of offensive doctrines on international politics. States are assumed to be sovereign units that wish to remain so. The environment in which they live is anarchic; each must look to its own security. Measures that one state takes to ensure its security can diminish the security of others. When this occurs, those threatened, mindful that they can rely only upon themselves should war come, tend to take countervailing measures. Whether by alliance building or arms racing, states engage in balancing behavior.

This description of states, their environment, and their behavior does not rely upon any peculiarities of particular states. It is more concerned with the environment of states than with their attributes.[51] As I conceive it, balance of power theory examines the nature of the international political system as a whole, and stresses the influence of the system on the behavior of individual actors. Thus, throughout this book I occasionally use *systemic* synonymously with *balance of power* (in its adjectival meaning).

The condition of anarchy, the absence of a sovereign, allows disputes to arise among states. These disputes frequently can be settled only by war. Due to the absence of a sovereign, violence is a constant and omnipresent possibility among states. In violent disputes two factors determine outcomes: capability and will. Wars are often won by those states that disarm their adversaries by dint of their superior coalitions, stronger economies, or more efficient military organizations. The allies won World War II this way. Wars are also won by superior willingness to pay the money or blood price of waging them.

[60]

The U.S. armed forces were not destroyed on the battlefields of South Vietnam. By virtue of the pain inflicted and the costs incurred on those battlefields, the will of the government and people of the United States was destroyed.

Although disputes among states are frequent, they do not always end in war. Capabilities for war and threats of war are often in the background, however. In the context of anarchy, capability and will are the final arbiters. War measures the relative capability and will of the parties to a dispute when one side or the other is either completely defeated or signals a willingness to quit. Thus, an understanding of relative capabilities and relative will in the context of a particular dispute reduces the tendency to resort to violence. There is no need for each side to measure the power and will of the other relative to its own through the medium of war, if such an understanding can be achieved in another way. States do not go to war for its own sake. Mindful of the costs and risks of war, they attempt through diplomacy to achieve a mutual understanding of one another's power and will—an agreement on who cares more and who has more.[52] This is a difficult process, in which each side does its best to convey an impression of great capability and concern, even as it must cast a cold analytical eye on its adversary's efforts to do the same. If this process fails to produce an agreement on relative power and will, then the task of achieving this "measurement" must fall to war.

The mustering of power—military capability and assets that contribute to military capability—is perhaps the most important task imposed on the state by the international political system. It is the means of survival in an anarchical environment. The mustering of power is a central concern of balance of power theorists and advocates of Realpolitik. In the context of anarchy, states take measures to ensure their security. They endeavor to increase their power. They do not necessarily do this single-mindedly or without limits. But even when a state tries to improve its power position out of defensive motives, frequently the things it does to ensure its own security reduce the security of others. If a given state is bent on expansion, its actions are still more likely to have this effect. Those threatened have a strong incentive to respond with attempts to increase their own power. This is called "balancing behavior."

States balance in two general ways: coalition formation and internal mobilization. Coalition formation has been the concern of most statesmen and academics who use the term "balance of power." Some of the discussions have been prescriptive, admonishing the wise statesman to preserve the balance of power. Others have been predictive, suggesting that the anarchical condition of international politics strongly encourages balancing behavior among states. Whether or not states explicitly pursue a balance, a balance will be the likely result. The emphasis has been on alliance-building among great powers.

An alliance combines the military power of a number of states for the purpose of fighting wars. In advance of a war, a coalition (or the hint of one) can serve the purpose of enlarging perceived power as well. In the late 1970s, the United States manipulated the "China card" in this fashion. Lord Grenville, the British foreign secretary, originally conceived the Second Coalition against revolutionary France as a diplomatic instrument first, a military instrument second. He wanted to present the Directory with a plan for a comprehensive settlement, backed by the threat of war.[53] This method of mustering real and perceived power is of little utility in a bipolar system. Although the threat of alliance with a third party may carry some diplomatic weight, the relative weakness of the third party mitigates the effect. Thus, in bipolar systems we should see greater attention to "internal" mechanisms both for mustering real power and for enlarging perceived power. The same should be true of politically isolated states in multipolar systems.

Internal mobilization is the second way states increase their power. In response to increases in the offensive capabilities of a single adversary or to the development of an offensive coalition, states can look inside their own borders for additional capability. The arms race or "competition" between the two superpowers is internal balancing behavior. States may extract more resources from their economies for military purposes. They may restrict consumption and promote investment to achieve high rates of growth. Through enhanced training, qualitative improvements in a state's military organization can be sought. Salaries can be raised and professional cadres expanded.

Just as coalition formation and the hint of coalition formation can enhance perceived power in peacetime, so can the mustering of internal capabilities. Arms racing in large and visible weapons systems is hard for adversaries to avoid. Such weapons are often taken as indices of relative power. Thirty-five years into the Soviet-American arms competition, and fifteen years after the Soviets obtained an inescapable second-strike capability, many analysts and high officials still regularly become disturbed over minor inequalities in numerical indices of particular components of military capability. Such indices evidently influence political perceptions of relative strength.

Military forces can also be used more directly to display both power and *will.* Forces can be moved, alerted, or mobilized. Small wars may be fought as indications of willingness to fight larger ones. This latter rationale arose frequently in defense of the U.S. presence in Vietnam, especially when no other rationale could be found. Such demonstrative uses of force have been a long-time adjunct of diplomacy. Frederick the Great once observed that "diplomacy without armaments is like music without instruments." The custom of armed demonstration arose in Frederick's time, with the emergence of the standing army.[54] A Brookings Institution study notes that the United States has alerted or deployed forces in this fashion over two hundred times in the Cold War.[55]

Several factors influence both the intensity of balancing behavior and the mix between coalition formation and internal mobilization. The degree of effort with which some states in a system attempt to improve their power position is the most important factor. Those states most often identified as history's would-be hegemons have elicited the most intense balancing behavior by their neighbors. Three other factors are also important: the distribution of power in the system; the geographical assets and liabilities of the various actors; and military technology.

The number of great powers in a given system is taken to be an important variable by many balance of power theorists because it affects both the mustering and measurement of capabilities.[56] The more great powers there are in a political system, the more complex these tasks become. A system of many powers provides opportunities for aggrandizing states because the responsibility for opposing expansion is unclear. Multipolar systems encourage "buck-passing." In bipolar systems the reverse is the case. The superpowers mainly have each other to fear, so they watch each other carefully. Neither can begin preparations for aggression without arousing the other's attention. The status quo superpower takes responsibility for opposing expansion because buck-passing is not an option—no other state is powerful enough to take over a passed buck. Each superpower is structurally constrained. The distribution of capabilities encourages wariness and discourages irresponsibility.

In multipolar systems, relative power is hard to calculate. Nobody can be quite sure who will side with whom. Even when two alliances face each other, the possibility of defection remains. This problem does not arise under bipolarity. The distribution of power is sufficiently unequal that, while each superpower can, on its own, do substantial harm to the other, no third party can do nearly as much harm to either. Bipolarity may encourage overreaction. It may cause a widening and deepening of conflict. On the other hand, it makes relative power easier to assess and disabuses both superpowers from the belief that piecemeal aggression can be successful.

In multipolar systems aggressors can get a head start because defenders bicker about the nature of the threat and who shall pay the price of opposing it. As Mancur Olsen has pointed out, and as Kenneth Waltz has reiterated, such dissension is, at least in the short term, sensible behavior for each autonomous self-regarding unit. Checking an expanding hegemon is a collective good. Whether one state creates that good, or all create that good, all benefit. Because there is no way to prevent a given state from enjoying this benefit, that state has an incentive to "free ride." Each state may view the world in this fashion, attempting to pay as little, and get others to pay as much, as can be managed.

Dissension of this kind will retard the formation of defensive coalitions, and will hamper their effectiveness even after they are formed. Disputes about risks and costs are endemic to alliances. Moreover, the knowledge that today's friend may be tomorrow's enemy encourages disputes over spoils. The war must not end with any member of the coalition more powerful relative to the others than at the war's outset. No state wants to lose more than the others. No state wants others to gain more than itself. These calculations mean that a less than "optimal" amount of the collective good—defense—is likely to be provided.

The question of relative capabilities among great powers is less often addressed by balance of power theorists. Theory is facilitated by simplifying reality. It is possible to generate relatively clear and explicit hypotheses about behavior in systems of either several equal powers (multipolarity) or two equal powers (bipolarity). It would be quite difficult to generate such hypotheses about the myriad real-world variations that could occur in the relative capabilities of two or more major powers. Unfortunately, it is easy to reify a theoretically useful assumption.

For instance, theorists correctly view the current international environment as bipolar, although the fact that U.S. GNP is roughly twice that of the Soviet Union, and the latter only roughly equal to the Japanese, subtly alters the behavior of each superpower away from what it would be in a strictly bipolar system. The Soviets probably compete with greater intensity and the U.S. with less intensity than would be the case if the two states were more nearly equal in overall power. Similarly, the case studies that follow show that real-world variations in the capabilities of the major powers within a multipolar

[64]

system do seem to matter, although they matter in ways that are broadly consistent with the predictions of balance of power theory. Particularly, in multipolar systems, the weaker a status quo major power is relative to an expansionist state, the greater is the tendency for that power to devote energy to seeking allies—indeed, it may devote a good deal more energy to that endeavor than to enhancing its own military power. Status quo states in a more favorable position may pay more attention to their own military capabilities and less to coalition building, because they perceive themselves as better able to go it alone, at least for a time.

Geography and technology can affect the intensity and character of balancing behavior. Where geography and technology are believed to favor the defender, balancing behavior of all kinds should be slower and less intense than if the offensive is believed to have the advantage. Given the characteristic preferences of military organizations suggested earlier, civilian policy-makers will be more likely than soldiers to hold such views.

The study of the influence of geography on international politics may have been the first attempt systematically to examine the influence of the environment on the national security behavior of states. For instance, observers have long stressed the impact of geography on the military strategies, indeed the foreign policies, of Switzerland, Britain, and Germany, almost independent of the influence of total capabilities and military technology.

Mountain barriers have presented the Swiss with strong defensive advantages, which that nation has long adapted its military organization to exploit.

The English channel provided a defensive advantage that allowed Britain to forego a large land army in favor of a navy. In wartime, the naval superiority this permitted, combined with a position astride the sea routes out of western Europe, allowed Britain to blockade the merchant and war fleets of her continental adversaries, and thus to dominate much of the world's trade. These advantages produced a characteristic foreign policy and military doctrine. Safe and rich, Britain was usually slow to anger, and waged war with blockade, coalitions, subsidies, and small land expeditionary forces.

Germany was denied this luxury. Relatively barren of natural defenses and surrounded by strong powers, she had no obvious tactical advantages. If troops could be moved quickly enough, however, Germany might enjoy the advantage of "interior lines," the ability to shift forces quickly from one threatened border to another. To some extent, Frederick the Great managed to exploit this advantage. The invention of the steam engine and construction of a dense rail net converted this geographical attribute into an even more important military factor—given an appropriate doctrine. German soldiers responded by placing a growing emphasis on mobility and the offensive. That combination would allow the German army to choose the place it wished to concentrate, deal quickly with one adversary, and then shift forces to deter or defeat attacks from other quarters.

These examples illustrate some of the ways geography is believed to have influenced military doctrine. Generally, it is not unreasonable to suggest that states with geographical defensive advantages will react more slowly and less intensively than other states to increases in adversary capability, and will more often stress defensive doctrines. The absence of such barriers should tend to produce the opposite effect. Where geographic factors seem to reward offensive military doctrines, states will be drawn to such doctrines whether or not they have status quo policies, and balancing behavior should tend to be quick and intense.

As illustrated by the case of Germany, more or less force will attach to these propositions depending on the interaction of geographic factors with the distribution of capabilities and the possibilities opened by military technology. Finally, although changes in military technology and the distribution of industrial power do affect the military influence of geographic factors in the long run, certain geographic factors tend to exert some influence on military practice for a very long time indeed. The defensive value of the Swiss mountains is an example already cited. The influence of the English Channel on British doctrine remained strong for almost three hundred years, through the end of World War II. The restricted access to the open oceans that limited Tzarist Russia's military options continues to plague the Soviet ballistic missile submarine force. Water transport, on the whole, remains so much more efficient than land transport that the United States can contemplate conventional war with the Soviet Union in southern Iran, even though the theater of operations in at least ten times as far from the United States as it is from the Soviet Union.

Complicating any theoretical inquiry into the influence of technology on military doctrine is the fact that technology appears sometimes as an independent or intervening variable and sometimes as a dependent variable. Statesmen often seem to treat technology as an immutable factor that intervenes between their raw power and that of their adversaries, influencing the effective military capability that each state can generate. For example, where military technology is perceived to favor the defender, an increase in an adversary's GNP may appear less threatening than it would if military technology were perceived to favor the offense. A technological defensive advantage effectively dilutes the raw power of an expansionist state, while a technological offensive advantage supercharges that power.

On the other hand, some geographical or political factors can make an offensive doctrine (or defensive doctrine) so attractive that a state will go to great lengths to reconcile technology with that preferred doctrine. Inasmuch as raw military technology, like civilian technology, is often quite malleable, and several military technologies may be combined and recombined to produce offensive (or, as the case may be, defensive) advantages where defense (or offense) may have seemed the only feasible option, states may innovate to change apparently immutable technological realities. Whether a single military technology or a combination of military technologies fixes overall advantages in favor of offense or defense is, therefore, often as much a matter of perception as reality. If the advantage to offense or defense in a given instance is real, and if that reality is uncomfortable, actors on the scene may make great efforts to change it, depending on the other pressures that they face. Whether these efforts will prove successful is never clear. As will be shown, for geographical and political reasons German and British statesmen and soldiers in the 1930s successfully intervened to change perceived technological realities. Soviet and American statesmen and soldiers, unhappy with a condition apparently inherent in the nature of nuclear technology—invulnerable retaliatory forces are easy for relatively rich countries to get, and therefore nuclear war is unwinnable—have sustained constant, fairly well-funded efforts to reverse this condition for the last three decades. These efforts have met with failure, but they continue.

Hypotheses—Offense, Deterrence, and Defense

Discussion of individual hypotheses on the causes of offensive, defensive, and deterrent doctrines must be prefaced with a defense of the overarching hypothesis that balance of power theory implies heterogeneity rather than homogeneity on this dimension. I have argued that organization theory suggests that most militaries will prefer the offensive. If balance of power theory also suggested homogeneity on this dimension—the predominance among doctrines of *one* of the three categories—that could make the task of competitive theory testing either simpler or more difficult. The task would be simple if balance of power theory implied that states would prefer defensive doctrines, since we could easily examine a large number of military doctrines and discover if they were usually offensive or usually defensive. On the other hand, if balance of power theory predicted offensive doctrines, then both theories would be predicting the same outcome, and one could hardly test them against each other. In cases where we found offensive doctrines, we would have an "overdetermination" problem—explanation of over 100 percent of the outcome. Of course, in cases where defensive or deterrent doctrines were found, both theories would be discredited. Balance of power theory does not predict homogeneous outcomes, however, although a misreading of the theory might suggest this.

Several students of state behavior whose analyses reflect the balance of power perspective have predicted state policies that would seem to demand offensive doctrines. Hans Morgenthau, John Herz, and to a lesser extent Robert Gilpin predict that states will generally try to expand their power.[57] States will seek not simply equality, but superiority. States are likely to behave this way because power is the key to survival in an anarchical system; since relative power is difficult to measure, the state never knows when it has enough, and it should therefore logically strive for a fairly wide margin of superiority. Basically, these theorists argue, as I have argued, that the security dilemma is always present. Effectively, they also argue, as I have *not*, that the security dilemma is usually quite intense. If this view of the system and its effects on actors were complete, then it would seem logical to deduce that all states will prefer offensive doctrines in order to be ready to expand their power. Because an offensive doctrine may allow the conquest of one's neighbors and the seizure of power assets that lie beyond one's borders, it might appear to be the military option that provides the most security.

This view, however, is not complete. It is *ahistorical* in the most fundamental sense, assuming that states are effectively newborn children, thrust into the jungle of international politics with nothing more than an orientation briefing on the "law of tooth and claw" to guide their actions. Under such conditions the security dilemma might indeed operate with extraordinary intensity. Robert Gilpin, however, admits that states make cost-benefit calculations when deliberating about whether or not to attempt expansion, and that perceptions of cost are affected by the state's historical experience.[58] Of particular importance are the consequences of its own or others' attempts at expansion, and the lessons learned from those episodes. While states, or those who act for them, frequently misread the lessons of history, balance of power theory itself suggests that expanding hegemons will be opposed and stopped. *We have ample his-*

torical evidence that this is the case. This is a lesson that is easy to learn. Indeed, such learning is consistent with Kenneth Waltz's prediction that states will become socialized to the norms of the system that they inhabit.[59] Not all states learn the lesson—not well enough to sustain perpetual peace—but enough learning takes place to make violent, unlimited, expansionist policies the exception rather than the rule. Status quo policies are the rule rather than the exception. France under Louis XIV and Napoleon, Germany under the Kaiser and Hitler, are already too many would-be European hegemons for those who have had to oppose them, but surprisingly few for a three-century game that has often involved as many as six major players.

A status quo policy, of course, need not lead to a defensive military doctrine, but it certainly need not lead to an offensive one either. Instead, status quo powers will assess their political, geographical, and technological positions and possibilities, and devise a military doctrine that preserves their interests at the lowest costs and risks. Thus, an inference from balance of power theory is that military doctrines will be heterogeneous along the dimension of offense-defense-deterrence.

Offense
1. States bent on conquest will prefer offensive military doctrines. This proposition is not deduced from balance of power theory, but rather is a matter of common sense. Louis XIV, Napoleon Bonaparte, and Adolph Hitler all had expansionist foreign policies, and required offensive instruments to pursue those policies.
2. States will try to pass on the costs of war to others. Offensive operations are one way to accomplish this. If war seems to involve high collateral damage, states will try to arrange that the war will be fought on the territory of the enemy, of neutrals, or even of allies. Nicholas Spykman once admonished, "Only in periods of weakness and decline have states fought at home. In periods of vitality and strength, they fight on other people's territory."[60] Of course, not all states have the option of fighting abroad, but those that do tend to avail themselves of it. Michael Handel offers another example: "It is an iron law of the Israeli strategic military doctrine that if a war breaks out, it must be transferred and fought on the opponent's territory as soon as possible."[61] Contrary as it may seem to what is popularly believed, this was a fundamental tenet of French doctrine in the inter-war period. (This is discussed at greater length in chapter 4.)
3. States will support offensive doctrines when power appears to be shifting against them. Offensive doctrines are necessary to fight "pre-

ventive" wars. It also seems probable that in environments where power might rapidly shift, statesmen will want to keep an offensive capability "in the hole." A particularly intense arms race would seem to promote offensive doctrines. (We have already seen how the reverse can be true.) Preventive war is a peculiar sort of balancing behavior. "Because I cannot keep you from catching up I will cut you down now." Israel's cooperation in the Franco-British attack on Egypt in 1956 is explained in part by the fear that Egypt's new claim on the arsenals of the Eastern bloc would give her a permanent arms-race advantage. Hitler preferred an offensive doctrine partly because he believed that he had rearmed more quickly than his putative adversaries, but that they would soon catch up. An offensive doctrine would allow him to prevent this by permitting Germany to strike the Allies before they could remedy their military deficiencies (see chapter 6).

4. Similarly, states without allies, *facing multiple threats*, will be attracted to offensive doctrines. An offensive doctrine allows the state to choose the time and place of battle. If the joint capabilities of the adversaries are superior, offensive doctrines will be particularly attractive. In an offensive move, an isolated state can attack and defeat its adversaries sequentially, minimizing the effect of the imbalance of capabilities. This is a variety of preventive war. Instead of waging one dangerous war against a superior coalition, the offender elects to wage what amounts to a separate war against each of the members of the opposing coalition in turn. An offensive doctrine is thus a method of power balancing.

5. The force of the preceding hypothesis is increased if the geographic factor of encirclement is added. The military history of Prussia and later of Germany reveals a constant affinity for offensive doctrines. This is explained in part by the frequent threats of multifront wars. Israel's offensive doctrine allows her to defeat the Arab states sequentially. It may be that the offensiveness of the Soviet military doctrine—both in the rocket forces and in the ground forces—is partially a response to the existence of hostile states on every border.

6. Statesmen will prefer offensive military doctrines if they lack powerful allies, because such doctrines allow them to manipulate the threat of war with credibility. Offensive doctrines are best for making threats. States can use both the threat of alliance and the threat of military force to aid diplomacy in communicating power and will. In the absence of strong allies, the full burden of this task falls on the state's military capabilities. This was the major characteristic of Hitler's early diplomacy (see chapter 6). It provided the motivation for former Secretary of Defense James Schlesinger's merchandising of

substantial nuclear counterforce capability in the guise of "flexible strategic options." To some extent, this motivation appears to have been behind the offensive aspects of Strategic Air Command doctrine in the 1950s. Military demonstrations and an offensive doctrine are also important elements of Israeli grand strategy.

7. A state need not be politically isolated or geographically encircled to find defensive doctrines unattractive. States with far-flung security dependencies may find it advisable to defend such allies by concentrating offensive, disarming military power, or deterrent, punitive military power, against its adversary (or adversaries) rather than dispersing its scarce military capabilities in futile denial efforts in many places. Such dependencies, like NATO Europe in the 1950s, may be far from the guarantor, close to a major power adversary, and too weak to contribute much to their own defense. The security of such states is difficult to guarantee by defensive/denial means alone. If the United States had had to secure postwar Europe with conventional denial means, there would probably have been a great many more American troops in Europe than there were. The Soviet adversary had to be dissuaded from going to war against U.S. dependencies. The same was true if French allies in eastern Europe were going to be protected during the interwar period.

How is dissuasion to be accomplished if defensive/denial means are ruled out? Only deterrence and offense remain. While the United States has relied mainly on deterrence in the Cold War, offense has also played an important role. Many have argued against reliance on deterrence alone, since the adversary could punish the United States in return for any strike we might deliver. Extended deterrence is difficult because, whereas a state's readiness to inflict punishment on an adversary that aggresses directly against it might be unquestionable, its willingness to punish the same adversary for offenses against far-removed dependencies, and so to draw fresh fire and suffering on itself, is less likely to be credited. The credibility of the commitment is believed to go up with an ability to limit damage to ourselves by disarming the adversary. Herman Kahn, Colin Gray, and Glenn Snyder have suggested this with varying emphasis.[62] The offensive aspects of "massive retaliation" are explained in part by these considerations. To this day, a good deal of the offensiveness of U.S. nuclear doctrine may be explained by the unspoken requirement for a "not implausible," damage-limiting, first-strike capability.

Deterrence

8. Far-flung security dependencies and powerful adversaries can lead a great power to either deterrent or offensive doctrines. Offen-

sive doctrines will be preferred, but often the sheer scope of the problem and the capabilities of the adversary (or adversaries) make offensive capabilities hard to get. Technology and geography are frequently the key determinants of the scope of the problem. Before World War II Britain hoped to hold possessions half a globe away. She lacked the raw capability to project much power such a distance—particularly after ensuring the homeland against more immediate adversaries. Even if she could have mustered the capabilities and mastered the distances, Britain lacked a military technology that could disarm Japan and keep her disarmed. When states face such a situation, they will accept, although they may not embrace, deterrent doctrines.

The political organisms that most often find themselves in this situation seem to be the great empires of history. The British found it advantageous in the 1920s and '30s to police Arabian tribesmen not by pitched battle, but by bombing from the air. They could either obey the rules or be punished.[63] A close examination of British defense policy in the 1930s shows a pronounced inclination toward deterrence. The politicians of the period frequently used the term. Due to economic, industrial, and technological constraints, the actual operations envisioned were more of the denial than the punishment variety. However, dissuasion was the goal, and one finds a constant concern with the manipulation of military capability and potential military capability to discourage aggression. Only with the short-lived commitment to the population bombing doctrine of Bomber Command were any punitive operations planned in the 1930s.

C. W. C. Oman finds a clear example of a deterrent strategy in the Byzantine Empire of the ninth century:

> Much could also be done by delivering a vigorous raid into his (the Saracen's) country and wasting Cilicia and northern Syria the moment his armies were reported to have passed north into Cappadocia. This destructive practice was frequently adopted, and the sight of two armies each ravaging the other's territory without attempting to defend its own was only too familiar to the inhabitants of the borderlands of Christendom and Islam. Incursions by sea supplemented the forays by land.[64]

9. As noted previously, small states threatened by powerful adversaries often make recourse to deterrent doctrines. The peculiar coincidence of doctrines among the very strong and the very weak is easy to explain. In both cases, insufficient capabilities drive states to such doctrines. When a state's capabilities fall short of its aims or needs, it

may throw its political "will" into the balance. Will is as much a product of a state's political cohesion as it is a product of any material source. Thus, whenever states face security threats and are, by reason of the magnitude of the task or their own poverty, short of resources, we can expect to see deterrent doctrines.

Defense

I have argued that coalition formation is a common method both of enhancing perceived power for diplomacy and mustering real power for war. Yet, coalition management has its problems. Napoleon once declared that if he had to make war, he would prefer to make it against a coalition. Alfred Vagts observes, "Of all types of war, this is the one in which it is most likely that political aims will crowd out and repress strategic aims. And even if this is not intended, the other partner or partners will still suspect it, will try to spare their own forces and sacrifice those of the ally."[65]

10. Defensive doctrines, or doctrines with strong defensive elements, will be preferred by statesmen with status quo policies who are preparing to fight in coalitions. Such doctrines give the states in the coalition more time to settle the division of costs and benefits of the war. This phenomenon will be particularly pronounced if the costs of going on the offensive are seen to be high. One paradoxical example is found in Egyptian behavior during the 1973 Arab-Israeli war. Although the Egyptians had mounted a successful offensive to cross the Suez Canal, after crossing they chose a low-risk strategy of staying behind their air and anti-tank defenses. By so doing, they allowed Israel the luxury of concentrating the bulk of her military capability on the dangerous Syrian offensive. Egypt passed on the costs of the war to the Syrians. Egypt only left her defensive positions when frenzied Syrian protests suggested Israel's imminent victory. When Egypt finally attacked, its offensive was shattered. Britain and France were guilty of similar "buck-passing" in the 1930s. In both the Egyptian-Syrian case and the British-French case, the costs of going on the offensive were seen to be high. In the case of the 1914 powers, the cost of the offensive was seen to be low. This explains the less cautious behavior in the earlier period.

11. The preceding hypothesis may be attenuated by another constraint. Although states may seek military doctrines that allow them to pass some of their defense costs onto coalition partners, they must in some measure please these present or potential allies in order to attract them.[66] Thus, alliance suitors may adopt the doctrines of their intended allies. A given military doctrine may fail to achieve both the

goal of buck-passing and the goal of alliance-making, and when it does, a state can face difficult choices. In 1973, Egypt appears to have portrayed her military doctrine one way to achieve Syrian cooperation in the initial attack; operated another to spare her own forces early in the war; and finally shifted back to a strategy more accommodating to the Syrians in the abortive offensive against Israeli forces in the Sinai passes. France in the 1930s, on the other hand, could both attract British support and control her own contribution to any ultimate war effort with a defensive doctrine. Britain did not want any provocation of Germany, and that was fine with France.

12. Status quo states will generally prefer defensive doctrines if geography or technology makes such doctrines attractive. They are more likely to correctly interpret such factors than are non–status quo states, and since their goal is to conserve power, they are more likely to exploit them militarily.

13. Status quo states may prefer defensive doctrines simply because those states know that they are unlikely to strike the first blow. Since they expect to suffer the first blow, it is reasonable for them to expend their military effort learning how to parry it.

Hypotheses—The Causes of Civilian Intervention and Its Effects on Integration and Innovation

I have discussed some causes of the character of military doctrine. Organization theory identifies external intervention as a key source of integration and innovation, but also predicts that such intervention will be very difficult. Balance of power theory predicts that, difficult or not, such intervention will occur if it is necessary to secure the state. If balance of power theory successfully predicts not only intervention, but also the circumstances under which it occurs, then the theory gains in credibility relative to organization theory. Thus, it is important to address the causes of civilian intervention into military matters.

1. Political leaders with aggression in mind will often take a look at their military forces to see if they are ready to go. Hitler was most attentive to his military capabilities and, as we shall see, was a prime mover in the development of Blitzkrieg. This is not so much a proposition deduced from balance of power theory as a matter of common sense. The anarchy of international politics permits mischief. The military value of the object in view may or may not be a motive for mischief. If political leaders contemplate aggression for the purpose of expanding their resources for security, then their intervention can

be loosely explained in terms of structural constraints. Otherwise, we must fall back on avarice and "bloody-mindedness" as an explanation.

For whatever reasons civilian policy-makers choose a path of aggression, soldiers must either carry out the orders of their chiefs or resign. The prospect of war can have a catalytic effect on the behavior of soldiers whose lives or careers will inevitably be put into jeopardy. The final steps to the Blitzkrieg doctrine were taken by the commanders of the Germany Army only late in 1939 and early in 1940, when it became clear that Hitler was committed to an offensive against the Allies.

2. If planned aggression for political ends is one general cause of civilian intervention in military matters, the other is fear. This is consistent with balance of power theory. It is easy for statesmen to become frightened by events in the international environment. Many different kinds of events may threaten the state's security. Just as states "balance" materially by arms-racing or coalition formation, they "balance" qualitatively by taking a close look at the doctrine, competence, and readiness of their military organizations. They do not do so all the time, but when they do, fear is most often the driving force.

3. The same fear increases military organizations' receptivity to outside criticism and also sharpens their own self-critical faculties. The force of this proposition is attenuated in multipolar systems, however, if a given state perceives itself to have alliance possibilities. Under conditions of threat, civilians may divide their energies between chasing allies and reviewing their military posture. This may so reduce the pressure on a given military organization as to allow organizational dynamics to triumph. More specific propositions on this matter can be generated.

4. In the face of any sort of security problem, states without allies will tend to pay a good deal of attention to their military organizations. This is true of states that are politically isolated. Israel is a good current example: military leaders retire to become key political leaders, and politicians are generally well versed in military matters. This sort of attention is also characteristic of both poles in a bipolar system. Since the dawn of the Cold War American leaders have paid more attention to military matters than in any prior period of our history.

Examples of military innovation caused by civilian intervention and stimulated by political isolation are the development of the standing army in France under Louis XIV and the mass army during the French Revolution. Recall the important role played by Cardinal

Richelieu and the civilian war minister Michel Le Tellier in the development of France's first all-professional, standing army. What had driven France in this direction? Historian Michael Howard writes, "On the death of Gustavus, . . . Richelieu saw himself faced with the necessity of improvising an army and entering the field himself if Habsburg power, Spanish and Austrian, was not to become dominant in Europe."[67] Le Tellier's son, the Marquis de Louvois, completed his father's work, creating the army with which Louis XIV waged war on nearly all of Europe.[68]

The case of Revolutionary France is similar. The Directory had accumulated six major adversaries, and by August 23, 1793, the danger had become so great that the Committee on Public Safety ordered universal conscription for the first time in any modern European state. By the following summer, the French army fielded three-quarters of a million men, the largest armed force in Europe since the barbarian invasions.[69] The Committee did not simply invent the mass army. Lazare Carnot, a former military professional and a man with new ideas about military organizations and tactics, had joined the Revolution. It was his hand that guided French military innovation.

While political isolation provides an added spur to civilian intervention, even states with alliance possibilities show tendencies to civilian intervention in the face of new or growing threats. The best example of this is found in British behavior in 1934–1940. The rising military power of Germany brought not only a return to substantial defense spending, but greater civilian attention to the plans of the military. In spite of a military organization committed to an offensive doctrine, civilians intervened to promote a major defensive innovation—the development of the country's integrated air defense system, the first of its kind in history (see chapter 5). While the RAF did not wholeheartedly embrace air defense, and jealously guarded Bomber Command, that organization's support for air defense increased as the possibility of war loomed larger.

5. Disasters fresh in a state's memory are great promoters of civilian intervention, even if no immediate threat appears on the horizon. (This proposition and those that follow have their counterparts at the organizational level.) If a threat is apparent, the tendency will be more pronounced. The most recent example is the apparently very thorough review by Israel's Agranat Commission of all the events leading up to and including the 1973 war. While the Commission included two former chiefs of staff, the chairman and the other two members were civilians. Most of the report remains secret, but it is

known to have generated wide-ranging reform in Israel's armed forces.[70]

Another example is found in the case of Prussia. Between October 7 and November 7, 1806, Napoleon Bonaparte completely destroyed the armies of the heirs of Frederick the Great. The "army with a country" was swept aside by the superior numbers and methods of the French. Following this disaster, both civilian and military reformers came to the fore. Before the war, reforms of either bureaucracy or army were practically impossible. After the war, under the leadership of the soldiers Gerhard Scharnhorst and Count August Gneisenau, a commission was set up to reform the army. Opposition was not wanting, and in fact was suppressed only by the direct intervention of the king, who removed the opponents of reform from the commission.[71]

6. Some civilian intervention is produced not by disaster but by the high costs expected of a particular military exercise. A victorious but very costly war can substantially weaken a state. Even in the context of a superiority that provided some damage-limiting capability, U.S. civilian policy-makers in the 1950s watched their nuclear forces more closely than they had ever watched military forces before. Though the United States might have "prevailed" in a nuclear conflict, the game was not likely to be worth the candle. (Another example of this sort of behavior is seen in interwar France—see chapter 6.)

The experience or expectation of military disaster provides a key avenue by which technology can influence military doctrine. Civilians especially are moved to interpret new technology and integrate such interpretations into military doctrine when the technology presents some very clear and unambiguous threat to the state's survival. The threat may be of defeat or the probability of high collateral damage. Civilian intervention is unlikely unless demonstration of the technology, by test or combat-use, is sufficiently stark and frightening to shake civilians' faith in the ability of their own military organizations to handle it. The attitudes of French civilians to any chance of a replay of World War I, British civilians to the spectre of bombs falling on London, and American civilians to nuclear weapons are all good examples. Even here, though, the impact of technology is not determinative. In the French case technology was seen to be largely immutable, a force to be accepted and dealt with. In the British case, technology was seen as something to be changed.

Simple fear of defeat provides another motivation for civilian intervention. If an adversary appears particularly impressive, potentially capable of a decisive victory, civilians will pay considerable attention to their military instrument. The intervention of British civilians into the doctrine of the RAF, for instance, was driven by fear of the German "knock-out-blow-from-the-air" (see chapter 5).

Summary: Balance of Power Theory Hypotheses

Offense, Defense, and Deterrence

In general, the theory predicts heterogeneity along the dimension offense-defense-deterrence.

1. Expansionist powers will prefer offensive doctrines.

2. States will prefer offensive doctrines when war appears to involve very high collateral damage, because offense allows the state to take the war somewhere else.

3. States with a favorable power position that is suffering erosion will prefer offensive doctrines. (Offensive doctrines are a vehicle for preventive war.)

4. States that face several adversaries may prefer offensive doctrines. (Again, offensive doctrines are the vehicle for preventive war.)

5. Similarly, geographically encircled states may prefer offensive doctrines.

6. States without allies will prefer offensive doctrines because they must exploit military power for diplomacy, a purpose best served by offensive capabilities.

7. States with widely distributed security dependencies will prefer offensive doctrines because they allow the concentration of scarce military assets.

8. States with far-flung security dependencies will accept deterrent doctrines when it is not feasible to sustain offensive or defensive doctrines. Deterrent doctrines are a vehicle for throwing political will into the military balance.

9. Similarly, small states may opt for deterrent doctrines because their capabilities are insufficient to support any other kind.

10. The possibility of coalition warfare can lead a state to a defensive doctrine because such doctrines permit a pace of warfare that allows allies to settle the division of the risks, costs, and benefits of war.

11. States preparing to fight in coalitions must also please their prospective coalition partners. This dilutes the power of proposition 10. If, for its own special reasons, a state adopts an offensive doctrine, its suitors may find it necessary to conform. By the same token, however, conformity to a defensive doctrine is likely if the state being wooed adopts a defensive doctrine.

12. Status quo states will generally prefer defensive doctrines if geography or technology makes such doctrines attractive.

13. Status quo states may prefer defensive doctrines simply because they know that they are unlikely to strike first.

Integration and Innovation

1. Statesmen contemplating aggression will tend to intervene in their military organizations.

2. Generally, anything that increases the perceived threat to state security is a cause of civilian intervention in military matters and hence a possible cause of integration and innovation.

3. Soldiers themselves tend to be more amenable to external prodding when the threat of war looms larger.

4. In states that are either politically isolated or geographically surrounded, civilians tend to intervene in military matters more frequently, and soldiers tend to approach war more seriously than in states with more favorable security conditions. Thus, both integration and innovation should be more frequent in such states.

5. Recent military disasters can be causes of integration and innovation.

6. Anticipated high costs of warfare can be a cause of civilian intervention. Because new technology (e.g., nuclear weapons) can greatly affect anticipated costs, this is one way technology can exert an influence on integration and innovation.

All of the preceding possible causes can be weakened in multipolar systems, where allies appear to be easy to come by. States and statesmen may spend too much time chasing allies, and not enough time auditing their war machines.

SUMMARY

In this chapter I have offered brief surveys of organization theory and balance of power theory, and from these theories I have inferred hypotheses about what causes military doctrine to vary along the dimensions offense-defense-deterrence, innovation-stagnation, and integration-disintegration. I have integrated with these hypotheses a small group of propositions that concern the influence of technology and geography upon military doctrine. Most of these propositions are consistent with one or the other of the two theories introduced.

As argued in the opening pages of this chapter, these are structural theories. They are appropriate for the examination of the cases that follow. These theories will be used in combination to explain the military doctrines of France, Britain, and Germany. Because in some of the cases contradictory hypotheses about doctrine are generated by the two theories, a comparison of these military doctrines allows us to examine and weigh the explanatory power of each theory.

In the broadest sense military doctrine should, according to *organization theory*, show a tendency to be offensive, disintegrated, and stagnant. This is suggested both by the character of military organizations and by their functional separation from the political decision-makers of the state. *Balance of power theory* predicts somewhat different outcomes, depending on the state's situation. In general, anything that makes the civilian leaders of a state more fearful should encourage political-military integration and operational innovation. Civilian preferences for offense, defense, or deterrence will be influenced by the international environment. Finally, if the two theories introduced here have any validity at all, we should find that *technology* and *geography* are rarely determinative in their own right, although they should often have an important effect on doctrine.

Under what conditions will organization theory enjoy its greatest explanatory power? Under what conditions will the international environment have the greatest influence? In times of relative international calm we should expect a high degree of organizational determinism. In times of threat we should see greater accommodation of doctrine to the international system—integration should be more pronounced, innovation more likely. Among states, doctrines should show more heterogeneity. However, even under such circumstances all will not necessarily be well. Multipolar structures, although they exert an important influence on doctrine, may so confuse decision-makers as to allow organizational determinants to come to the fore once again. The effects can be disastrous.

[3]

The Battles of 1940

Two great battles were fought in 1940. During May, in Belgium and northern France, Germany destroyed the cream of French and British land forces, so opening metropolitan France to complete conquest. The second battle, the Battle of Britain, was fought between the Luftwaffe and the Royal Air Force (RAF) from mid-July to late September 1940. While Hitler's objectives and strategy in this second battle seem to have fluctuated, Germany's fundamental goal was to destroy the RAF and seize control of the airspace over southern England and the English Channel. This was seen to be the necessary prerequisite for any successful invasion of Britain. Some historians doubt the strength of Hitler's commitment to such a course. However, the effort expended in the air battle itself, as well as the substantial ancillary efforts to prepare an invasion force, indicate that an invasion might have been attempted had Germany won the air battle.[1] The Luftwaffe was not successful, and Hitler turned his attention to the Soviet Union, a continental power more vulnerable to the Wehrmacht's specialty—coordinated air/ground operations.

These were important battles. Hitler's defeat of France brought Germany industrial, financial, and geographical advantages guaranteeing that whoever opposed past and future German expansion would have a rough time. World War II would be a long war. The Battle of Britain guaranteed that past and future German expansion would be opposed, and preserved the possibility of a future assault on the German homeland. Had Britain collapsed, one wonders if such an assault would ever have taken place. The resources freed might just have tipped the scales in Germany's favor in a future war with the Soviet Union.

Historians have offered many explanations for the outcomes of these two battles. Social, political, technological, and military explanations can be found. However, I would argue that each battle was won by the side that had prepared for it. For years Germany had directed her industrial and military resources toward fighting short, decisive wars of aggression against those immediate neighbors who had most profited from her 1918 defeat, and who would most oppose a resurgence of her military power. France, expecting this resurgence, had planned a careful, initially defensive war that would allow her the time to coax maximum military contributions from former World War I Allies, particularly Britain. Because the Germans both outnumbered and out-produced the French, it was believed that no offensive against Germany could be mounted without Allied help. Without such help, the prospects for success would be low, and the costs high. For reasons that still remain unclear, France adopted a war plan that eroded her ability to fight the careful, initially defensive war for which her soldiers had planned and trained since 1918.

Britain, having hoped to avoid participation in future continental land conflicts, found herself committing a small, undertrained, and inadequately equipped expeditionary force to a campaign for which it had not prepared, but which nonetheless suddenly seemed to be essential to British security. On the other hand, two months later, the RAF found itself fighting a battle that British statesmen, and to a lesser extent British soldiers, had both feared and prepared for since 1934.

These battles, and the manner in which they were fought, are matters of military doctrine. Before summarizing and explaining the peculiarities of French, German, and British doctrine, however (the subject of chapters 4–6), I will examine the two battles of 1940 in greater detail to highlight the ultimate impact of these peculiarities.

THE BATTLE OF FRANCE

The Forces

There is substantial agreement that the German victory cannot be explained by superiority in numbers of men, in numbers of major combat formations (divisions), in quantities of heavy equipment (tanks, guns, etc.), or in the quality of that equipment.[2] (See table 2.)

As Table 2 shows, Germany and the Allies fielded roughly equal numbers of major formations. Infantry divisions, both walking and motorized, were very similar on both sides—15,000 or so men, 70 or 80 artillery pieces, 40 or 50 anti-tank guns, dozens of mortars, and hundreds of machine guns. Armored divisions, as will be seen later,

Table 2. German and Allied Forces Available in the Battle of France, Phase 1

Resource	Germany	Allied Coalition
Men	2.5 million	3 million
Divisions:		
Armored	10	6
Motorized Infantry	7	8
Infantry	117	108
Other	2 (1 airborne, 1 horse cavalry)	11 (fully or partially motorized cavalry)
Total	136	133*
Equipment		
Tanks	2,700	3,000 (Fr. and Br.)
Guns (Artillery)	7,710	12,200 (11,200 Fr., 1,000 Br.)
Anti-Tank Guns	12,800	8,050 (7,200 Fr., 850 Br.)
Anti-Aircraft Guns:		
Medium and Heavy	9,300	3,800 (plus 850 miscellaneous
Light	no data	2,300 Br.)

*103 French, 9 British, and miscellaneous Belgian, Dutch, and Polish.
Sources: Few accounts of the Battle of France offer comprehensive order of battle data. This table was assembled from the following sources: R. Ernest Dupuy and Trevor N. Dupuy, *The Encyclopedia of Military History* (New York: Harper and Row, 1977), pp. 1057–1058; Colonel A. Goutard, *The Battle of France, 1940*, trans. Captain A. R. P. Burgess (New York: Ives Washburn, 1959), pp. 21–31, 37, 39–40; Jeffrey A. Gunsburg, *Divided and Conquered: The French High Command and The Defeat of the West, 1940* (Westport, Conn.: Greenwood Press, 1979); Roger Parkinson, *Dawn on our Darkness: The Summer of 1940* (London: Granada, 1977), p. 5; R. H. S. Stolfi, "Equipment for Victory in France," *History* 52 (February 1970): 1–20.

differed markedly. The German Panzer division was the largest and most effective armored formation of the period.[3]

Generally, quantitative and qualitative advantages in ground weaponry were offsetting between the two sides. Allied artillery outnumbered that of Germany, and since it included a much greater proportion of large-caliber, heavy guns, should probably be credited with qualitative superiority. It is true, however, that much Allied artillery dated from World War I, while the German guns were fairly new. German anti-aircraft artillery was quantitatively and qualitatively superior to that of the Allies. The numbers for engaged anti-aircraft artillery are probably the least reliable numbers in table 2. This is particularly unfortunate since the Germans also employed these guns for direct-fire ground missions against tanks and bunkers, a role for which they were highly effective—especially the famed 88 mm gun. Germany enjoyed an advantage in numbers of anti-tank guns, but French guns were probably better able to pierce German armor than German guns the French armor. The Allies enjoyed an advantage in numbers of tanks, armor thickness, and gun caliber. German tanks enjoyed offsetting advantages in communications gear and optics. They averaged larger crews and larger fuel tanks.

Although the statistics on air forces involved in the battle are less clear, they tend to show an Allied inferiority in engaged aircraft that may help to explain Allied reverses. It appears that the French and British air forces engaged were outnumbered by two to one. German aircraft were, on the whole, somewhat superior to their enemy counterparts. These facts do not tell the whole story, however. Mysteriously, a large number of combat aircraft—perhaps 1,500—were scattered around France unused.[4] Six hundred may have been in combat units.[5] Equally mysterious is the relatively small number of British aircraft committed to the battle, some 400 out of a total of 1,800 combat aircraft in the RAF.[6] Especially odd is the limited contribution made by some 300 or more medium and heavy bombers based in Britain, but well within range of the battle; while all of these bombers were used, it does not appear that they were used very well. Bomber Command scattered its attacks against a multiplicity of "quasi-strategic" targets, most of them too far in the German rear to affect the battle in the Low Countries and northern France.[7]

Bombers aside, in the critical single-seat fighter category the disparity between the two sides—roughly four to three—was much less than the overall force ratio would suggest. Facing such odds, admittedly under different circumstances, the RAF Fighter Command was to do a creditable job during the Battle of Britain. In short, while the Allied air forces did face an adversary that flew slightly superior machines, the quantitative imbalance seems to have been partially of their own making.[8]

Table 3. German and Allied Aircraft Engaged in the Battle of France, Phase 1

	Germany	Allies (Fr. + Br.)
Single-Seat Fighters	850	635
Multi-Seat Fighters	200	100
Dive Bombers	280	49
Light Bombers	0	45
Medium Bombers	1,100	414
Reconnaissance	500	300–400

SOURCES: Goutard, *Battle of France*, pp. 31–36; Gunsburg, *Divided*, 1:269–271.

Neither an inequality of ground forces nor one of air forces provides a sufficient explanation for the Allied defeat. Rather, those forces were in sufficient equilibrium that one is immediately drawn to doctrinal and strategic explanations for the battle's outcome.

Military Doctrine

Military historians have come to believe that some combination of doctrine and operational plans best explains the Allied defeat. Few credit the once popular explanations based on German quantitative superiority. Explanations based on the failure of French morale have also become somewhat less popular.[9]

It is important to note that the German war plan reflected and improved upon existing German military doctrine. The French war plan deviated in important ways from French military doctrine—at least from that doctrine's implications for the first phase of any great war. The French Army (as well as the British) was thrust into a type of engagement for which it was not prepared. The French gave up the opportunity to fight the war for which they had planned, and allowed themselves to be drawn into the type of war that they knew the Germans sought. Although historians agree that General Gamelin's war plan—Plan D and its "Breda variant"—was instrumental in the Allied defeat, they have not adequately explained its origin. Nor has its weight in explaining the French defeat been assessed. Although this book does not settle the latter question, it will be argued that some of the same factors that explain the nature of French doctrine may paradoxically explain the peculiarities of the French war plan in 1940. Less paradoxically, the same is true in the case of Germany.

While the conventional caricature of French doctrine as backward-looking—mired in the mud, trenches, and massed artillery barrages of World War I—is exaggerated, it is fair to say that the French were *much* more conservative in their approach to changes in air, armor, and communications technology than were the Germans.[10] Although the French armed forces had acquired these new technologies, and even created some new organizations and plans to use them, the doctrine, training, and command style tended to favor slow-paced, conservative operations.[11] The stress was on firepower over movement, defense over offense, and "tactical security" over risk. Concerning the latter, commanders were taught to minimize risks rather than take risks to exploit opportunities. Of particular importance was the avoidance of "encounter battles." Today called "meeting engagements," these battles take place unexpectedly, between forces on the move. They are fought from unprepared positions and occur frequently in mechanized warfare. They are risky, violent, and often costly. The French and British shunned such engagements and knew that the Germans had mastered them.

French Air Force cooperation with the French Army was more limited than Luftwaffe cooperation with the German Army. It does not appear that the French Air Force was well integrated with the French ground forces, although they were more or less subordinate to army command. All could agree that fighters were necessary to keep enemy bombers away from army formations and lines of supply. There was some thought and planning for cooperation between bombers and ground forces, but by May 10, 1940, few bombers appropriate to the task had been built, and no system for air-ground cooperation had been developed.[12]

German military doctrine was quite different from French and British doctrine. Unlike the French, who had given up most of their pre–World War I offensive proclivities, the Germans had reaffirmed their historical commitment to the offensive. Moreover, by a laborious and uncertain process, Germany had created and deployed a new operational arm—the Panzer divisions. Additionally, by 1940 elements within the German Army had created (though the army had not yet fully adopted) a new doctrine—Blitzkrieg. For the Blitzkrieg advocates, fast-paced air-armor combinations would now aim more to "unravel" an enemy army than to destroy it. The doctrine stressed mobility and speed over firepower, although in the form of the tank, the dive bomber, and the high-velocity anti-tank or anti-aircraft gun it aimed for great firepower at decisive points. Blitzkrieg welcomed encounter battles. It employed concentrated air power offensively and defensively, to prepare the way for advancing armor. Like German doctrine at the end of World War I, Blitzkrieg stressed infiltration tactics and flanking movements for both infantry and armor. As in the classic pre–World War I German doctrine, the new doctrine sought single and double envelopments. Unlike the earlier doctrine, it aimed as much at the disorientation and dislocation of the enemy command system as it did at the annihilation of enemy forces. This was to be achieved by deep penetrations into the rear areas of an enemy army. It was believed that if dislocation could be achieved, the battle of annihilation might be avoided, or at least easier.[13]

War Plans[14]

Because of the difficulties that the Germans would encounter in an operation through Switzerland, and the strength of the Maginot Line, it had long been believed by the French that any German attack on France would have to move through Belgium. Indeed, the Maginot Line was built to encourage such an event (see chapter 4). From September 1939 to May 1940 the war plans of both sides for Belgium shifted. France started out with a war plan that reflected her military doctrine and capabilities, and shifted to one that did not. Germany started out with a war plan that did not reflect either her classical military doctrine or the new Blitzkrieg doctrine, and that did not fully exploit the new German Panzer arm. Unfortunately for the Allies, the Germans shifted to one that did.

In the fall of 1939 the French Plan E (Escaut) called for an advance to a defense line on the River Escaut in Belgium. The Escaut roughly parallels the Belgian coast, about 100–150 km inland, from the French interior to Antwerp. This would not have been a difficult move for the French and British armies on the Franco-Belgian border. It would probably have allowed ample time for the preparation of fortified positions. It was a conservative strategy which put little stress on the defensive doctrine of Britain and France, and ameliorated the command and control problems that afflict coalition warfare. The plan was fairly consistent with French military doctrine of the previous twenty years, which had aimed at fighting an initially low-cost battle, in Belgium, with British help. This would keep the war away from much of France's border industrial region. On balance, Plan E was well suited to French military doctrine and military capabilities.

The German war plan of 1939 was a pale imitation of the German war plan of 1914. It was similar in that it concentrated the bulk of its formations, including Panzer and motorized divisions, on the German right—in central and northern Belgium. It differed in that it called for the conquest of Holland, and it did not hold out any hope for a decisive operational victory. The Low Countries would be conquered, the Dutch and Belgian armies destroyed, and some French and British troops killed. Germany might acquire some industrial and geographical assets useful for an attrition war. Had this plan run into Plan E, it is doubtful that the Germans would have destroyed the cream of the French and British armies. The Escaut Line might have held. The ultimate major battle necessary for German conquest of France might have occurred under vastly different circumstances than it did. The Allies could have caught up with the German lead in combat experience. Combined British and French industrial mobilization for war, probably equal to or greater than Germany's in the spring of 1940, might have generated (at least temporarily) an across-the-board Allied materiel superiority.

Due to bad weather, widespread dissatisfaction with the first plan in the army leadership, and Hitler's own uncertainty, the German offensive did not materialize in 1939. Gradually, the original war plan, which had been hastily contrived after the Polish victory, was abandoned. General Erich von Manstein, chief of staff to Army Group A (the weaker and southernmost of the two army groups aimed at Belgium), opposed the original plan from the first. He believed that it held no hope for a decisive victory and guaranteed an attrition war that Germany could not win.

From the end of October 1939, Manstein and his chief, General Gerd von Rundstedt, pressed an alternative plan on German Army headquarters. This plan, ultimately implemented, called for a reconcentration of German armored forces away from northern Belgium and Holland (Army Group B) and toward southern Belgium and northern France (Army Group A). This armored concentration would attempt to breach the Ardennes, cross the Meuse, and dash for the channel, cutting behind the large Allied formations that the Germans were convinced would enter Belgium. To make sure, the Germans would do everything possible to create the impression that the main effort was still on their right, and to obscure their attack on the left. The Allied forces would be cut off in Belgium and annihilated.

As Manstein promoted his plan, others were coming to similar conclusions. Hitler is said to have been "instinctively" drawn to some sort of a major armored thrust similar to Manstein's, long before learning of the soldier's plan. At the same time, the Army High Command (OKH) seems to have paid more attention to Manstein's plan. Hitler's intuition, support, and intervention converged with OKH's grudging agreement in mid-February. On February 20 Manstein's plan was codified in the Operations Order for the assault on France and the Low Countries.[15]

This new plan capitalized on all the traditional strengths of the German General Staff in mobile warfare. It embodied that organization's classical commitment to encirclement battles of annihilation. More important, it exploited the German Army's new mechanized warfare capability to achieve a deep penetration into the Allied rear areas. Germany's Panzer forces, supported by the Luftwaffe, would be unleashed in the kind of daring, unexpected, rapid operation envisioned for over a decade by their creator, General Heinz Guderian. Guderian himself would lead the key Panzer corps of the operation.

As the Germans altered their operational plan to one that would better suit their skills and capabilities, the French changed their plans in an ever more adventurous direction. These changes would draw

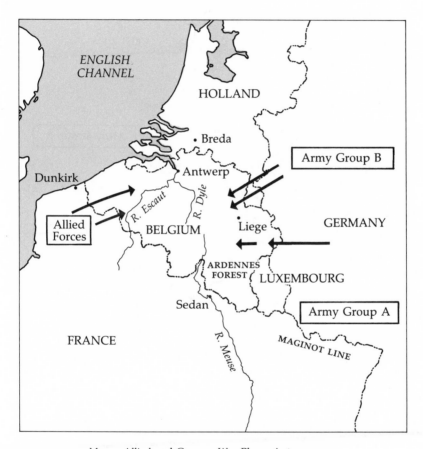

Map 1. Allied and German War Plans, Autumn 1939

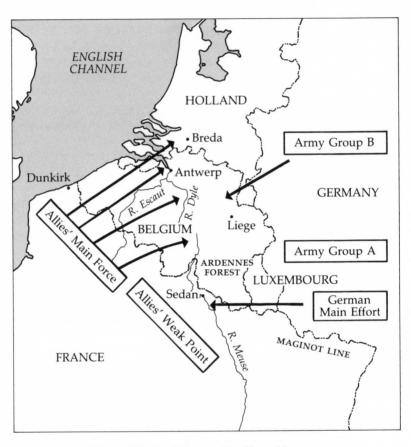

Map 2. Allied and German War Plans, May 1940

her army and her allies' armies into operations for which they were ill prepared, and would greatly accentuate the command, control, and coordination problems normally associated with coalition warfare.[16] These problems were complicated by the refusal of the Belgians and Dutch to concert war plans with the British and French before a German attack. Belgium and Holland justifiably feared that such co-operation would erode the neutral status that they claimed and somewhat naively hoped to preserve. This also meant that French and British units could not enter Belgium to prepare defensive positions until the German attack was under way. France and Britain depended on the Belgians to do so, but the Belgians did a poor job.[17]

As noted above, Plan E put relatively little strain on officers and men trained for slow-moving, defensive warfare. Its successor, Plan D (Dyle), called for an advance by the British Expeditionary Force and the bulk of the remaining French mechanized and motorized formations to a line much farther forward, running along the Dyle River (northern and central Belgium), across the Gembloux Gap (between the Dyle and the Belgian Meuse), and then along the Belgian Meuse down to northeastern France. This advance tacked almost 100 km onto the distance that some of the Allied formations would have to travel, increasing the probability of encounter battles and reducing the time available to prepare defensive positions.

For reasons that have never been adequately explained, General Maurice Gamelin, commander in chief of the French armed forces, almost single-handedly pressed for and settled on the even more daring Breda variant to the Dyle Plan. This committed a substantial portion of French mobile forces, equivalent to two motorized infantry divisions and two mechanized (armored) divisions, plus three high-quality marching infantry divisions, to an advance into southern Holland (to Breda). These forces, perhaps two-thirds of which had originally been part of the Allied central reserve (held to cope with unexpected contingencies), were to be sorely missed later in the campaign.

Although the northern and central parts of the front were to be held by first-class formations, the hinge of the Allied advance in the area of Sedan and the Ardennes forest was held by General Corap's weak Ninth Army. It comprised only seven infantry divisions and two light cavalry divisions. Of the seven infantry divisions, two were underequipped and undertrained Series B formations of elderly reservists, one was a barely mobile fortress division, one was a first-class motorized infantry division, and the other three were good-quality marching infantry. The cavalry divisions each contained a brigade of horse cavalry and a light mechanized brigade. (This is but one example of the French habit of parceling out scarce motorized assets across the front, in contrast to the German habit of concentration.) The Ninth Army and its southern neighbor, the five-division Second Army, were both rather weak formations. French soldiers have explained this deployment in two ways. First, the Ardennes was believed by some to be impassable for large forces, particularly mechanized forces.[18] Second, it was believed that this area could easily be reinforced by the French reserve. This reserve was, however, denuded by implementation of the Breda variant and other ill-advised decisions. In retrospect, the French reasoning seems strikingly faulty, because we now know of substantial intelligence available to Gamelin that suggested German reinforcement of Army Group A in accordance with the Manstein Plan.[19] Gamelin not only failed to take precautions to reinforce this area, he stripped his operational reserve for the southern Holland adventure. Having done so, he compounded his error by failing to restore the reserve with high-quality formations that were—again for some unknown reason—held behind the Maginot Line.

Plan D and the Breda variant included two major flaws. First, they stretched, if they did not violate, the fundamental tenet of French interwar doctrine—avoid encounter battles.[20] This lapse was challenged at the time, but the risk apparently was perceived to be worth the possible benefits. Paul Reynaud, then premier of France, opposed the advance, and was on the verge of relieving Gamelin just as the war commenced. Although the history is a bit vague, many of the French troops did not have quite enough time to dig in before coming into contact with the Germans. This appears to have been particularly important in the Belgian sector of the Ninth Army, whose southern wing on the French side of the border bore the brunt of the German breakthrough effort. It is true, of course, that since this sector was in France, the French army had had plenty of time to prepare fortifications. These were not fully completed, however, because of the prevailing French view that large German forces could not pass through the Ardennes Forest. The combination of lack of time in the north and insufficient effort in the south left the Ninth Army highly vulnerable to the concentrated striking power of the seven Panzer divisions that it and the neighboring Second Army ultimately had to meet.

Second, the Breda variant stretched, if it did not violate, a fundamental, commonsense "rule of war": maintain a strategic reserve force against unexpected contingencies. Plan E and Plan D maintained such a reserve; the Breda variant did not. Commanders on the

scene protested this lapse, but only weak efforts were made to reconstitute the reserve.[21]

Plan D apparently included sufficient perceived advantages to disarm the ill-organized internal opposition. Some advantages may have
appealed mainly to the soldiers. The plan offered the Allies greater
defensive depth. It provided a shorter front. Although the armies
would have a longer advance, the shorter front would either allow for
a more dense defense or it would free additional formations for the
operational reserve. The Breda variant undid both of these advantages. However, although Plan D was agreed to in November, the
Breda variant was not ordered until March. Hence, the opposition to
the plan was temporarily disarmed.

Other benefits of the plan may have appealed to soldiers and
statesmen alike. The farther the Allies advanced, the greater was the
possibility of linking up with the retreating Belgians and possibly the
retreating Dutch. While these two armies were certainly less well
trained and equipped than the British and French, they amounted to
almost a million men. Considering the costly attrition war envisioned
and the perceived manpower advantage of the Germans, it was hard
to abandon such resources. Similarly, the Dyle advance offered some
additional Belgian industrial resources and raw materials for the war,
and further removed the battle from French border industrial regions.
It also brought the Allies closer to Germany—facilitating the ultimate
1918-style offensive against Germany that many expected.[22] These
calculations must have appealed to all parties involved. Additionally,
British leaders may have been attracted to the scheme out of their
traditional concern for the security of the Low Countries. The French
may have believed that the British would commit more resources to
the war if Belgium and Holland were being protected. Finally, there
may have been just a touch of political-military embarrassment involved in the new Anglo-French daring. They had watched Hitler
bully, bluff, and battle his way into five independent countries—
Austria, Czechoslovakia, Poland, Denmark, and Norway. It may be
that Allied political and military leadership were moved by some
residual sense of "Great Power" pride or prestige to rescue two weak
neutrals.

In sum, the Allied strategy became more daring, thrusting ever-
increasing numbers of high-quality formations farther and farther
into Holland and Belgium and weakening the operational reserve. At
the same time, this reserve was not reinforced by formations with-
drawn from the Maginot Line. (Such action was apparently dis-

[93]

cussed, but not implemented.) The Germans simultaneously strengthened their left, opposite the Franco-Belgian border. With intelligence that revealed the Allied plan, the Germans saw that the cream of the Allied forces could be drawn deep into Belgium; cut off from their rear by powerful, fast-moving, mechanized formations; and surrounded and destroyed.[23] The German right wing (Army Group B) would do everything possible to convince the French that the main effort was in the north and to divert French attention from the critical attack out of the Ardennes.[24] This is what occurred in May 1940.

THE BATTLE OF BRITAIN

The most notable of the great differences between the Battle of France and the Battle of Britain is that in the later case neither side's forces were destroyed as were those of the Allies in Belgium. When Hitler called off his plans for Sea-Lion, the amphibious assault on Britain, both sides were still capable of combat operations. The Germans had simply been persuaded by the resistance of the RAF Fighter Command that further attempts to gain sufficient control over British airspace to allow a seaborne invasion were likely to be both costly and unsuccessful.

The Forces

How had the British achieved this outcome? As with the Battle of France, numbers cannot by themselves provide a sufficient explanation. The British were outnumbered in frontline aircraft, though not overwhelmingly. In the summer of 1940, the RAF had about 2,913 aircraft of all kinds, the Luftwaffe 4,549. Of course, not all of these were engaged in the battle. Table 4 presents a count of aircraft available for combat in the battle as of mid-July 1940.

Single-engine, single-seat fighters were the key elements of both forces. This was less apparent in the beginning to the Germans than to the British; moreover, British operational strength in August and September sometimes exceeded 600 Hurricanes and Spitfires, and seldom dropped below 575, whereas German fighter strength probably declined a little in the course of the battle. While the British were producing close to 500 fighters per month during the battle, it is unlikely that German production of Bf 109s exceeded 200 per month. Although I have included British bomber strength in table 4, most

Table 4. German and British Combat Aircraft Available in the Battle of Britain, July 1940

Aircraft	Germany	Britain
Single-Engine Single-Seat Fighters	656[a] (Bf 109)	500[a] (Hurricane & Spitfire)
Other Fighters	202[a] (Bf 110 2-eng.)	80–85[a] (2-engine Blenheim, 1-engine Defiant, night fighters)
Dive Bombers	248[a] (Stuka)	0
Medium Bombers	864[a] (various)	300[b] (Blenheim)
Heavy Bombers	0	400[b] (various)

[a]Operational aircraft, combat-ready.
[b]Total number, some of which were not combat-ready.
SOURCES: Len Deighton, *Fighter: The True Story of the Battle of Britain* (London: Jonathan Cape, 1977), p. 151; Parkinson, *Dawn*, pp. 27, 29–211.

historians agree that they played a small part in the battle—attacking German invasion shipping as it was collected. They might have done more but for Bomber Command's doctrinal preferences. The RAF commanders preferred to send their bombers against industrial targets in Germany.

To summarize the quantitative balance, between 550 and 650 British fighters had to deal with some 1,700 German fighters and bombers. In the early phase of the battle, the approximately 520 Stukas also played a role. While the combat interaction between a defending force of fighters and a combined offensive force of fighters and bombers is complex, it is fair to say that the British were somewhat outnumbered. British success certainly cannot be explained by the quantitative balance.

In terms of aircraft quality, most students of the battle agree that the Spitfire and the Bf 109 were the best aircraft, and evenly matched. Hurricanes were somewhat inferior. Bf 110s were the least capable of all the day fighters. In terms of sheer weapons quality, the Germans may have had a slight edge, since the number of Spitfires in Fighter Command seldom exceeded 250 and was often closer to 200.

Doctrine

As in the Battle of France, quantity and quality of weapons alone do not explain outcomes. Any attempt at explanation must include consideration of military doctrine and organization.

As noted in the discussion of the Battle of France, the Luftwaffe had specialized in direct cooperation with the German Army.[25] It was

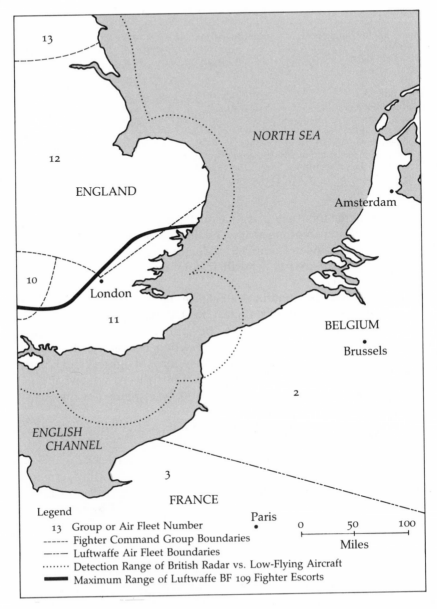

13   12   NORTH SEA

ENGLAND   Amsterdam

10   London   11   BELGIUM

Brussels

2

ENGLISH
CHANNEL

3

FRANCE

Legend   Paris

13   Group or Air Fleet Number   0   50   100
------ Fighter Command Group Boundaries
– – – Luftwaffe Air Fleet Boundaries   Miles
········· Detection Range of British Radar vs. Low-Flying Aircraft
▬▬ Maximum Range of Luftwaffe BF 109 Fighter Escorts

Map 3. The Battle of Britain, Summer 1940

a balanced force of fighters, dive bombers, twin-engined medium bombers, reconnaissance aircraft, and transports that aimed to create the conditions for successful ground operations. German ground forces were oriented toward rapid operations with early decisions. So was the Luftwaffe. It had to seize control of the air over selected areas of the battlefield for limited periods. In military parlance, the task demanded "shock power" rather than staying power. Thus, the Luftwaffe emerged in 1940 as a force capable of high-intensity operations for short periods. It was mainly a "frontline" air force, with few aircraft in reserve. Even the successful Battle of France weakened the strength of some units by 50 percent in a matter of weeks.[26]

Because the Luftwaffe was designed for support of land campaigns, its aircraft had limited range and payload. They were meant to sortie from bases in the German Army's immediate rear against military targets on the front line or in the rear area of the enemy army. The Luftwaffe had not planned for, nor had it been designed for, a "strategic" campaign which called for pursuit of an autonomous strategic goal, such as the destruction of an enemy industrial base. It was not set up to defeat a *major* adversary air force by itself. (Even the French Air Force had continuously replenished its strength during the Battle of France. At the time of the Armistice it had a greater frontline strength than on May 10.)

The Luftwaffe was set up for short wars, not attrition campaigns. With no reserve stocks of aircraft and relatively low stocks of spare parts, it was hard put to keep squadrons at full strength during limited periods of intense combat. With the German aircraft industry turning out only small numbers of fighter aircraft, it was difficult to keep fighter squadrons at full strength over a longer period of intense combat. In every way, the Luftwaffe was ill suited to the campaign it was to undertake against Britain. It is doubtful that the Luftwaffe had ever *seriously* entertained the possibility of such a campaign.

Once Hitler began to consider the invasion of Britain, he had no choice but to order the Luftwaffe to spearhead the attempt. Moreover, since bad weather in the channel made a seaborne invasion of Britain impossible beyond early autumn, the Luftwaffe had only three months to develop a strategy for defeating the RAF, and, in some measure, to reconfigure itself for that strategy. This is a short time for any large organization to learn or to change. Perhaps this explains why, contrary to popular belief, some serious students of the battle conclude that the Luftwaffe was never close to the level of success necessary for an invasion attempt.[27]

The purpose or doctrine of Fighter Command was clear; it differed markedly from that of the Luftwaffe.[28] (It also differed from the doctrine preferred by Bomber Command, the preeminent branch of the Royal Air Force. This very separation of the RAF into functional commands differed from the Luftwaffe practice of organizing aircraft of different types into "air fleets" for specific campaigns.) As Sir Thomas Inskip, minister for the coordination of defense, put it, "The role of our air force is not an early knockout blow . . . but to prevent the Germans from knocking us out."[29]

Although the British government had worked on the air defense problem since 1934, the emphasis on fighter defense did not become official policy until December 1937. By the summer of 1940, the first integrated air defense system in history was in place. Its centerpiece was the radar system "Chain-Home," which warned Fighter Command of an impending attack and allowed ground controllers both to plot the paths of incoming raids and to vector British fighter squadrons onto intercept courses. The radar was crude and the ground instructions frequently inadequate, but "Chain-Home" gave Fighter Command a big edge. It appears that at least two other intelligence assets contributed to early warning: an elaborate communication intercept program called Y-service,[30] and the Ultra information provided by the breaking of German's Enigma codes.[31] Radar was supplemented by an elaborate system of visual observers. All this information was fed into a single Fighter Command "Filter" center which, in its turn, passed the information out to the appropriate Group headquarters (Britain was divided into four Groups, numbered 10–13). These allocated the targets to particular Sector Headquarters, which organized and controlled the actual squadron interceptions.

Integrated in this system were the critical fighter squadrons, dispersed among a large number of airfields, and the anti-aircraft artillery, both high- and low-altitude. As time passed, and as the Germans grew more adept at attacking RAF airfields, more and more low-altitude anti-aircraft guns were concentrated on the defense of airfields. On the whole, however, the anti-aircraft artillery were not of great importance.

Fighters and fighter pilots were the central elements of British air defense. In the supply of fighter aircraft the British were better prepared than the Germans. During the late 1930s money had been appropriated for the construction of "shadow factories" that could be expanded to full production in the event of war. In May 1940 Churchill appointed Lord Beaverbrook to oversee aircraft production. Beaverbrook understood Fighter Command's need for fighters and produced them with a vengeance. The one area in which Britain seems to have been insufficiently prepared was the provision of fighter pilots. As the campaign progressed, pilot attrition forced Sir Hugh Caswall Dowding, the chief of Fighter Command, to scrounge pilots from other commands and to commit poorly trained pilots to the fray. The origin of this problem has never been adequately explained, and some dispute its seriousness. If there was a problem, it may not have been one of numbers, but rather of the organization and training of the pilots on hand.[32]

Strategy

The different military doctrines and force postures of the two sides were reflected in the "strategy" or lack of it exhibited by each side. As noted above, the Luftwaffe was not set up for the job it was to undertake. Yet, if Germany were to have any hope of invading Britain, the Luftwaffe would have to destroy the RAF. Within the German armed forces the navy was the weakest service; within the British armed forces it was the strongest. No invasion of Britain could succeed unless the Royal Navy were neutralized. Moreover, to maximize the chance of success, the attempt would have to be made before the British ground forces recovered from their costly defeats in Belgium, France, and Norway. This meant that the invasion would have to take place within a short time. Finally, such an invasion would have to exploit the good weather of the summer months. In short, the Germans had relatively little time to exploit the short-term advantage gained as a result of Britain's early defeats and late start at rearmament. Small though that advantage was, it might prove decisive in an inherently risky invasion attempt, and in its absence the "window" might never be open again.

Within the June–September time frame the small and badly damaged German Navy had no hope of neutralizing the British Navy without maximum help from the Luftwaffe. The Luftwaffe could only provide this help if the RAF were completely driven from the English Channel and the channel coast. This meant the destruction of Fighter Command. Moreover, if Fighter Command could be destroyed, then German bombers alone might intimidate the British into surrender, or terms, altogether obviating the need for an invasion.

British strategy was exactly the reverse of the German. If Fighter Command could be kept alive through the summer, no invasion attempt was likely. If an invasion occurred, there was good reason to hope that the RAF in cooperation with the Royal Navy would be able

[99]

to defeat it. If Fighter Command could survive the summer, the weather in the channel would buy Britain the time to replenish her strength and make herself impregnable.

For purposes of discussion, the Battle of Britain is usually divided into four phases.[33] During phase 1 (July 10–August 7), each side's strategy was vague. The Germans wanted to close the channel to British coastal shipping and establish some sort of air superiority over the water. They allocated only a part of their force to this task, and its actual relevance to the invasion of Britain is unclear. Anti-shipping attacks drew some British fighter squadrons into the air, allowing the Luftwaffe to begin the task of destroying Fighter Command. Dowding was canny, however, contributing as few aircraft as possible. Some coastal shipping was sunk, encouraging the British to make a relatively easy shift to rail transport. For a time, however, in spite of Dowding's resistance, Fighter Command was ordered to protect these coastal convoys. Fighter Command had not prepared for this mission. On the whole, the Germans lost more aircraft in the channel fighting than did the British. The British gained some valuable combat experience, but at a cost in combat aircraft that outweighed the value of the shipping. British civilians and sailors who persisted in the channel fighting had not yet fully grasped their strategic objective—the preservation of Fighter Command. It took Dowding a few weeks to teach it to them.

The second phase of the battle was August 8–23, and the third August 24–September 6. In both phases the Luftwaffe aimed more or less directly at Fighter Command, although the third phase was more successful than the second. Air attacks were mounted against radar installations, airfields, and the aircraft industry in the hope of disabling the whole Fighter Command organization. Additionally, the Germans hoped to draw the British into air battles that would destroy the bulk of RAF fighter strength. In this they were unsuccessful. The Germans did not understand the structure of Fighter Command, and their intelligence did little to improve the situation. As a result, their targeting was erratic and unfocused. Coordination among the three German air fleets was poor. Moreover, German fighters had insufficient range to escort German bombers to all of the major RAF sectors. As a result, they concentrated on Number 11 Group, guarding the invasion routes and the city of London. While this group was badly damaged in the fighting, the Luftwaffe itself suffered heavy casualties. The other British Groups, 10, 12, and 13, remained relatively undamaged.

It is widely believed that had the Luftwaffe continued concentration on 11 Group and its ground infrastructure it would have soon achieved "air superiority" over Britain. However, Fighter Command seems to have had the aircraft, pilots, and alternative bases to ensure its survival in sufficient strength to stubbornly oppose a German invasion. Under serious pressure, the RAF might have redeployed 11 Group's fighters north of London, just out of range of the Bf 109. There they could have rested and refitted, and still been able to operate at their own discretion.[34] Moreover, 11 Group airfields and infrastructure might have been repaired to a level that would support a southward surge by Fighter Command in opposition to any German invasion attempt. In any case, the move proved unnecessary.

The British did not cooperate with the German strategy. During phases 3 and 4, Fighter Command, particularly 11 Group, followed a very conservative and careful strategy. Keith Park, the 11 Group commander, husbanded his fighter resources. He committed his squadrons to combat gradually, with the intention of disrupting each individual German bombing raid. This would limit German damage to his airfields and ground control system. Fighters were instructed to avoid direct clashes with German fighters if possible, concentrating on the bombers. Thus, Park tried to limit his own losses and punish the Germans—even if German raids were not decisively stopped. Historians agree that Park and Dowding understood their mission to be the preservation of Fighter Command. This they achieved during the second and third phases of the battle, although with very high casualties.

Phase 4 of the Battle of Britain (September 7–30) exhausted both the time and the creativity of the Luftwaffe. By early September the Germans had become convinced that a substantial portion of Fighter Command resources were still intact, although they greatly underestimated British strength. Moreover, they themselves were taking high casualties and time was running out for Sea-Lion. Many in the Luftwaffe had long argued that attacks on London would draw a major effort by Fighter Command, allowing the Luftwaffe a chance to finish it off. A decisive aerial battle was being proposed—wholly consistent with the Luftwaffe's origins. British bombing of Berlin brought Hitler's approval and support for this plan.

The focus on London actually seems to have helped Fighter Command in three ways. First, it took pressure off the 11 Group ground infrastructure. Second, the Germans lost the element of surprise, allowing the British to take more time to concentrate their squadrons. Third, German fighters were operating at their extreme range limits, so they had limited fuel reserves for dog-fights. These changes increased German casualties. Nevertheless, the Germans continued and increased their effort. On September 15, now celebrated as Battle of Britain day, the Luftwaffe seems to have made a maximum effort. Again Fighter Command dashed German hopes; while it lost twenty-five planes and thirteen pilots, it destroyed sixty enemy aircraft in the battle. The German High Command acknowledged the Luftwaffe's failure. On September 17 Sea-Lion was postponed until further notice. The aerial assault tapered off gradually into a campaign of night terror bombing.

SUMMARY

Germany won the Battle of France and lost the Battle of Britain. She won the battle for which she had prepared and lost the one for which she had not. Her military doctrine had long envisioned major land campaigns on the European continent. Operations beyond its shores had been given little thought. For the most part German military doctrine was offensive, innovative, and integrated with Germany's political strategy. Had that doctrine been held by a state with more limited aims, the Battle of Britain might never have been fought. However, German grand strategy contained the seeds of its own "disintegration" because its ends were infinitely expansive and they expanded at a rapid rate. No military doctrine, much less a force posture, could keep up with such a policy. In a way, Germany was a victim of its own too rapid successes. These made new enemies for Germany more quickly than her military organization could adapt to them. In a world of limited means and widely distributed power, it may be that such a hidden brake would operate on any open-endedly imperial policy. No doctrine can keep up.

French military doctrine was defensive, stagnant, and not fully integrated with the state's political strategy. Both operationally and politically, it looked backward to World War I. Stationary, defensive, attrition warfare, waged in the company of a powerful coalition, was both the French fear and the French aim. The main goal was to get others to share the costs of French defense. Until such cooperation could be assured, French military doctrine would aim to limit possible damage to France and to the French Army.

This strategy was clear to France's potential allies, all of whom reciprocated by passing the burden of their own defense back to France. None would risk German animosity for the sake of French goals. For this reason, interwar military cooperation was weak.

Belgium, Holland, Britain, and France, the 1940 coalition, had few military discussions in the late 1930s. Yet, French doctrine called for limiting the damage to France, keeping the war away from her frontiers. This demanded a move into Belgium, a move that could only be a nightmare for the uncoordinated, defensively oriented, mutually suspicious Allied armies. Nevertheless, Gamelin plunged foreward, chasing the chimera of a stabilized front, far from the French border, manned and paid for—at least in part—by France's allies.

British doctrine was somewhat similar. It was defensive, yet it was more innovative. It was well integrated with the political aspects of British grand strategy. Like France, Britain sought to transfer the costs of her defense to her allies. Geographically, she was better set up for this. Britain was hard to conquer, except by sea, and the Royal Navy had that bet covered. When emerging technology cast doubt upon the channel's eternal military value, British politicians responded by giving increased support to Fighter Command. What they temporarily forgot, because it was convenient to do so, was that a successful German occupation of the channel coast, even if only of the "mouth of the Scheldt," would provide an amphibious and aerial springboard against Britain.

Defending the channel coast would demand a major ground force commitment and potentially high casualities such as those Britain had suffered in World War I. Until 1939, the British hoped that the French would pay these costs. With the channel and British airspace defended, Britain's bets were covered. She hoped to commit just enough ground forces to the continent to get the French to fight. Who could imagine a change in land warfare so decisive as to allow the conquest of France? Hence, in May 1940, Britain fought a land battle that her grand strategy had for years sought to avoid. The peculiar British euphoria after Dunkirk may be explained by the fact that the British Expeditionary Force had both preserved British "honor" and avoided the disaster of the trenches at the same time. Beside these gains, a military defeat was a smallish matter.

In the summer of 1940, on the other hand, the British found themselves fighting the battle that they had both feared and planned for during the preceding six years. The casualties of that summer were puny compared to the astounding losses of World War I. British fighters successfully bought the time for the next phase of the long-planned British war effort. For just as the French had counted on transferring a portion of their defense costs to the British, the British had counted on transferring some of their defense costs to anybody and everybody. With the time bought by Fighter Command, a new ally or two might be found. In this sense, British grand strategy was perhaps the most successful of the 1930s.

The peculiarities of French, British, and German military doctrine are explained in part by their unique historical experiences. However, the remainder of this book is concerned with explanations of a different kind. In the next three chapters, the military doctrines of France, Britain, and Germany will be examined along the dimensions of offense-defense-deterrence, integration-disintegration, and innovation-stagnation in terms of organization theory and balance of power theory. In this way, the causes of the events of 1940 can perhaps be illuminated in a different and more systematic fashion than that found in conventional histories. At the same time, the two theories can be tested for their utility in explaining complex matters of national security.

[4]

France

French grand strategy during the interwar period aimed to preserve the political and territorial settlement of Versailles. The French
recognized that the Versailles restrictions on German military power
were the most fragile elements of the postwar settlement. They constructed their military doctrine to deal with an *expected* resurgence of
German industrial and military power, which was identified as the
main threat to French security. The army would play the key role in
French strategy toward Germany, with the air force in support. (I am
omitting discussion of the French Navy. Although it was a fairly
powerful force, its role in the struggle against Germany was ancillary.
The navy's mission was to help protect French access to her colonies,
as well as to other possible extra-European sources of military support. The navy had a strong Mediterranean orientation, focusing
more on the threat posed by the Italian fleet than on that posed by the
German Navy.) French military doctrine was largely *defensive*; its purpose was to deny the German Army entry into France. Offensive or
disarming operations were a distinctly secondary mission. The only
major military move envisioned was the advance into Belgium, and
even this had the initial purpose of holding assets rather than beating
the Germans.

When it emerged in the mid-1920s, French grand strategy represented a relatively well-integrated approach to French security problems. Nevertheless, from its inception, the strategy gradually began
to unravel. The defensive French military doctrine became less and
less capable of supporting the French alliance system. Following the
events of 1936 the doctrine may be considered as substantially,
though not completely, disintegrated from the political elements of
French grand strategy. The Belgian declaration of neutrality ended
joint military planning between Belgium and France. This maximized

the possibility of a battle of movement in Belgium for which the French Army had not prepared. German fortification of the Rhineland ended even the pretense of a French offensive capability to support eastern European allies threatened by a resurgent Germany. French military doctrine, particularly its stress on defensive tactics and prepared positions, would have benefited from a serious review after 1936. While efforts were made to improve the French military position in a general way, there is little evidence to suggest that such a review was undertaken.

French military doctrine was not innovative during the interwar period, although political circumstances changed rather quickly during the 1930s. The Maginot Line, the first fortress system of its kind, can be looked upon as an innovation. However, when set against the static attrition battles of World War I, the Line seems more evolutionary than revolutionary. Similarly, although the French Army became more motorized and mechanized during the late 1930s, and the French Air Force acquired new aircraft, new equipment was not associated with any deeply held revolutionary view of modern warfare. The French Army and Air Force were organized for the first phase of a future war with Germany. This phase would stabilize the fronts preparatory to the mobilization of French and especially *allied* industrial assets for total war.

In this chapter the defensive, disintegrated, and stagnant character of French doctrine will be discussed in greater detail. I will evaluate and compare the contributions to French doctrine of systemic constraints and incentives, organizational pressures, and technology and geography. Of these, I will argue that systemic factors loomed largest; technological, geographical, and organizational factors played important though subsidiary roles. In many respects, it was *interactions* of all these forces that produced the complex and distinctive military doctrine of interwar France.

The Role of Technology

Much of the defensiveness of French doctrine can be explained by France's experience in World War I. French civilians and soldiers drew important and similar lessons from the war. Initially, civilians seem to have been more willing to translate these lessons into a markedly defensive military doctrine. Civilians and soldiers agreed that the war had demonstrated the decisiveness of modern firepower.[1] Some soldiers, such as Marshalls Ferdinand Foch and Joseph Joffre (prewar advocates of the offensive), were unwilling to translate this experience into an endorsement of defensive over offensive tactics and operations. Marshall Henri Pétain, on the other hand, with the apparent support of French political leaders, turned immediately to long-term planning for French security, based on defensive warfare in fortified positions.[2] During Pétain's tenure as peacetime chief of the French Army, his views, given the support of civilian leadership, prevailed both in written doctrine and in that doctrine's physical manifestation—the Maginot Line.

In chapter 2 the proposition was advanced that civilians will impose a judgment about technology on military doctrine when the implications of the technology are sufficiently stark. Soldiers may also draw conclusions under these circumstances. For France, World War I's firepower lessons were particularly stark. In that war France lost 1.4 million dead and missing, or 10.5 per cent of her "active male population."[3] Perhaps another 4.2 million soldiers were wounded.[4] This casualty rate produced the mutinies of May 1917, in which "collective indiscipline" occurred in 54 of the 110 French divisions on the Western Front.[5] The subsequent military decisions of French civilians show a determination to avoid the repetition of such casualties. Those decisions bound the French state and the French Army ever more tightly to a defensive strategy.

The second major lesson, stemming in part from the first was that the effectiveness of modern firepower could produce a *stalemate* very costly in terms not only of human but of industrial resources. When such a stalemate developed on the Western Front in World War I, it was discovered that modern weaponry could only be sustained by huge commitments of resources. Still greater resources were required for attempts to overwhelm enemy defenses in order to end the war,[6] attempts that were usually unsuccessful. Due to early reverses, France had been particularly disadvantaged in terms of industrial and natural resources. Before and after the war most of these resources were concentrated along her northern and northeastern frontiers.[7] Because the offensive Plan Seventeen, executed at the war's outset, included no provisions for defending these areas, they were lost, substantially weakening the subsequent French war effort and increasing French dependence on Britain. French interwar military planning would strive to secure these vulnerable areas from land attack.

Two major decisions, taken mainly by French civilians, determined the subsequent defensive character of French grand strategy and military doctrine. Both decisions reflected the technological lessons of the war. The first was to drastically reduce the term of conscription; the second was to create the Maginot Line—an ambitious system of fortifications along the northeast frontier. These decisions were closely related.

French statesmen and soldiers were not alone in drawing lessons from the war. In the aftermath of World War I, there was throughout French society a turning away from things military. French leaders were faced with a widespread and overwhelming desire for a substantial reduction in the length of a conscript's period of service.[8] To succumb to these demands was to push the French Army to think largely in terms of defensive operations, because the offensive had previously been closely identified with a *three*-year term of service.

In 1913 the term of service in the French Army had been raised from two to three years. This was attributable in part to increasing international tension, and in part to the declining French birthrate. Less well known is that at the highest levels of the French Army the shift to a more offensive tactical doctrine was used to support demands for the third year. Offense was said to demand highly skilled and highly motivated troops. It was believed that this higher-quality army was impossible unless conscripts spent three years with the colors.

The term of service was reduced to eighteen months in 1924 and to twelve months in 1928, and there it remained until 1935.[9] The number of fully ready divisions dropped from twelve to six; fourteen divisions at partial strength were added; and twenty divisions were to be formed as before by mobilized reservists. This allowed but a thin *couverture* (covering force) against a German surprise attack. The French Army was now unsuited for offensive action and barely suited for defense. The one-year term was a major impetus for the construction of the Maginot Line.[10]

The small couverture would need defensive works to stop a sudden German attack. Compared to prewar French conscripts, the postwar conscript would have little time to develop his military skills. If thirty-six months had been necessary to produce an "offensive" soldier before the war, then twelve months certainly could not do so in the 1920s. Fortifications would be a valuable aid to the postwar conscript. As much was said during the debates on reducing the term of service to twelve months.[11] The new French Army would, at least during the initial stages of a future war, fight defensive engagements.[12]

The decisions by French statesmen to shorten the term of service and build the Maginot Line were quite deliberate steps away from an offensive doctrine and toward a defensive one. These steps were taken, in part, as a reaction to the carnage of World War I. They also reflected a belief that France might not escape another war with Germany, and that such a war would demand human and industrial mobilization equal to that of the last. Therefore, France would have to maintain some sort of conscription to give minimal training to her young men. Hence, the twelve-month term. It was just as important to protect the critical industrial mobilization resources that had been lost to Germany early in the previous war. The Maginot Line would not only allow France to defend a dangerous invasion route with limited forces, it would help France defend her critical long-war resources in the northeastern part of the country.[13]

Reading the technological lessons of the war, French statesmen and soldiers came to reasonable conclusions. Modern firepower meant that offensives could be very costly. Manpower and industry had to be husbanded until the decisive moment when materiel superiority had been achieved. For French civilians and, as time passed, for French soldiers, this meant defensive operations and fortifications. At least one of France's greatest soldiers, Marshall Pétain, was a powerful advocate of this view.[14]

The Distribution of Power in Europe: Constraints and Incentives Affecting French Strategy

The French interpreted the technological lessons of the war in light of the overall balance of power between France and interwar Germany. Even after the Versailles Treaty Germany remained industrially and demographically superior to France, inherently more capable of waging an extended attrition war like World War I. This superiority may actually have increased during the interwar period.[15] In the 1930s Germany's population was a third again that of France. A comparison of relative industrial potential for modern war shows Germany with 2.5–3.5 times French mobilization capability by 1937–1938.[16] Such a massive disparity could prove decisive in an attrition war. From the first, French doctrine viewed the addition of Allied (especially British) industrial resources to her war effort as a prerequisite to any successful encounter with Germany.

Even a hypothesized defensive advantage might be overcome by German resource superiority. At the same time, an industrially inferior France would never overcome German defenses to end a war. If France had to face Germany unaided, she might ultimately be worn down and defeated. This had nearly been French experience in World

War I, even with British aid. Hence, the *imbalance of power* encouraged France to seek allies. Experience with modern technology sharpened the French perception of an imbalance of power and raised their fears of its implications for French security, but a real and serious imbalance did obtain.[17]

The imbalance of power might not have encouraged a defensive military doctrine. In some cases (as argued in Chapter 2) such imbalances encourage offensive doctrines. This was the case in Germany (see chapter 6). Two important systemic factors intervened to make defense attractive to France: the distribution of capabilities in the European political system, and the tendency of threatened states to defend their sovereignty. There were potential allies in Europe with enough strength to tip the balance against Germany if they formed a coalition with France. Given German expansionism, these states would soonor or later have to join France to ensure their own survival. With a defensive military doctrine France could avoid appearing bellicose herself, and thus enhance the legitimacy of her claim for assistance; remove the necessity for precipitate and potentially costly offensive military action before a new anti-German coalition pulled itself together; and, in the event of war, economically buy the time necessary to negotiate the substantial military contributions from her allies that would be needed for the ultimate decisive battles with Germany.

In the aftermath of World War I, there were many states with meaningful, if not substantial, military capability in Europe. For instance, by 1938 the mobilized Czech Army was a little over half the size of the mobilized German Army, and was nearly as well equipped.[18] Not only were capabilities widely distributed in interwar Europe, but states controlling those capabilities might ally themselves with France. Most European states had reason to fear a resurgence of German expansionism if only because so many of them had profited from Germany's downfall. France could exploit these fears. The central question would be how quickly and easily these states could be brought into an anti-German wartime coalition.

Although eastern European allies were cultivated by the French, for most of the interwar period Britain was perceived as the most important and powerful prospective ally. With two and a half times the industrial resources of France, Britain was an especially critical factor.[19] Yet, her geographical defensive advantage allowed her the luxury of waiting—both to determine the extent of a given aggressor's hegemonic ambitions and the extent to which other European states might oppose those ambitions. French experience with Britain immediately after World War I did not bode well for a future alliance. Britain had refused to help enforce certain provisions of the Versailles Treaty, and had undermined French efforts to do so. She successfully opposed an effective security plank in the League Charter. She declined a direct alliance with France, and refused to guarantee the postwar status quo either on the Rhine or in eastern Europe. Indeed, Britain thwarted French anti-German actions at every turn. All the same, Britain's unique capabilities and attributes made her the focus of French strategic and diplomatic efforts in the 1930s.[20] British hesitancy would simply demand a more careful and cunning French diplomacy and military doctrine than had originally been envisioned.

In sum, France had potential allies, but bringing the most important ally into a future anti-German coalition was recognized as difficult. French decision-makers viewed British industrial and military resources as critical to their national security. No offensive against Germany would be contemplated until combined British and French resources were mobilized. Britain and other allies would have to pay a share of French defense costs. The French constructed a defensive military doctrine and posture in the belief that by doing so they would maximize the probability of this outcome. The same sort of decision—a decision predicted by balance of power theory (see chapter 2)—was made in Britain in the 1930s, as shall be argued in the next chapter. Both France and Britain constructed military doctrines that facilitated "buck-passing," because the Germans appeared so formidable and because prospective allies were there to receive the buck.

Students of French doctrine agree on the connection between its defensiveness and the desire to extract large contributions from French allies. The French Army's mission was to *prevent defeat* while French and allied resources were being mobilized. The military history curriculum of the École Supérieure de Guerre concentrated mainly on the lessons of World War I, stressing how the French Army had exploited the stabilized front without excessive losses and waited until enemy attrition and American aid resulted in decisive quantitative superiority. In a future war, an initially defensive strategy would similarly serve to elicit military contributions from France's allies at a minimum cost to France.[21]

After the war, Édouard Daladier, the French minister of defense in 1940, summed up his opposition to early offensives in Belgium by noting that they would have killed "one or two million of [France's] sons without the allies assuming their share of the common sacrifice."[22]

French doctrine depended upon Britain bearing part of the burden of any future war. A 1935 document from the War Ministry to the Haut Comité Militaire read, "From the practical point of view it is England which could assist us most effectively, not only in the long term, thanks to her great imperial potential and to her control of the seas, but even at the start of hostilities. Therefore, and above all, we must regain and marshal the immediate support of England."[23] In late 1938 the Army Staff echoed these sentiments, connecting a defensive strategy with burden-sharing in a memorandum to Daladier, then premier and war minister.

> In a word, the *only* chance the Anglo-French coalition has for victory, and for marshaling its hidden strength in the form of its great war potential, rests on two conditions: (i) that an early and very serious effort be made to *thwart* any attempt by future enemy to end a war quickly by means of a sudden and overwhelming blow; and (ii) that a continual and prolonged collaboration between the two Governments be anticipated and that preparations be made in advance for the *sharing* of their respective *resources*.[24] [my emphases]

Regular joint military staff conversations were the peacetime symbol of the wartime collaboration envisioned by the French. These the British constantly declined. Yet, every time there was some sort of crisis—in the Rhineland, in Spain, or with the Belgian declaration of neutrality—the French attempted to cement their military ties with the British.[25]

Much of French interwar diplomacy should be viewed as an attempt either to expand her alliance with Britain or to compensate for British coquettishness by alliances in the east or by flirtations with the Soviet Union and Italy. Historian Judith Hughes views the Locarno Pact of 1925 as a major example of such French machinations. Though it did not achieve the French goal of a first-class military alliance with Britain, it did attain more limited objectives.[26] Locarno safeguarded the international-legal basis of any future French reoccupation of the Rhineland in defense of Versailles, and obtained Britain's pledge that France would not be diplomatically isolated if she did so.[27]

The Maginot Line was the centerpiece of interwar French military doctrine, and played a critical role in French schemes to transfer war costs to her allies. The borders of France were all fortified to some degree, but the impressive Maginot fortifications, extending roughly one hundred miles from Lauterborg to the Belgium-Luxembourg border, were of a different order. These fortifications protected a great natural invasion route and the substantial industrial assets that lay astride it.

The Line would protect French soldiers from the horrible effects of firepower. It would protect the soil of France and the critical industrial resources required for a long war. It would also allow the French to fight a low-cost defensive action while negotiating the contributions of her allies. Thus, the Maginot Line would seem to have represented an adequate response to the technological lessons of World War I, the interwar Franco-German imbalance of industrial and demographic power, and the alliance possibilities of the interwar European political system. This is not quite correct. As is well known, the Line was not extended along the Belgian border to the channel coast, even though important industrial resources were concentrated in this area. Indeed, this sector remained weakly fortified throughout the period.

Popularly, this is often seen as a mere blunder. It was not. Some historians have explained the inadequate fortifications by French fear of alienating Belgium—her ally until 1936.[28] Quite the reverse seems to have been the case: the Belgians demanded strong fortification of the border and viewed its absence as an invitation to the Germans and a grave threat to their own security. This was the Belgian position from 1932 onward.[29]

If the weak fortifications on the border were no mere oversight, nor a consequence of Belgian sensibilities, then how is the French decision to be explained? If France was interested in protecting her soldiers from modern firepower, preserving her border-concentrated industry, and buying the time to extract contributions from her allies, why did she not fortify the border? This question looms especially large when one considers that the contrast between the strength of the Maginot Line and the weakness of the Belgian border could be counted on to encourage a German end-run through Belgium. *This is exactly what the French wanted to have happen.* Paradoxically, an unfortified Belgian border would actually make it easier for France to achieve two out of three of the strategic objectives outlined above.

First, the industry in northern France was closer to the border than the industry in northeastern France. Fortifications along the Belgian border would only allow German invaders to shoot this industrial region to pieces from Belgian territory.[30] Thus, although fortification of the border might make France easier to defend in the short term, it would also occasion the loss of a good deal of her mobilization capability to enemy shellfire. Hence, in the event of a German attack *and a Belgian request for assistance*, the French planned to advance into central Belgium to establish a defense line that would keep the battle away from French territory and industry.[31] This operation would of course depend on a timely Belgian request for aid, and careful advance planning and cooperation between the two militaries. Such cooperation was tenuous during the period of the Belgian-French alliance and would all but evaporate in 1936.[32]

Second, German violation of Belgian territory was almost certain to bring Britain into the war on the side of France. The security of the Low Countries had long been a British concern, since an invasion of Britain would be facilitated by the rivers and seaports of Belgium and the Netherlands. Hence, France's fortification of the German border and neglect of the Belgian border increased the probability of British aid.

General Maurice Chauvineau became one of the foremost exponents of French defensive doctrine, publishing in 1939 the famous and ironic *Une invasion, Est-elle encore possible?*[33] In the 1920s, he taught the fortifications course at the École Supérieure de Guerre. His explanation of the purpose of the Maginot Line, as recounted by Donald Harvey, was:

"To incite the Germans to invade through Belgium," in order to by-pass a strongly fortified Franco-German border, "is at once to alienate England and to lead the Belgians to intervene. Even more importantly, it marks the direction of the offensive which is most advantageous for us, since it increases the distance from Paris to the frontier by the whole depth of the Belgian territory."[34]

This ploy seems to have worked very well, although it had the unavoidable consequence of poisoning relations with the British. By the spring of 1938 the British Committee of Imperial Defense was becoming concerned about the weakness of the frontier fortifications facing Belgium. In the words of one report, this was suspected to be a "deliberate inducement to compel us to intervene on land in order to safeguard an area which we have regarded as vital for centuries."[35]

What the unfortified Belgian border failed to accomplish was the protection of French soldiers from the effects of firepower. If Belgium cooperated, the French Army *might* be able to advance quickly and efficiently into prepared or partially prepared Belgian fortifications and make whatever additional defensive preparations were necessary to meet a German onslaught. If not, as became a near certainty after the Belgian 1936 neutrality declaration, then French soldiers would face defensive combat from poorly prepared defensive positions at best, or a violent "encounter battle" or a confused war of movement at worst.

Thus the decision not to fortify the Belgian border seems to have been at least as much a response to systemic constraints and incentives as to narrow technological ones. The French were trying to "export" damage by an "offensive" into Belgium (a plan consistent with balance of power theory; see chapter 2):[36] as General Gamelin remarked after the war, "the occupation of the front Namur-Antwerp ([in Belgium]) diverted the war from our northern province. . . . If one considers the devastation that a modern battle entails in the region where it takes place, isn't this argument [that it was desirable to keep the war out of France] even more convincing?"[37] France would seek to establish a defense line somewhere on Belgian territory. At the same time, the German threat to Belgium was the best guarantee of British aid.

How then are we to weigh the relative influence on French military doctrine of the stark technological lessons of World War I, on the one hand, and the systemic constraints and incentives inherent in interwar European politics, on the other? Unquestionably, the firepower technology of the previous war had taught many lessons—that battles in the open were risky and costly; that collateral damage was heavy; that victory required quantitative superiority. In varying degrees, French doctrine responded to all of these lessons. However, the imbalance of power and the availability of allies heavily influenced the overall character of French doctrine.

In the northeast, the Maginot Line not only was calculated to buy time to negotiate Allied contributions in the event of war, but represented a rational response to all the technological lessons of World War I. Along the Belgian border, however, it was deemed wise to discount some of those lessons as the price for avoiding high collateral damage, for saving French industrial resources, and for increasing the probability of Britain's early entry into a future war.

A move into Belgium would expose French troops to the effects of firepower and the risks of encounter battles. Furthermore, the Franco-Belgian border had to be left weakly fortified if the Belgian battleground and British resources were to be exploited. The Germans had to be drawn into Belgium. This meant that if the battle in Belgium did not go well, France herself would be left vulnerable. As long as Belgium remained a French ally, such a calculated risk may have been sensible. After the 1936 declaration of Belgian neutrality, the French plan became more risky, and deserved a serious review. While the French moved after 1936 to shore up their overall military position,

[115]

especially in the areas of fortifications, industrial mobilization capability, and armaments, the plan itself appears to have received little serious attention. Neither the military nor its civilian leaders seem to have considered the possibility that French military doctrine had become inadequate for one of the fundamental military missions identified by the state's grand strategy. It appears then that some of the narrow technological lessons of World War I took a backseat to systemic constraints and incentives. The overriding concerns seem to have been to export war damage and export war costs. Opportunities existed for doing both, and French military doctrine reflects a readiness to accept risks in order to seize those opportunities.

Organizational Influences

How was the French Army brought to accept this defensive doctrine? Among the hypotheses derived from organization theory (chapter 2) are that military organizations prefer offensive doctrines because they help reduce internal and external uncertainty, and because they contribute to organizational size, wealth, and autonomy. In chapter 1 I discussed the highly offensive character of pre–World War I French Army doctrine. The commitment to this doctrine was so strong that it survived long into a war that was daily demonstrating the defensive advantages bestowed by modern firepower.

The thinking behind France's pre–World War I offensive doctrine had included an important qualifying assumption: offensive warfare could be successful only with high-quality, well-trained troops. This had been a central argument in the successful prewar campaign to extend the term of service to three years, a move that gave the French Army a great deal of control over its personnel. They could be thoroughly prepared for the offensive battle. The offensive doctrine reduced external uncertainty by increasing the likelihood that the battle would be structured according to the French Army's battle plans. Finally, the offensive doctrine seems to have reduced the uncertainty that arises from fear of civil intervention. Anticipation of a short war was so pronounced that upon the outbreak of World War I the Chamber of Deputies adjourned with no plans to exercise any wartime functions whatsoever. The soldiers of France were in control.

With this history in mind, it seems strange that the defensive doctrine outlined in the preceding pages could so easily have been adopted by the French Army. Though the army had become highly respectful of modern firepower during World War I, its apparent embrace of a doctrine that was as much a defensive caricature as the prewar doctrine was an offensive caricature requires some explanation. I will argue that the French Army's choice grew out of a confluence of forces that made a defensive doctrine a better device than an offensive doctrine for uncertainty reduction. The army came to prefer defense in part because of its World War I experience. Of equal importance were those civilian preferences and critical decisions favoring defense outlined in the preceding sections of this chapter.

After World War I French soldiers did not believe that offensives were impossible; they concluded, rather, that an offensive would require a quantitative superiority which France was unlikely to enjoy at a war's outset. Marshall Foch seems to have thought that the demilitarization of the Rhineland would allow offensives early in a war.[38] Even Pétain, the "high priest" of the defensive, recognized that the offensive spirit had to be preserved. However, offensives would require careful planning and overwhelming quantities of materiel.[39]

Moreover, some important French political leaders were willing to consider an early offensive as a device to avoid a repetition of World War I. In the debates of the 1920s on army reorganization and service reduction some suggested that the couverture had to be sufficiently strong to attack. Both André Maginot, the defense minister, and Édouard de Castelnau, the president of the Chamber Army Commission, made such arguments. A very strong couverture might be able to disrupt German preparations for an offensive against France and thus avoid a long attrition war.[40] If the technological lessons of the war did not inevitably imply a defensive doctrine for civilian decision-makers, then why should they have had such an effect on soldiers?

French civilians did not complete their drift to an overwhelmingly defensive doctrine until the end of the 1920s. By then the combination of the one-year term of service and the commitment of French regulars to the colonies had substantially reduced the size of the couverture. At the same time, the French withdrew from the Rhineland, lengthening the distance and difficulty of an offensive against Germany. The combination of a small couverture and greater distance encouraged the final flight from the idea of an early offensive action in a future war.[41] Indeed the reverse occurred. France began to fear the German General Hans von Seeckt's *attaque brusquée*.[42] These fears were a major impetus to the fortification of the northeastern frontier.[43]

Even granting a defensive predisposition among French civilians, the character of the Maginot fortifications themselves was not predetermined. Originally, the French Army hoped to use them as an *offensive* base. Within the army, there had been a debate between two opposing factions. It was fought out over a five-year period in the Conseil Supérieur de la Guerre starting in May 1920. One faction advocated a 1918-style defensive system that stressed a series of well-prepared battlefields with continuous lines of barbed-wired light defensive works. Another faction advocated a series of heavily defended concrete fortifications at locations carefully chosen to facilitate maneuver, offensives, and counteroffensives. The Conseil favored the latter position. When Paul Painlevé became war minister in 1925 he advanced the "concrete" approach over the "barbed wire" approach. It is not clear, however, that Painlevé accepted the "offensive" uses of these forts favored by some of the generals.[44]

Historian Judith Hughes contends that the French Army began to abandon its offensive plans almost as soon as work had begun on the fortifications. Another historian, Donald Harvey, contends that the High Command continued to view the forts as counteroffensive and maneuver aids until well into the 1930s. The forts were believed to allow for economy of force on the defense and the creation of a "mass of maneuver" for the offense. Hughes admits that such elements were present in the army's declarations, but argues that the *plans* called for stabilization in the northeast, an advance to a defensive line in Belgium, and the slow mobilization of alliance resources for an ultimate counteroffensive.[45]

The different readings of French doctrine reflect its internal tensions. The French Army formally retained a classical interest in the offensive and wished to keep the offensive spirit alive. At the same time, all factions, within and without the military, could agree on one lesson from the previous war—"le feu tue" (fire kills). Offensives would thus require quantitative and qualitative superiority to overcome defensive firepower. Such superiority would take time to muster. As Germany rearmed and fortified her border, and as the French officer corps gained more experience with the one-year term of service, the ability to muster superior strength for offensives and counteroffensives early in a war seemed more and more problematical. In any case, as argued earlier, civilian interest in such offensives rapidly disappeared.

The French Army accepted a defensive doctrine because it reduced uncertainty in three ways. First, it helped the army protect what it perceived to be a vulnerable political position in the aftermath of World War I. Second, a defensive doctrine would allow the army to fight the kind of battle it had learned to fight in the earlier war. French officers would not have to "retool." Third, French officers distrusted the military skills and morale of one-year conscripts. Defensive operations would put the least stress on what were perceived to be poor human resources.

As noted earlier, the military legislation of 1928 provided for a one-year term of service for French conscripts. The general staff was not at all happy with this decision and demanded a number of important provisions to rectify the perceived dangers of the 1928 law. These provisions did not reconcile the High Command to the one-year term, or cause them to view it as any less of a threat to the professional army's existence and efficiency. Rather, the soldiers accepted the new legislation, tempered with their amendments, in order to "create a stable organization as a solid bulwark for and as a psychological encouragement to the military profession."[46] In short, the military was striving to reduce uncertainty for itself.

The army was serious about the amendments it had proposed. Later foot-dragging by the civilians on the implementation of these and other provisions of the legislation both reduced the confidence of French professional officers in the combat capability of the army and rekindled fears for the very survival of a professional officer corps in France.[47] From the professional officer's perspective, the various decisions and actions of the interwar governments of France threatened the survival, autonomy, and combat efficiency of the French Army. In order to defend the army, the High Command did what was necessary to build the defensive capability that the civilians seemed to want. A one-year term and the construction of fortifications were the two major commitments to national security that the civilians were willing to undertake. Within this context, a substantially defensive strategy was almost inevitable.[48]

Although the threat to the autonomy of the military institution provided a major stimulus to the army's acceptance of the defensive doctrine, that doctrine satisfied two additional requirements. Defense reduced battlefield uncertainty in two ways.

Defense allowed for the assumption of a slow-paced war, similar to the familiar methods of World War I, in which commanders would have time to command, and in which previously developed battle plans could be carefully employed. As remarked earlier (chapter 2), an hypothesis from organization theory is that military organizations generally try to reduce uncertainty by structuring the battle through the offensive (the German Army's inclination to adopt this solution is discussed in chapter 6). However, we have seen how the technological lessons of World War I and the political preferences of French governments militated against such a solution. Once the basic parameters were set, a rigidly defensive doctrine became perhaps the only logical way for the French Army to reduce battlefield uncertainty. In the end, military thought became rigid and dogmatic.[49] The notion that an adversary might wreck one's defensive plans was somehow lost.

Finally, the defensive doctrine helped the French Army resolve the uncertainty about its own personnel. The professional officers did not regard the one-year conscript as a competent soldier.[50] Concrete forts would allow the small couverture to fight more efficiently and compensate for the one-year conscript's supposed lack of offensive spirit. Consistent with this view, as early as 1929, Maginot began to amend some of the ideas that had originally spawned the fortifications. He conceded the need for smaller forts in-between the large fortifications.[51] These spaces had first been thought of as areas for maneuver. They too would become fixed positions. By the mid-1930s the basic tactical doctrine of the French Army would reflect this static view.[52]

The French Army's acceptance of a defensive doctrine can thus be explained in large part by its desire to reduce internal and external uncertainty. Partly, too, the army's acquiescence was owing to a common mechanism of control over the military exercised by French civilians: finding a general who agreed with them and putting him in charge of overseeing major military decisions. As war minister in 1922, Maginot interposed Pétain as "Inspector General" between himself and the army High Command. The chief of staff had to submit all decisions on "military-technical" questions to Pétain, who in the French system would assume actual command of the military only in time of war.[53] Pétain's inclinations—especially his willingness to organize the reduction in conscripts' term of service—were very much in harmony with the desires of the civilians.

Maginot in effect co-opted one of France's greatest heroes in order to lend technical credibility to a fundamentally political/grand-strategic decision. Giving Pétain review power over all military decisions would allow more effective control over the military organization that would have to implement the strategy. Pétain could see to it that the critical "technical" decisions of the period favored defense, regardless of the preferences of other members of the French High Command.

This mechanism of civilian control over the instrumental tasks of a military organization is a common one. Political actors who find the preferences of their military organizations troublesome will often reach into the organization, select an individual who can fulfill their needs, and promote that individual to an important position. This mechanism was employed in interwar Britain and Germany. The

[120]

placement of Pétain in a key decision-making position during a period of military restructuring should have allowed him to set the terms by which the organization would subsequently function.

Pétain's position was doubly influential inasmuch as later French war ministers, like French governments, did not enjoy long tenure. They often came to power with little defense expertise and had scant time to develop more. The War Ministry was largely staffed by the military. The chief of the French General Staff became the key source of military information.[54] Thus, political instability may have increased the impact of functional specialization on French military doctrine. French civilian leadership of the 1930s was probably too unschooled in military matters even to consider major alteration of the defense decisions of the 1920s.

STAGNATION AND DISINTEGRATION

We have seen how French civilian and military decision-makers addressed in their military doctrine the technological lessons of World War I, relative French weakness, and the political alliance possibilites of the peace. They produced an integrated, defensive doctrine which was more evolutionary than innovative. The proposed advance into Belgium created one major problem for the doctrine: it might force French soldiers into military actions of the kind that modern weapons technology had made so costly in World War I. This possibility was mitigated but not eliminated by the formal defensive alliance with Belgium.

A second major problem for the doctrine stemmed from France's alliances in eastern Europe—with Czechoslovakia, Poland, Romania, and Yugoslavia. The defensive cast of French military doctrine would make it difficult to lend aid to any of these allies if they were attacked by Germany. France was, of course, more concerned with their aid to her if she were attacked. However, piecemeal German conquests in the east could, by virtue of the resources seized, increase Germany's short- and long-war capability against France.[55] Consciousness of this problem would have been wholly consistent with French doctrine. Yet, it does not seem to have played a great role in French thinking. The problem of guaranteeing the security of French allies may not have appeared serious while the Rhineland remained unfortified. Even a defensively oriented French Army might hope to attack under such advantageous circumstances. But how could German adherence to the Rhineland demilitarization provisions of Versailles and Locarno be enforced with a defensive doctrine? This question did not receive serious attention either. Thus, the seeds of French doctrinal disintegration were contained in the doctrine all along. Political events could and would turn small problems into big ones. The remilitarization of the Rhineland and the Belgian declaration of neutrality in 1936 were to put French military doctrine in the position of having to innovate or disintegrate.

In addition to problems with French ground doctrine in the 1930s, France had problems with the role of her air force. From World War I through the mid-thirties the French Air Force was a modest collection of qualitatively indifferent aircraft. It lacked a well-defined doctrine. Its command structure and relationship to the rest of France's armed forces fluctuated. Even with these problems, its aerial capability remained superior to that of Germany, since the latter was strictly limited by Versailles; but in 1935, when Germany revealed the creation of the Luftwaffe, and in subsequent years as that organization grew in strength and experience, little was done to alter the confusion that reigned in the French Air Force. Even without the benefit of hindsight, it would have made sense in terms of German progress to develop some sort of coherent conception of the air mission vis-à-vis Germany. This was not done. The absence of attention to the air problem is particularly striking in the context of French dependence on short-term mobilization of the army and long-term mobilization of industry. At minimum, one would expect a substantial commitment to air defense to protect the mobilization process.

Although the political and military circumstances surrounding French doctrine changed substantially during the mid- to late 1930s, surprisingly little change occurred in French military doctrine. There was little innovation. French military doctrine grew less and less capable of achieving French foreign policy goals. Moreover, this is no mere hindsight. At least some Frenchmen were cognizant of these problems at the time. What then explains the stagnation and disintegration of French military doctrine?

The Distribution of Power: An Enduring Factor

One reason French doctrine did not change in the late 1930s is that French politicians remained more interested in transferring the costs of their defense to others than they were in assuring France's ability to defend herself. This is explained in part by overall French weakness relative to Germany, and in particular by the perceived continued relevance of the World War I experiences with modern military technology that had enhanced the impact of this imbalance. There was little if any striking evidence from actual combat in the interwar period to suggest that the World War I lessons needed revision. French doctrine, however, is as much explained by the opportunities for alliance building or buck-passing within the European political system. As noted earlier, there were plenty of countries in Europe with something to fear from a resurgent Germany. Even the reluctant British might be coaxed into a new anti-German coalition; they had always opposed the hegemonic ambitions of any European aggressor. French politicians concentrated their balancing efforts abroad, rather than at home, *both* because without powerful allies France could not expect to prevail in an attrition war with Germany, *and* because there were powerful allies out there to be had. The defense might have the advantage, but in a one-to-one slugfest Germany's large population and resource superiority might overwhelm French defenses. Thus, even when rearmament was undertaken, one of its chief purposes was to reestablish French credibility with allies. There was little if any effort to give France a unilateral military option against Germany.

France had three ways to pass the security buck. Great Britain was the first priority. She continued to be seen as the fundamental alliance requirement for any future war. France's cluster of eastern allies was of second priority—an insurance policy against British recalcitrance. Alliance with either the Soviet Union or Italy was of third priority; it was a speculative venture with a potentially high payoff. To say that Britain enjoyed number-one priority is still to understate her importance. It was believed that war against Germany without Britain was out of the question.

French leaders focused their energies on their political opportunities. For the most part, military organizations were *left with insufficient guidance.* The relative stagnation of their doctrine was not of great concern, because the doctrine remained consistent with the political priorities of French leadership. While some political conditions changed in the mid-thirties, the most important political influences on French doctrine did not change. Germany outnumbered and out-produced France. Allies must be sought to equalize the contest. Risks must not be taken that might draw France into an unequal contest without the assistance of allies. In this, the French may have been correct, but French military doctrine needed adjustment if it was to have a high probability of success in Belgium once that nation returned to neutrality. Similarly, preserving the security of French eastern allies in the context of a fortified Rhineland would demand a more offensive doctrine. While some recognized the requirement for such changes, most notably and vociferously Charles de Gaulle, the political impetus for change was not forthcoming.

That the political will was not present reflected the French concern that her allies pay a "fair" share of future war costs. The French were concerned not to scare off the British, who were perpetually afraid that the French would draw them into a new war. French strategic defensiveness eased relations with the critical British ally. This is in line with an important balance of power theory prediction. In multi-polar systems, states construct their strategies to attract allies. France had reason to doubt British willingness to support a vigorous anti-German policy. In the immediate postwar period, aggressive French behavior to enforce the provisions of Versailles had damaged relations with Britain. British policy-makers in the 1930s, with the fearful casualties of World War I fresh in their memory, were very reluctant to field the military forces needed to play a continental role. Britain enjoyed a natural geographical buffer against continental aggressors. British continental foreign policy was thus not only defensive, but sluggish. Anything in France that smacked of aggressiveness, such as an offensive military doctrine, might alienate Britain, and put off the day when she could be brought into an anti-German coalition.

At the same time, a more offensive French doctrine might have encouraged the eastern allies to engage in impetuous acts out of excessive confidence in France. The French feared being drawn into a war that they had no desire to fight—particularly without Britain. The eastern Europeans were meant to help France if she were attacked.

Thus, it is hard to see any overwhelming impetus for French civilians to tamper with the doctrine of their military organization. They would have had to carefully encourage offensive arms, doctrine, and training while at the same time obscuring these developments from everybody but the Germans—whom such measures would have been designed to dissuade. Moreover, French civilians would have had to keep careful watch on their soldiers to guard against any backsliding in the direction of pre–World War I offensive optimism. (Indeed, one may hypothesize that Gamelin's advance to Breda was an example of such offensive backsliding.)

The French case is suggestive of limits that may apply to active civil control of military doctrine in general. At least in pre–World War II France, civilians were much better at controlling the broad parameters of military doctrine than they were at controlling some of its more subtle aspects. Of course, the French may have had no satisfactory solution open to them. It may also be, as organization theory would suggest, that there are simply limits on the time, energy, and expertise of civilians. (In subsequent chapters, however, we will see civilians transcending their apparent limits.) These should be especially pronounced when the energy of civilians is absorbed externally, in the forging and management of a large coalition. Hitler, who was less concerned with allies, paid more attention to his forces.

While the causal forces identified by balance of power theory and organization theory seem to have worked in tandem to produce an ineffective French doctrine, the French case still contains a lesson for those who might wish to do better than did the leaders of interwar France. For it is clear that the civilians' preoccupation with external events, and the military's preoccupation with preserving its autonomy and traditions, allowed little communication between civilians and soldiers. These factors were exacerbated by a political and social civil-military schism that dated from the dawn of the Third Republic. The state could not solve a doctrinal problem as delicate as that outlined above when its statesmen and soldiers communicated so poorly with each other. While direct policy relevance is only an implicit goal of this essay, the lesson that follows from the French case is that close civil-military relations are a prerequisite for an effective military doctrine. Civilians and soldiers must talk to each other *in detail* about the military operations that each imagines that the state will have to undertake. Such relations may never be amicable, but they must be close.

Alliance Diplomacy

In chapter 2 I argued that a central task of a state's diplomacy is the projection of an image of effective power in time of peace. States may accomplish this through the manipulation of external coalitions, military capabilities, or some combination of the two. In time of war, states must marshal capabilities through some combination of alliances and internal mobilization. In the 1930s the leaders of France concentrated on their external possibilities, both for peacetime diplomacy and in anticipation of a future war. Internal capabilities played an important but decidedly ancillary role.

The manipulation of internal capabilities for diplomacy might have demanded a more offensive military doctrine and posture. Such an offensive appearance would have contradicted the pattern of French strategic thinking outlined thus far. It would have raised the risk of a solitary France becoming involved in a war with Germany. Diplomatic alternatives offered lower risks and the possibility of greater gains. Hence, European political possibilities again encouraged

France to preserve her defensive military doctrine. Moreover, as noted above, the exploitation of these possibilities tended to absorb a great deal of political attention. French military doctrine was thus deprived of the sort of scrutiny that German doctrine received from Hitler. The same constraints and incentives that encouraged a defensive doctrine for war-fighting also discouraged an offensive doctrine for short-of-war coercive diplomacy. Hitler, with few alliance possibilities, structured his forces as much for bully and bluff as for war. Conditions promoting civil intervention and its concomitant pressure toward innovation in the German case were not present in the French case.

The French pattern was set in 1934 when France left the Disarmament Conference. In 1933, when Hitler accelerated German rearmament, the British and French put forth more strenuous disarmament proposals. Hitler responded by withdrawal from the Conference and the League of Nations.

Here was a clear signal that Germany was initiating military developments ultimately threatening to France. The decision of French leaders to leave the Conference indicates that they understood this well. Yet, no new measures were taken to increase France's military capabilities. Instead, defense expenditures were cut, and Jean Barthou, the foreign minister, went off to search for allies in the Soviet Union and in Italy.[56]

Rather than make any effort to increase French offensive capabilities to dissuade the Germans or improve the cohesion of her coalition, French leaders turned to Italy. In 1935, Pierre Laval was moved to describe Italy as "the bridge constructed between France and all those countries of central and eastern Europe which were allied with our country."[57] Such considerations gave rise to the short-lived Stresa Front (an anti-German coalition comprising France, Italy, and Britain). In their search for an eastern version of the Locarno Pact, their flirtations (admittedly restrained) with the Soviet Union, and their wooing of Italy, French governments sought to counter rising German military capability with a show of coalition-building. By 1936 these efforts had run their course, ending either in failure or, as in the case of Russia, in success so qualified as to be almost meaningless. Only the alliances of the 1920s with Belgium and the eastern allies remained intact, along with the Locarno Pact.

The events of 1936 put a still greater strain on French grand strategy and prompted a new burst of coalition-building. March saw the German remilitarization of the Rhineland, reducing the credibility of French security guarantees to her eastern European allies. August

1936 saw the outbreak of the Spanish Civil War. The early involvement of Fascist Italy in that conflict alienated Leon Blum, Popular Front prime minister of France. The policy of using Italy as a "bridge" to the east was dropped. In October, Belgium returned to neutrality. This act soon rendered joint military planning for the long-sought defensive engagement in Belgium impossible. Each of these events prompted new French efforts to draw Britain into the joint military staff talks that would provide the essential preliminaries for the sort of war the French intended to fight.[58]

The British remained coy. Yet, from this point to the war's outbreak, cementing the tie with England remained the fundamental goal of French policy. Indeed, French willingness to sell out Czechoslovakia, the most capable of her eastern allies, is explained in part by the clear British disinterest in the Czech problem. Given a choice between joining forces with Czechoslovakia, but without Britain, or with Britain, and without Czechoslovakia, the French, consistent with their grand strategy, opted for Britain.[59]

From 1936 to 1940 France declined to take risks to ensure the security of her allies.[60] Indeed, throughout the period, French policy was to reassure her allies without increasing tangible commitments.[61] Even after France and Britain conceded parts of Czechoslovakia to Germany at Munich, General Gamelin was to advocate further alliance diplomacy to counter increasing German capability and bellicosity. In October 1938 he argued for strengthening French ties with Spain, Turkey, and the Balkans. How this was to be achieved after France had so recently sold out one of her most important allies is unclear.[62]

Repeatedly, from 1934 to the outbreak of the war, we see a well-defined emphasis in French responses to Germany. When Germany took any initiative that threatened France, the French scurried around trying to collect allies. While France managed to hold on to her treaty relationships of the 1920s, she was not able to expand them. Neither did she take military steps that would allow her to lend support to allies in eastern Europe. France was more interested in what her allies could do for her than in what she could do for them.

Of course, alliances are not charities; they are generally attempts by each party involved to transfer its defense costs to some other party or parties. In terms of French doctrine, however, it did not make sense to allow the Germans to take "long-war" resources piecemeal. This would put France at a disadvantage in terms of her own strategic calculations. Yet, this is what happened. Were French leaders completely unaware of this lapse?

Offensive Advocates

Even before France's final withdrawal from the Disarmament Conference on April 17, 1934, General Maxime Weygand, commander in chief of the French Army, and General Gamelin, chief of staff, were concerned about the German violations of the Versailles Treaty disarmament provisions. They overstated the extent of these violations to support arguments for a general increase in French defense spending, with special emphasis on the need for heavy tanks and artillery. These would permit the offensives necessary to aid French allies.[63] One should not leap to the conclusion that anything like Blitzkrieg was being proposed. The desired weaponry was destined for offensive uses, but in the slow and methodical manner developed at the end of World War I.

On April 17 the French cabinet approved a policy statement that advocated a much stronger line against Germany. The note foreshadowed Barthou's energetic alliance policy discussed above. The policy statement called for a more offensive cast to French military planning. The generals had argued for this previously. Yet, the only additional funding made available to the military in 1934 was dedicated to further work on the fortification system. The original plans for the Maginot Line were nearing fulfillment in 1934. Rather than shift expenditure to new programs, the government allocated more money to defensive works. French behavior was contradictory. While the policy statement of April 17 implied a requirement for greater offensive mobility, the army preferred greater mobility within an overall defensive context. One doubts that offensives were really in anyone's mind. Neither the subsequent behavior of the government in power in 1934 nor of later governments suggests any concern for offensive capability.[64] General Louis Maurin, the minister of war, summarized the position of the French government in a statement to the Chamber of Deputies on March 3, 1935.

> How could it be believed that we are still thinking of the offensive when we have spent billions to establish a fortified barrier? Should we be such fools as to go beyond that barrier, seeking some God knows what kind of military adventure? This I say to show you the thought of the government, that at least as far as my person is concerned, knows the war plans perfectly well.[65]

The Maginot Line signaled to friend and foe alike French unwillingness to undertake any kind of military action unless she were directly threatened.[66] This judgment is borne out by French behavior

[128]

in 1936 and remarked by observers on the scene. The structure of the French Army was one of the principal internal arguments against resisting German remilitarization of the Rhineland. In a note to the Conseil Supérieur de la Guerre, Gamelin stated flatly that no troops were immediately available for use in the Rhineland. France's military system did not give this capability, since the active units were simply the nucleus of a mobilized national army. Gamelin opposed even a symbolic action. Nothing should be done unless the entire couverture were put on a war footing, implying a call-up of a million men.[67] Due to internal political conflict at the time, the government deemed such action out of the question.

Lessons were drawn from this experience but were never applied in the forces. Later in 1936 Gamelin himself admitted that the form of the French Army was too defensive, and that to preserve her alliances the military forces had to be capable of some intervention beyond the frontiers.[68] In 1937 Lt. Col. Jean Fabry wrote in the *Revue Militaire Générale* that France's military organization did not allow any sort of bold diplomatic response to Hitler's occupation of the Rhineland.[69] Critics outside the center of government recognized the problem. De Gaulle argued for his armored and mechanized "armée de metier" on the grounds that it would prevent the piecemeal destruction of the French alliance system. Such a standing force would make possible limited military action to dissuade or defend, as opposed to total mobilization.[70] Paul Reynaud, later to become prime minister, shared de Gaulle's views and explained many of the failures of French foreign policy by the dearth of intervention capabilities.[71]

In 1936 the Popular Front government of Leon Blum recognized that an increased military effort was necessary to counter German actions and support French diplomacy.[72] Yet, none of the measures taken by France over the next two years, important and extensive though they were, directly served to increase France's capability to help her allies. The measures taken were completely consistent with the military doctrine evolved during the 1920s. First, a new program of light defensive works along the Belgian border was begun. This was meant to provide an insurance policy against the failure of the Belgian maneuver. The forts were not on the scale of the Maginot Line and were incomplete in the fall of 1939. Second, the system of economic mobilization for the long attrition war was improved. Third, an overall program of rearmament was begun. Although this program involved the purchase of substantial numbers of tanks and planes, no attempt was made to alter the army's predominantly defensive plans for the use of these weapons.[73] No major preparations for offensive operations of any kind were made.

French war plans and preparations never improved "the speed and effectiveness of their aid to the east." General LeLong's remarks to the British on the subject of aid to Poland in 1939 show that the defensive French doctrine of the 1920s had undergone little change. LeLong noted that "the Maginot Line and the Siegfried Line faced each other, and France could not seriously attack Germany on land without long preparation."[74] The sacrifice of Poland would contribute to French security. One factor contributing to Gamelin's approval of the declaration of war in 1939 was his belief that mobilization could proceed without interference, while Germany was busy destroying Poland.[75]

Summary: Balance of Power Factors and the
Stagnation and Disintegration of French Military Doctrine

The continuing obsession of French civilians and soldiers with passing the costs of French defense to potential allies militated against major innovations in military doctrine during the 1930s. French civilian leadership during the period concentrated its energies on preserving or expanding alliances. Of primary importance was the alliance with Britain. A more offensive military doctrine could only complicate the task of winning British support. Consistent with the priority assigned to British aid, France was willing to pay little in the coin of her own offensive capabilities to preserve her eastern alliances. France walked a tightrope between doing just enough to preserve her eastern alliances and at the same time maintaining a primarily defensive capability that would both satisfy the British and allow France, once war came, to pass the costs of war to all of her allies, great and small.

The unintended consequence of this policy was to produce a military organization insufficiently prepared for some of the important contingencies identified by French grand strategy, especially the French advance into Belgium. Civilians looked outward rather than inward for solutions to French security problems. Had the French political situation been more like that of Germany in the 1930s, or Israel today, one suspects that more sustained political attention would have been focused on military means. Unfortunately, the military was left to its own devices.

Organizational Influences

During the 1930s, both the French Army and Air Force failed to achieve innovations in military doctrine. In the wake of the political changes of 1936, this failure became a prime cause of the disintegration of French grand strategy.

The defensive doctrine that had evolved in the 1920s and early 1930s put French civilians and soldiers in an unfavorable position to absorb improvements in tank and aircraft design. Consistent with Brodie's generalization, the armed forces "accepted" the new weaponry without "adapting" to it.[76] The simplest lessons of World War I governed the army's behavior.[77] The French always stressed firepower over maneuver.[78] The requirement for a heavy firepower offensive with a massive preliminary bombardment fostered a slow and deliberate style of warfare. New techniques and machines were fitted to this model.[79] Ten years after World War I the École Supérieure de Guerre was teaching this view of war to its students, students who were to be commanding officers ten years later. Moreover, French officers were taught abstract principles of war in a "formalistic and routine" way. Instruction in the actual conduct of complex military operations seems to have been sparse.[80]

The evolution of French thinking on the tank provides a useful illustration. As early as 1920 the first subjugation of the tank to the rhythm of the infantry had occurred. By 1929 this was formalized in *instruction sur l'emploi des chars de combat* (instruction for the employment of tanks) issued by Paul Painlevé. This basic field manual declared that tanks were "only a means of supplementary action temporarily set at the disposal of the infantry. They considerably reenforce the action of the latter, but they do not replace it."[81]

By the late 1930s the tank course at the École Supérieure de Guerre attempted to teach the mass use of tanks and combined arms operations. Yet, in 1937 the École des Chars de Combat (the Armor School) still stressed the subjugation of the tank to the infantry, and the necessity for massive artillery support to suppress anti-tank guns.[82] (It is worth nothing that this last idea has come to have considerable validity.) The tank manual of 1937, signed by General Gamelin, deliberately forswore the discussion of mechanized divisions and the mechanized exploitation of breakthroughs.[83] Generally, there was a dogmatic subjugation of the tank to the infantry and an unwillingness to exploit any of its maneuver possibilities. Unlike German Panzer units, French tank units were usually not provided with mechanized organic support elements, such as infantry, artillery, and engineers, which could help commanders exploit the full maneuver possibilities of the tank.[84]

As early as 1932 the French Army had experimented with an all-mechanized force. A tactical error by its commander was seized upon to end the experiment. Instead, old-style formations were gradually motorized and mechanized.[85] The horse cavalry division of 1932 gradually metamorphosed into the DLM (Light Mechanized Division) of 1940. Giving a new technology to the most traditional branch of a service is perhaps the worst way to assure its effective exploitation.

By 1936, the thought patterns and organizational structures were set. When Hitler began his depredations, few were willing to embark upon risky innovations. Weygand concluded that the speed of German rearmament did not allow anything revolutionary. Though many French writers continued to harp on the dangers of the attaque brusquée, few suggested that the French Army adopt its techniques.[86] While the *Instruction sur les grandes unités* of 1936, the official statement of French tactical doctrine for the late 1930s, extolled the speed and mobility of modern weaponry, it simultaneously stressed careful planning and the avoidance of encounter battles. The infantry manual of 1938 stressed firepower and "tactical security."[87]

In May 1939, in a speech at Chatham House (Britain's Royal Institute of International Affairs), Weygand reaffirmed his faith in the defensive and in firepower. "On this basis, he then outlined for his listeners a picture of stabilization on the western front in the coming war, with the decision to be reached elsewhere—in Eastern Europe or the Balkans."[88] In the end, French doctrine and forces were specialized for this hope.

How is the stagnation of French ground doctrine to be explained? As argued earlier, the French armed forces were brought to accept the defensive doctrine as a way to salvage their autonomy and identity. Throughout the 1930s, the civilian preference for a cautious defensive doctrine did not change; civilians did not intervene to promote innovation. They gave the soldiers little reason to believe that another doctrine would find official favor. Indeed, Philip Bankwitz offers this consideration (perhaps over-sympathetically) as the fundamental reason General Weygand would not consider major doctrinal reforms in the mid-thirties.[89]

Second, the doctrine's assumptions about the character of a future war continued to be based chiefly on French World War I experience. The veteran World War I French Army commanders were disinclined to seek changes that would render their own skills obsolescent.

Third, from 1928 through 1935 the French Army had its conscripts for only a year. This was believed to be an inadequate training period. It was feared that when such conscripts were ultimately mobilized and recalled for active service, they would be unfit for all but well-planned defensive actions. Even after the two-year term was restored in 1936, the army perceived the standard of training as low for the majority of mobilizable reservists.

After 1936 an additional fear forestalled change. International politics was heating up. Suppose the army was caught during a major reorganization. If it were in transition between doctrines when war broke out, the question would be not whether it could fight well, but whether it could fight at all.

Thus, none of the factors hypothesized in chapter 2 as contributing to innovation were at work in the French military during the 1930s. There was little direct experience with new technology; new technologies were in the custody of very traditional services and service branches. There was little civilian pressure to innovate. The military hierarchy was inflexible and populated by elderly veterans of World War I. Conversely, in almost every way, an absence of doctrinal innovation reduced uncertainty for the organization.

The doctrine of the French Air Force (l'Armée de l'Air) in 1940 remains something of a mystery, but it too played a role in the French defeat. Historians agree that its contribution to the war was insufficient. It began the war with a miscellaneous collection of largely mediocre fighters. It deployed even fewer bombers. Some of these were obsolete; others were new but ineffective. Overall coordination of air operations was weak. Targets were frequently hit too late or with insufficient strength. The air force often failed to concentrate its fighters over critical points on the battlefield.

On the other hand, it does not seem that the air force was decisively defeated, but rather that it was improperly used, and in some ways scarcely used at all. While its goals and purposes were never clear, the French Air Force was, in the words of its commander, General Joseph Vuillemin, "at the time of the Armistice . . . ready to carry on, as it had a greater front line effective strength than on May 10."[90] On the one hand we have an air force that accomplished very little in the war. It lost over 500 planes in combat. Yet, it had sufficient reserves of personnel and machines to remain at full strength during sustained combat. Technically, then, the air force could fight. The problem was the failure to develop a coherent and appropriate doctrine.

Explaining the failure of the French Air Force is a complicated task, and one that historians have yet to complete. The following discussion relies heavily on the work of Robert Young.[91] His explanations ring true in organization theory terms.

First, the French Air Force did not gain its independence from the army until 1933. Hence, it could not, as most organizations are known to do, promote any sort of independent task for itself. The army forced it into a mold that made it a mere appendage.

Second, even after the air force achieved nominal autonomy, it remained under the close control of the army. Independent developments had to be cloaked in the guise of the army's traditional preferences. Until 1936, the air force seems to have lacked an effective civilian minister either to fight for it or to push it along. When it finally got such a minister, Pierre Cot, his schemes were opposed by the army and went unsupported by the remainder of the government.

Like many of the French Air Force officers prior to his term, Cot had a modest preference for the counter–city strategic bombing advocated by Giulio Douhet, the famous Italian airpower theorist. Neither Cot nor his officers were fanatical about this; Cot paid attention to air defense, but he built bombers. This is understandable if it is seen as the search by a young organization for a mission that could preserve its newly won autonomy. Strategic bombing would get the air force out of the army's clutches. Because of the army's institutional clout, this doctrine was a key element in Cot's demise as civilian minister.

When Cot was driven from office in January 1938, his successor, Guy La Chambre, found it necessary to race hard to catch up with an increasingly threatening Germany. Like the British, he saw the shift of resources to the production of single-engine aircraft (the easiest to produce) as the simplest solution to his problem. Although the French resource shift to fighters was not as dramatic as the British, the decision gave France what little air power it had in 1940. La Chambre also abandoned any notion of strategic bombing in the early stages of a future war.[92] Why risk planes against and provoke retaliation by a superior adversary?

Generated in a haphazard way and without clear goals, l'Armée de l'Air was not much more than a pile of aircraft. When the war began, the fighters were parceled out to the commanders of large ground formations. Where the French Air Force fought, it gave the Luftwaffe as tough a time as could have been expected from an inexperienced and technically inferior force. But it was usually a case of too little and too late.

The tragedy of the French Air Force is partially explained by organization theory. As argued in chapter 2, it is difficult for a group of services to construct among themselves a unified military doctrine consistent with a state's grand strategy. Services are more likely to bargain with each other in pursuit of their separate parochial interests. Each service will attempt to impose its own view of war on the others. Civilian intervention is required to coordinate the contributions of different services. French civilian leadership did not at first take an active hand in managing the air force because, as noted earlier, its energies were largely spent on coalition diplomacy. When Cot and La Chambre did take a hand, they drove the air force first one way and then another, each precipitating a destabilizing reorganization. La Chambre may well have been on the right track, but he had a late start compared to the Germans.

By 1940 the French Air Force was interested in almost every imaginable mission, from strategic bombing to air defense. However, with few priorities set by civilians, none of the missions were done well. In light of Britain's successful mastery of air strategy, the absence of strong civilian control in France is not adequately explained by the sheer technical difficulty involved. It may be explained, but only in part, by the outward-looking obsession of French statesmen. A definitive solution to the mystery has yet to emerge.

CONCLUSIONS

Determining the relative value of balance of power theory and organization theory in explaining French doctrine is a complicated task. Often the two theories seem to point to the same outcome. Balance of power theory does, however, emerge with a slight edge.

On first appraisal it appears that both balance of power theory and organization theory predict a defensive military doctrine for France. The country faced an imbalance of power; the imbalance was getting worse; allies were available to redress it. Yet, Britain, the most useful ally, was loath to risk a return to continental warfare. A defensive doctrine would thus serve two purposes. In peacetime it would conform to the political and military cautiousness of the ally being courted. The legitimacy of the French claim to assistance would be high. Once war came, a defensive doctrine would buy time to negotiate the distribution of the great risks and high costs associated with the offensive that would ultimately be required to defeat Germany.

Geography and technology influenced the doctrine in more subtle ways. Because the modern weapons technology employed in World War I increased the possibility of another attrition war, it magnified the value of industrially powerful allies. It also magnified the importance of French industry, which was mainly located in the northeastern and northern parts of the country. The technological lessons of World War I increased the attractiveness of a tactically defensive military doctrine. Because the northeastern industries near Germany and Luxembourg were farther from the border than were the northern industries near Belgium, and because they possessed local terrain with greater natural defensive value, the French perceived them as more amenable to defense from fixed fortifications. Hence, the Maginot Line was built to cover these areas. On close examination, however, it appears that some of the industry of Lorraine remained vulnerable to artillery fire that a German invader could bring to bear from Luxembourg.

Maybe because the new technologies threw off various and in some cases contradictory implications for military doctrine, the conclusions drawn from them by the French were not wholly consistent. In the northeast, defense from prepared positions would help protect some essential mobilization resources, but some would remain vulnerable. In the north, it was argued that such resources could only be protected by moving forward into Belgium, with the associated risk of violent encounter battles. Arguably, some of the industrial resources of Lorraine could only be protected by a similar move into Luxembourg, but this does not seem to have been a high priority, judging from available accounts of French strategic thinking. Given French views, the requirement to avoid encounter battles and the requirement to protect industrial resources in the north contradicted each other. They could do one, or the other, but not both. It is also difficult to avoid the impression of at least some inconsistency between French views on the defense of the Belgian frontier and French willingness to install fixed defenses on the Luxembourg frontier.

The risks of an advance into Belgium were not excessive if the alliance with Belgium held together and the French could advance to reasonably well-prepared defensive positions. Once the alliance collapsed, French soldiers ran a higher risk of a battle of movement for which their doctrine was unprepared. What accounts for French acceptance of this risk?

Balance of power calculations tipped the scales in the north toward forward movement. Fortification of the northeastern border and an open Franco-Belgian border would induce Germany to move through Belgium. If Belgium cooperated, the Germans would be stopped far from the French border, saving the industries of the north. Furthermore, because Belgium had long been identified as an invasion springboard against England, a German attack would help draw that country into continental battle, redressing the imbalance of power with Germany. This perhaps clears up some of the mystery about the Luxembourg frontier. Offensive action in Luxembourg might help protect some industry, but it would not yield any other significant dividends. This would suggest that it was precisely these other dividends that loomed largest in French plans for Belgium. In the end, France took some risks in terms of the narrow technological lessons of World War I for the sake of potential gain in gross capabilities.

Organization theory offers contradictory predictions for the attitudes of the French Army toward offense and defense. On the one hand, the slow-paced, largely defensive war of attrition had been the army's major World War I experience. Conservatism should have drawn it to a defensive doctrine. On the other hand, the French Army entered World War I with a strong offensive bias, and ended that war marching toward Germany. One could argue that this background, and the organizational incentives for offense discussed in chapter 2, should have been enough to keep the offensive spirit alive in the French Army. Close students of French interwar military doctrine have debated whether or not this was the case. The burden of the argument has been that offensive thinking received short shrift, and that the army really had no interest in the offensive.

A careful reading of the history, however, shows why the debate on French Army doctrine continues. In the early post–World War I period the French General Foch continued to believe that a rapid offensive might subdue German military resurgence. As the French lost support for aggressive enforcement of the Versailles Treaty and began to build the Maginot Line, French generals argued that the border forts should be constructed in such a way as to facilitate maneuver and counteroffensives. The original plans for the Line conformed to these wishes. The field manual of 1936 retained a good word for offensive action, so much so that some students of the manual have tried to make the case that French doctrine was not so different from the German. Finally, General Gamelin's Breda variant has the look of the 1914 French Army's daring offensive lunge. The offensive spirit did not simply vanish from the French Army.

It must be admitted, however, that these offensive strains were muted. The offensive tendency was weak partly as a function of organizational inertia and partly as a result of institutional doubts about the offensive élan of the one-year conscript. But the principal cause of the great defensiveness of French doctrine was the army's awareness that offense would find little favor with the civilian leaders

[137]

of France. This is not to argue that the French officer corps showed a particularly strong desire for a more offensive doctrine. Rather, the doctrinal parameters set by civilians, largely for balance of power reasons, reduced to zero the probability of independent military advocacy of any kind of offensive doctrine.

In the areas of integration and innovation, balance of power theory just narrowly provides a better explanation for French military doctrine than organization theory. Organization theory predicts that soldiers and statesmen will have difficulty reconciling policy and military doctrine. Before the Belgian declaration of neutrality in 1936 this was not the case. Afterwards it was. Why? Organization theory suggests that lack of mutual technical understanding between soldiers and civilians should produce disintegration. This tendency is exacerbated by the military's pursuit of organizational autonomy. These tendencies did not produce disintegration while the French military position remained relatively simple—before the problem of French entry into Belgium grew in tactical complexity and subtlety. Before the Belgian declaration of neutrality, the French Army could hope for an early and safe entry into Belgium, perhaps to occupy defensive positions already prepared for them. Defensive tactics developed for the northeastern frontier would not be taxed. After 1937, the move involved a higher risk of a war of movement, for which the military doctrine of France was unprepared. But how could the French Army get ready for a war of movement without appearing to return to the offensive and so to subvert the overall objectives of French grand strategy? Such a doctrine might have been possible with closer civil-military relations. Yet, as the threat increased, civilians remained preoccupied with the balance of power, which could only be rectified by strong allies. Civilians spent their time and energy trying to rebuild the old World War I coalition. There was little time left to address the details of military doctrine.

The preoccupation with forging and managing an external coalition also affected the chances for innovation. After nearly eighteen years of a defensive doctrine, the French officer corps would have been hard put to grasp independently for a more offensive, mobile-warfare, doctrinal innovation. As German strength and belligerence grew, it seemed that war could occur at any time. What if it came in the middle of a doctrinal change, leaving the army without any coherent guidance for combat? If innovation consonant with the changed political circumstances of 1936 were to occur, civilian pressure would have to be applied. Had civilians not seen so many alliance options to pursue, such pressure might have been forthcoming. Had the imbalance of power not seemed so great, civilians might have paid more attention to their national military capabilities, and less to coalition diplomacy. But the imbalance did seem great, and civilians saw their greatest problem to be righting that imbalance. Moreover, a mobile-war doctrine might have appeared offensive, and jeopardized the possibility of timely British support. Civilians reacted to the balance of power, the constraints and incentives inherent in their environment, and created conditions in which organizational inertia could prevail.

Which of the two theories, balance of power theory or organization theory, better explains French interwar doctrine? Balance of power theory explains the broad defensive tendencies of French grand strategy. French soldiers were constrained to operate within these parameters. Once they had evolved a largely defensive doctrine, they had little incentive to change. Once the events of 1936 created the need for such a change, civilian intervention was required. Civilians kept their eyes on gross power disparities, however. The pursuit of allies occupied their time and energy. The details of the subtle changes that French doctrine required were probably beyond their understanding. The changes suggested by French military reformers such as de Gaulle had an excessively offensive appearance that would have undercut the broader purposes of French grand strategy. The constraints and incentives of the European political system thus created the conditions for organizational factors to produce stagnation and disintegration.

Perhaps the developments in actual French war planning in late 1939 and early 1940 can help clinch the argument that balance of power calculations were the determining factors in French grand strategy. By then, France had achieved its original overriding purpose of binding Britain to the French war effort. Would France concentrate on collecting her winnings or on acquiring more? Would she, in effect, return to those technological lessons of World War I that had influenced her doctrine in the direction of caution and conservatism? Or would she continue to respond to the constraints and incentives inherent in the European political system?

The Escaut Plan would have covered all the narrow military lessons of World War I. Its cautiousness might have compensated for the German lead in military experience, the absence of prewar Belgian cooperation, and the almost willful French ignorance of mobile warfare. It allowed the soldiers more time to prepare defenses; it took the battle away from the French border; it maintained an operational reserve against unforeseen contingencies; and it involved the British in the initial fighting. There were, however, other chips to be won, chips useful in an attrition war. Why not try to gather in a million Belgian and Dutch soldiers? Why not try to save some Belgian industry for the Allied cause? Why not take the war even farther from the French border? Why not try to increase Britain's contribution? Would she not be more likely to make an ever-widening commitment to a long and costly ground war if that war were securing the Low Countries, with which she had a traditional obsession? The conclusion seems warranted that the same political constraints and incentives that had so driven French doctrine in the twenties and thirties permitted the remarkable war plan of May 1940. Those narrow technological lessons of World War I that played such an apparently important role in the early postwar period seem to have been discounted when the crunch came.

With British cooperation finally assured, French civilian leaders were less cautious and restrictive. Their long-sought diplomatic objective had been achieved. Under these conditions, French soldiers could allow their few surviving offensive inclinations freer rein. The overall balance of power had at last been partially equalized, but this only opened up new prizes for the French to seek. Ironically, these would require more offensive military action, which the French commanders, at least General Gamelin, were suddenly willing to contemplate. It was easier, however, to change the plans in a more offensive direction than it was to change the army's doctrine. For years balance of power considerations and organizational tendencies had meshed to produce a defensive, disintegrated, and stagnant military doctrine. By 1940, those same factors paradoxically allowed France to drift in the direction of a more offensive war plan, which would sorely tax forces trained and organized according to her defensive military doctrine.

To some readers this case might only suggest that the two theories capture causal forces of equal power, which worked in tandem to produce the distinctive doctrine of interwar France. I have argued, however, that balance of power theory better explains the broad parameters of the doctrine. A comparative perspective further illuminates the relative power of the two theories. In the two cases that follow, balance of power constraints and incentives differ from those faced by France, although the organizational ones are quite similar. Different doctrinal results emerge, results consistent with the different political and geographical circumstances faced by Britain and Germany. In comparative perspective, balance of power theory appears more decisive than it does in the admittedly complicated and murky case of French interwar doctrine.

[140]

[5]

Britain

Britain entered World War II with a defensive, innovative military doctrine, moderately well integrated with the political aspects of her grand strategy. The doctrine had only emerged in this form during the two years immediately preceding the outbreak of the war. Before that time, although the doctrine was defensive, and in some ways innovative, it poorly served British political ends.

Britain tried to preserve both her global empire and her European interests with economic and military resources that her elites understood to be insufficient. Because of this weakness, British leaders expected a new war to destroy the empire, even if England proper were to survive. To save the empire, they had to dissuade potential aggressors from attack. World-wide dissuasion was difficult to achieve with the military capabilities at Britain's disposal. Hence, the British ultimately chose to rely on the dissuasive effect of the threat to fight their traditional attrition war of industrial mobilization and naval blockade—in spite of the obvious fact that the entire British Empire could not match the combined resources of Germany, Italy, and Japan. Strong defensive naval and air forces would protect the industrial homeland and the sea lanes of empire from any sudden attack. Behind this shield imperial resources would mobilize. Finally, potential aggressors could not ignore the possibility that Britain would in the future, as she had in the past, seek and find powerful allies. Reliance upon continental allies to do most of the expected brutal ground fighting was an important component of British strategy.

By the 1930s, this dissuasive strategy was perhaps Britain's best bet, at least for the purpose of preserving the empire. Yet, the difficulty of defending the empire fed the emphasis on avoiding war, which in turn fed the policy of appeasement. Britain incrementally sacrificed both the credibility of her threat to wage an attrition war and assets useful to her enemies in the event of such a war. By the fall of 1939, Germany had captured too many assets and seen too many British concessions to be easily dissuaded by British threats. In the end, the attempt to hold the British Empire put Britain herself at risk.

British military doctrine was poorly integrated with this grand strategy for much of the interwar period. First, British naval forces remained inadequate to protect the sea lanes to the Pacific, much less the Pacific dependencies and dominions. Britain sized her navy for equality with the world's largest fleet—the U.S. Navy. Although this might preserve British prestige, it was an artificial standard. When rearmament began in 1934, Neville Chamberlain warned that the country simply could not afford a navy capable of simultaneous operations against Germany and Japan, much less Germany, Japan, and Italy.[1] Such a navy was not built, but the commitment to dispatch a fleet to the Pacific in wartime was sustained. As threats in Europe mounted during the 1930s, British resources to deal with them were made adequate only by the tacit write-off of her interests in the Pacific. Yet, to some extent the damage had already been done. The effort to fortify Singapore and maintain some semblance of a Pacific naval capability had swallowed scarce military resources from the lean defense budgets of the 1920s and 1930s—resources that might have strengthened Britain's hand in Europe and the Mediterranean. The sacrifice of the battleships *Repulse* and *Prince of Wales* to the Pacific chimera in 1941 was the final futile act of a futile policy.

Until the late 1930s, British military doctrine was *qualitatively* inadequate in two areas. One problem was largely rectified by 1940; the other was not. First, throughout the 1920s and 1930s the Royal Air Force (RAF) was allowed to maintain an offensive doctrine that was both unworkable and inconsistent with the overall grand strategy of the state. This doctrine either demanded a risky British first strike (something never said aloud) or implied a high risk that Britain might be knocked out of the war in an overwhelming enemy aerial first strike. Neither of these possibilities was consistent with the more general defensive, long-war premises of British grand strategy. Ultimately, British leadership got fed up with the RAF offensive bombing doctrine and intervened to change it, at least temporarily.

Various government officials and some "insurgents" within the air force began working together in 1934 to reverse the maxim that the bomber would always get through. Overcoming great resistance from the chiefs of the RAF, this coalition designed, funded, and built the major elements of the air defense system that was to serve Britain so well in 1940. It was only in 1938, however, that the major impetus for massive production of the all-important Hurricane and Spitfire fighters was provided. The earlier developments in air defense, as well as the final push for fighter production, were a result of civilian intervention into the doctrine of the RAF. British civilian leadership became more concerned with British military capability as war seemed to draw near. They investigated the claims of their military advisors and found them wanting. In late 1937 the RAF was to admit that it had no idea how to bomb Germany. Fighter Command was an operational innovation of the first order. This innovation was perhaps the fundamental element in the integration of British strategy in the late 1930s.

Britain's second mistake was to invest little effort in maintaining a continental intervention capability.[2] The army was not authorized to maintain even the most rudimentary capability for combat in Europe until 1939. Cooperation between the RAF and the army for continental land war was poor. The British and French armies had not been allowed to preserve or strengthen their World War I habits and mechanisms of coalition warfare. We have already seen some of the consequences of this omission (chapter 3). This decision was, in the main, consistent with Britain's overall long-war strategy, and with her preference for passing war costs to allies. The absence of a continental intervention capability created two problems. In the first place, Germany, the most probable adversary, could not be prevented from expanding eastward. Such expansion could (and ultimately did) circumvent the British long-war blockade strategy. Many of the resources that Germany would require for a long war were in eastern Europe for the taking, and neither Britain nor (we have seen) France did anything to protect these assets. This problem was only occasionally admitted by British decision-makers; it may have been one of the elements which brought the 1939 Polish guarantee.

The lack of a ground intervention capability would also contribute to Britain's air defense problem. Britain had no way to ensure the security of the Low Countries. Yet, if they were lost to Germany, both the air and sea routes to Britain would be shortened dramatically. This possibility was occasionally broached. It was not, however, a decisive element in British thinking. It does not even appear to have been the decisive factor in the ultimate commitment of the British Expeditionary Force to the continent in 1939.

How is the evolution of British interwar military doctrine to be explained? The rest of this chapter will show that British military doctrine was largely driven by balance of power considerations, reinforced by World War I experiences with military technology and by Britain's natural geographic defensive advantage. Organization theory helps explain the early disintegration of British military doctrine from the political aspects of her grand strategy. During the immediate postwar period Britain was relatively secure, and British military organizations were allowed to pursue whatever parochial doctrines they wanted. British civilians could forego difficult defense decisions, including decisions about the military viability of the British Empire. As the international political system heated up in the 1930s, circumstances drove British decision-makers to supervise their military organizations more closely, and belatedly to diminish the scope of British military objectives.

DEFENSE AND DISSUASION

Technology

British civilian decision-makers were deeply influenced throughout the interwar period by the lessons of World War I. Two themes emerged. First, the general carnage of a war among industrial powers amounted to a major disaster. Like the French, the British were particularly struck by the costs of the war's land battles. Three-quarters of a million Englishmen, 9 percent of all men under 45, were killed, and one and one-half million were wounded or gassed. British leaders desperately wanted to avoid any repetition of such continental carnage.[3] Prime Minister David Lloyd George's attitude to the war in late 1917 can be taken to reflect attitudes that were to become widespread in the interwar policy-making community.

> I listened last night, at a dinner given to Philip Gibbs on his return from the front, to the most impressive and moving description from him of what the war in the West really means, that I have heard. Even an audience of hardened politicians and journalists was strongly affected. If people really knew, the war would be stopped tomorrow. But of course they don't know and can't know. The correspondents don't write and the censorship would not pass the truth. . . . The thing is horrible beyond human nature to bear and I feel I can't go on with the bloody business: I would rather resign.[4]

The people were ultimately to find out about the nature of the First World War and its costs, and British leaders were to have the war etched in their memories. The combination of elite and public horror

[144]

contributed to a universal desire for peace. Moreover, if war were to occur again, political and popular sentiment demanded that Britain not commit improvised mass armies to the field. Her goal would be to fight a more classically British campaign, which exploited sea-power, industrial and commercial strength, and allies.[5] Neville Chamberlain was to declare in 1936, "I cannot believe that the next war, if it ever comes, will be like the last one, and I believe our resources will be more profitably employed in the air, and on the sea, than in building up great armies."[6]

The second theme that influenced British strategic thinking was the expected horror of strategic bombing. Britain's unsavory behavior at Munich is often blamed on this fear.[7] This worry stemmed in part from direct experience with bombing at the end of World War I, and in part from the RAF's self-interested, systematic misinterpretation of those experiences.[8] Whether the lessons drawn from World War I were correct or not, they exerted an important influence on British civilian thinking.

During the First World War the Germans managed to drop 300 tons of bombs on Britain, producing 4,820 casualties, out of which 1,413 died. These raids spawned a number of panics in London. The government was forced to divert fighters from the front to the defense of Britain. The RAF emerged as an independent service after the war as a direct result of these raids. British leaders hoped to avoid a repetition.

In 1921 the RAF was asked to make a study of the World War I raids. By 1923 this study had produced some remarkable results.[9] It was concluded that the French Air Force of 1923 could make London uninhabitable in short order. Each ton of bombs would produce fifty casualties, one-third of them fatalities. By 1925 the French Air Force was given a "steady state" bombing capacity of 100 tons a day. These numbers were not scientifically derived.[10] Nonetheless, the fifty per ton casualty rate became the accepted number for all planning purposes for the next seventeen years, and was cranked into subsequent discussions of growing German capabilities. These figures proved to be overly pessimistic. During the peak of the Battle of Britain the larger and more modern Luftwaffe was able to deliver 150 tons of bombs a day.[11] The British casualty rate per ton was closer to seven than fifty.[12]

In sum, the experience of World War I strategic bombing and the ostensibly objective technical lessons drawn by the RAF from that experience combined to produce in British leadership a great fear of bombing in a future war. The notion of a "knock-out blow" was taken quite seriously until 1939.

The fear of bombing was added to the general fear of war outlined above. The two fears were logically somewhat mutually exclusive. The first projected a rapid *decisive* air offensive of great destructiveness, the second a long attrition campaign of great destructiveness. The inconsistency between the two fears was never resolved; they were simply added together to produce an intense desire to avoid another war. If that war should occur, Britain would try to find a way to fight it that would minimize her own costs. For many years both of these goals contributed to a willingness to indulge the strategic bombing fantasies of the RAF. Britain would try to maintain a bombing capability that would frighten others into not starting a war—a strategy of deterrence. At the same time, the British would maintain a force of sufficient capability, if the bombing advocates were correct, to win rapidly any offensive exchange with future adversaries. If the more extreme predictions of the bombing advocates proved wrong, if "knock-out blows" were unachievable, strategic bombing would at least give the British a way to attack their adversaries without recourse to the feared, casualty-intensive, ground operations of World War I. Bombing would be an addition to Britain's traditional blockade strategy. Under the pressure of events, these ideas were ultimately to erode.

The Global Distribution of Power: Constraints and Incentives

British national security problems during the interwar period went through two distinct phases. During the 1920s Britain faced few if any threats. Germany was disarmed; Italy and Japan were relatively quiescent. The 1922 Washington naval agreement limited the size of those fleets that could threaten Britain. British defense policy was dominated by the Ten-Year Rule (August 15, 1919), an assumption adopted for budgeting purposes to the effect that Britain would face no war for the next ten years. The assumption was reaffirmed on a rolling basis, and was retained until 1932. British foreign policy concentrated on various disarmament schemes, the League of Nations, and treaties such as the Locarno Pact, all aimed at the general pacification of Europe.

In the 1930s German, Italian, and Japanese foreign and military policies began to evolve in potentially hostile directions. Britain's classical security problem reemerged, as did her classical methods for dealing with this problem. The problem and the solution were systemic in nature. The first was a constraint. British interests around the world clashed with those of Germany, Italy, and Japan. Britain had most of what there was to get; these others wanted what Britain had. Because Britain had world-wide interests, she had world-wide adversaries whose total power exceeded her own. British commitments and interests exceeded British capabilities, relative to the capabilities of the adversaries who threatened these interests. Britain faced an imbalance of power.

In the past, Britain had coped with this power imbalance in two ways. First, she had attempted to get on "good terms" with some of her potential adversaries. In the early twentieth century she had been on good terms with Russia, France, and Japan, so as to cover her imperial assets. This freed her to concentrate on the greatest threat—Germany. That Russia and France had also seen Germany as their principal adversary had contributed mightily to the development of the Entente. Britain was not to be so fortunate in the 1930s. Although Italy was an early opponent of Germany, their mutual hostility to France and Britain drove the dictators to an understanding. Japan had no fear of Germany or Italy. Britain could not make common cause with any of her potential adversaries, try as she might throughout the 1930s.

Alliances were the second mechanism traditionally employed by Britain to cope with power imbalances, and they assumed heightened importance in the straitened circumstances of the 1930s. There were other powers in the European and international political system with something to fear from Germany, Italy, and Japan. France was a particularly obvious candidate. The United States might ultimately be of assistance in the Pacific in spite of the isolationist policy that ruled her approach to foreign affairs. Until the late thirties even Italy was considered as an alliance candidate. The Soviet Union, with a social system and an army held in little regard in England, was also approached, albeit tardily and with little enthusiasm.

As threats emerged around the world, particularly in Europe, Britain returned to her traditional strategy, pithily summarized by Winston Churchill in remarks to the Conservative Members Committee on Foreign Affairs in March 1936.

> For four hundred years the foreign policy of England has been to oppose the strongest, most aggressive, most dominating power on the continent, and particularly to prevent the Low Countries falling into the hands of such a power . . . it would have been easy and must have been very tempting to join with the stronger and share the fruits of his con-

quest. However, we always took the harder course, joined with the less strong powers, made a combination among them, and thus defeated and frustrated the continental military tyrant, whoever he was, whatever nation he led. Thus, we preserved the liberties of Europe, protected the growth of its vivacious and varied society and emerged after four terrible struggles with an ever-growing fame and widening Empire, and with the Low Countries safely protected in their independence.[13]

Mr. Churchill may be forgiven for concentrating on the nobler elements of the policy—the opposition to expanding hegemons. He says less about the character of British balancing behavior.

While Britain was the classic balancer, she was until 1914 a "buck-passer" as well. Britain usually found a way to pass a good portion of the cost of balancing to her continental allies. Until 1914 this was particularly true of manpower costs; Britain seldom committed large land armies to the continent, preferring instead the financial subsidization of her allies' land armies. Similarly, the British manpower kept at home could be profitably employed building the industries necessary to support the armies of the continental allies. A good deal of continental manpower was not merely drained from the civilian economy, it spent its days at best bleeding those economies and at worst destroying them. British territory, trade, and industry could be secured by the channel and the fleet. Britain had been permitted this beneficial form of defense by virtue of the tendency of threatened continental states to balance more often than bandwagon, and the natural geographic defensive advantage that allowed time to assemble the unwieldy coalitions with which she waged war.

The imbalance of power was keenly felt by British statesmen and soldiers during the 1930s.[14] The twin themes of insufficient capability and the tendency for trouble to spread from one part of the world to another were to dominate British policy. The first high-level civilian discussions of British rearmament in 1934 were plagued by the question of whether Britain had sufficient economic resources to defend the entire empire.[15] In 1936, after the Abyssinian crisis, Sir Ernle Chatfield, the First Sea Lord, noted that the empire was "disjointed, disconnected, and highly vulnerable. It is even open to debate whether it is *in reality strategically defensible.*"[16] Chamberlain's support for attempts to appease Italy in 1937 stemmed from his belief that Britain lacked the resources for multifront war. Neither he nor the chiefs of staff doubted British ability to defeat Italy. Rather, the concentration of capabilities against Italy would weaken other areas of vital interest, inviting attack by Britain's other opponents. Neither Chamberlain nor the chiefs of staff believed that Britain could manage the ensuing global war.[17] The geographic breadth of the empire precluded the "German" solution to this problem—the rapid shifting of forces from one threatened front to another. This worry among soldiers and sailors provided constant support for the policy of appeasement.

Sir Thomas Inskip, the minister for the coordination of defense, was to declare in February of 1938:

> The plain fact which cannot be obscured is that it is beyond the resources of this country to make proper provision in peace for defense of the British Empire against three major Powers in three different theaters of war. . . . the burden in peace-time of taking the steps which we are advised—I believe rightly—are prudent and indeed necessary in present circumstances, is too great for us. I therefore repeat with fresh emphasis the opinion which I have already expressed as to the importance of reducing the scale of our commitments and the number of our potential enemies.[18]

In sum, there was a rough consensus among British civilian and military decision-makers that Britain lacked the resources for global war, and that a war in one area would so denude British forces in other areas as to invite "preventive" attacks by other opponents. The prescription adopted was to reduce commitments and reduce enemies, but without conceding any part of the empire. Attempts to reduce enemies led to the policy of appeasement. Commitments were reduced only tacitly, and late in the game.

Deterrence

In chapter 2, I argued that balance of power theory suggests that states in the position outlined above will prefer offensive doctrines if they can get them, deterrence doctrines if they cannot. During the interwar period Britain flirted briefly with an offensive doctrine, hoping to knock Italy out early in a future war. For most of the 1930s Britain groped for a deterrence strategy. She did not achieve it, due in part to the absence of creative doctrinal thinking, and in part to a very primitive understanding of deterrence as a strategy. A true deterrence strategy attempts to dissuade an adversary from aggression through a credible promise to inflict pain upon him. Thus, it requires a political campaign to convince an adversary of one's will, and military capabilities that appear highly capable of destroying adversary values—punitive operations. The British never clearly defined deterrence in this way, although they used the term in reference to their strategy.

[149]

Britain's quest for a deterrence strategy was motivated by the fear that war anywhere would mean war everywhere. As Arnold Wolfers observed, and as many of the contemporary British statesmen declared, Britain had an overwhelming interest in peace.[19] The overriding goal of British military preparations was thus the preservation of peace—not victory in war. Indeed, the notion of how victory would be achieved in a future war was remarkably vague. It was generally assumed that somehow Britain would fight her traditional coalition-attrition war and emerge victorious. British deterrence strategy aimed to convince potential adversaries that this was true so that they would not attack. Britain strove for operational military capabilities that would allow her to fight such a war should the occasion arise.

British "deterrence" strategy had three major elements. First, Britain hoped to use the empire, and the image of power it conveyed, as a means to protect the empire. The British attempted to sustain their "prestige," their "reputation for invincibility."[20] Ironically, Britain's prestige depended upon the very empire that they sought prestige to defend. The empire's reputation as a source of British wealth, and hence of her long-war capability, was also thrown into the deterrence effort.[21] In 1938 the United Kingdom sold 62 percent of its exports, and took 55 percent of its imports from the Commonwealth and sterling bloc countries.[22] The image of British control over all this wealth was believed to contribute to potential adversaries' perceptions of British power.

Second, the image of imperial power and wealth was closely allied to a far more important and explicit theme of British interwar deterrence policy—the notion of British economic health as a "Fourth Arm" of defense. Sir Thomas Inskip vigorously argued this position in December 1937 as part of the Cabinet's consideration of future defense programs. Current rearmament programs had to be balanced against the capability of the economy to support them. Britain was generally dependent upon imports, and the manufacture of modern armaments had a particularly high import component. Thus, high arms spending could easily upset the balance of trade and damage Britain's credit position. Britain could not hope to win a new war against a major power by means of a "knock-out blow"; she had to "contemplate a long war." Germany especially was likely to begin any future war with an attempted "knock-out blow," since she was not "well placed for a long war in which the Sea Powers, as in the past, are likely to have the advantage."[23]

We must therefore confront our potential enemies with the risks of a

[150]

long war, which they cannot face. If we are to emerge victoriously from such a war, it is essential that we should enter it with sufficient economic strength to enable us to make the fullest uses of resources overseas, and to withstand the strain . . . seen in its true perspective, the maintenance of our economic stability would more accurately be described as an essential element in our defensive strength; one which can properly be regarded as a fourth arm in defense.[24]

Inskip went on to argue in what seems to be a more general sense, but bearing directly on the appearance of soundness in the British economy, that

nothing operates more strongly to *deter* a potential aggressor from attacking this country than our *stability*, and the power which this nation has so often shown of overcoming its difficulties without violent change and without damage to its inherent strength. This reputation stands us in good stead, and causes other countries to rate our powers of resistance at something far more formidable than is implied merely by the number of men of war, aeroplanes and battalions which we should have at our disposal immediately on the outbreak of war. But were other countries to detect in us signs of strain, this *deterrent* would at once be lost.[25]

Inskip's views were shared by the prime minister, Neville Chamberlain, and the chancellor of the exchequer, Sir John Simon.[26] While it is tempting to see these concerns as a hollow justification by weak-minded appeasers for criminally insufficient defense spending, there is much to be taken seriously in their argument. We often forget that the British had liquidated most of their foreign investments to fight World War I, that they had borrowed heavily from the United States to finance that war, and that the United States' Johnson Act of 1934 had denied Britain future access to American capital markets because she had defaulted on previous loans.[27] In May 1939 the Treasury was to make clear that Britain's position for waging a long war was greatly inferior to that in 1914.[28] Had the United States not come to the rescue in late 1940, the British might have been forced to cut back their war effort.[29] British attempts to balance the dissuasive and defensive value of immediate military preparedness against that of visible economic health should not, therefore, be dismissed out of hand. One may, however, criticize British leaders for putting excessive weight on the external political impact of British economic health, long after Hitler had demonstrated that he feared and respected only visible military power.[30]

[151]

British decision-makers believed that the appearance of national economic health contributed to the image of British military mobilization potential, and that this image helped "deter" aggressors. Therefore, they were committed to an arms program that would not unduly affect that healthful image. At the same time, Inskip is careful to point out that for Britain's long-war potential to function as a deterrent, adversary powers would have to be persuaded of Britain's ability to ride out and parry attempted "knock-out blows." Such military capability was the third element of Britain's deterrence strategy. It was important that Britain "be seen to be strong"; otherwise her "all important influence for the maintenance of peace" would suffer. Inskip argued that the Cabinet had to strike a balance between financial stability and military preparedness.[31]

British decision-makers spoke of their military preparations in "deterrence" terms. Again it must be stressed that their use of the term was often vague. As noted earlier, Inskip believed that the image of British "stability" was a great deterrent. Britain also wished to create the image of military power. In 1934, when the rearmament programs were initiated, disputes arose as to whether the RAF should strive for substantial "first-line" air strength, without the reserves necessary to sustain intense combat, or for fewer "first-line" assets backed by the reserves necessary to support sustained combat. The Cabinet opted for the former policy, buying what was called "window dressing." Great first-line strength was believed to "inspire respect in the mind of a possible enemy."[32]

The term "deterrence," and the policy, are often associated with the Royal Air Force—particularly though not exclusively with its bomber striking power. The famous Baldwinism, "The bomber will always get through," was part of a broader set of beliefs including the notion that Britain could secure herself under such conditions only by maintaining a bomber force that could rapidly and effectively destroy enemy values in response to any attack.[33] Here we see some of the *punitive* elements of modern deterrence theory.

The stress on counter-value punishment was not the rule, however. Lord Philip Swinton, secretary of state for air, spoke of deterrence as a result of Britain's general ability to win a future air battle: "We cannot create an effective deterrent and we cannot pretend that we could meet an opposing force on equal terms unless we are satisfied that our ground defenses will bear adequate comparison with those of the enemy."[34] Chamberlain was also to speak of deterrent military forces in relatively undifferentiated terms, supporting "a deterrent force so powerful as to render *success* in attack too doubtful to be

[152]

worthwhile."[35] At one point the government would ask the services to do a cost-benefit study of the deterrence value of land versus air forces.[36]

In short, Britain's deterrence doctrine did not depend mainly on punitive military operations. Only in the air, spurred by the civilian memories and Air Staff "lessons" of World War I, did the British flirt with reliance upon a true deterrence strategy. They sought dissuasion as an end without understanding that purely punitive military means were probably the best way to solve a security problem of global dimensions.

To deter her adversaries Britain had to rely on the threat of somehow defeating them with the imperial resources that she could ultimately mobilize. In order for her adversaries to be persuaded that Britain would mobilize these resources, these adversaries had also to be persuaded of her ability to deflect a knock-out blow. This had the effect of driving the British toward a denial or defensive military doctrine.[37] In short, British decision-makers hoped that a clear capability to ride out an attempted knock-out blow, coupled with the image of economic potential for a long, imperial, attrition war and an appearance of political, economic, and social stability, would convince Britain's enemies that she could and would impose a long and painful war on her enemies if she were attacked. Presumably, the blockade would be the main military instrument, perhaps supported by strategic bombing if RAF promises were borne out.

For most of the rearmament period only the air force was allowed to contemplate offensive operations of any magnitude. Even the offensive capabilities of the air force were gradually cut back in favor of defensive capabilities as the threat of war loomed larger. Moreover, the chiefs of staff believed for most of this period that Britain should fight a defensive war if war were to break out in any one of the three critical theaters. Although offensive action might knock an enemy out of the war, it also ran the risk of great losses. Such losses would reduce British ability to "deter" the outbreak of war elsewhere.[38]

Only for a brief time did Britain flirt with the "offensive," disarming strategy predicted in chapter 2. In the spring of 1939 the idea of holding two adversaries with minimum strength, and "delivering a crushing blow against the third," was temporarily adopted.[39] The victim would be Italy, rightly deemed to be the "soft spot of the axis." By July 1939, however, the risks of such a strategy came to appear to outweigh the benefits.[40] Once again the security of the other theaters drove Britain in the direction of caution. Even a rapid and successful war against Italy might leave the Japanese with a "window." Royal

Navy losses in such a war might further weaken British ability to deter Japanese aggression in the Far East, and all but eliminate any lingering possibility of substantial reinforcement there.

An offensive somewhere should have been quite attractive to the British. Britain, of course, lacked a "knock-out" capability against two of her adversaries—Germany and Japan. Italy, on the other hand, can plausibly be said to have been vulnerable to such a blow, at least in North Africa and at sea. This is why it was considered. If such an offensive had been successful—and given Italian performance in the war, there is some reason to believe it would have been—Britain's position in the Atlantic and the Far East would have been greatly strengthened. During such a campaign, however, there is no denying that the Japanese would have had an opportunity to attack British interests, perhaps decisively. Britain might finish with Italy too late to halt Japanese depradations in the Pacific. The difficulties and distances were perceived to be too great for an offensive to succeed in the triple goal of knocking out Italy, dissuading Japan, and defending the Pacific should dissuasion fail. Unlike Germany, the British Empire could not quickly shift forces from one front to another.

In sum, the magnitude of British interests, the extent of the threat to those interests, and the insufficiency of British capabilities drove Britain to a rudimentary deterrence strategy. It relied on a multiplicity of factors to dissuade adversaries from aggression. The punitive operational capabilities appropriate to a genuine deterrence strategy were barely present, in the form of RAF bombing capability.[41] Generally, Britain relied on defensive-denial operational capabilities, and the diffuse long-term threat of ultimate imperial mobilization and blockade. This would, in theory, lead to victory. It was a ramshackle doctrine, but under the circumstances the best that could be managed *if Britain were to try to preserve the empire.*

Exploiting Allies

A hypothesis from balance of power theory is that states preparing to fight in coalitions will prefer defensive doctrines because such doctrines facilitate the passing of war risks and war costs to an ally (see chapter 2). In the preceding chapter we saw how the goal of "buck-passing" helped propel the French in the direction of a largely defensive doctrine. The same can be said of the British, although they perhaps stated their goal somewhat less clearly than the French stated theirs.

In the postwar period British statesmen believed, consistent with their classical concern for preserving a balance of power on the continent, that their frontier was on the Rhine. At the same time, however, they were uninterested in providing a large land army to defend that frontier. The question then was who would do so, and the obvious answer was France. Throughout the 1930s the British counted upon an alliance with France in a major war.[42] With the exception of the Soviet Union, little trusted or respected by the British between the wars, France was the only major land power in Europe capable of opposing a new German effort to establish a continental hegemony. Thus, for the most part, British decision-makers understood that French security was important to British security. At the same time, they were loath to undertake explicit commitments to the French, since these would inevitably lead to the question of British participation in a land war.[43] The British hoped to console the French and defend their own interests with a wartime commitment of air and sea power. The efficient organization of even such restricted collaboration demanded close military cooperation and planning in peacetime. The British avoided this because they feared that it would commit them to support any and all French efforts to oppose and suppress Germany.[44]

Sir Robert Vansittart, permanent undersecretary at the Foreign Office in 1935, commented on both the extent of the belief that France would be a British ally and the paucity of British effort to ensure such an outcome:

> We should surely wish to avoid too great dependence on the defensive assistance of any other Power. I have often heard it said that we should never be exposed to a war in Europe without French assistance.[45]

> The other main point is our confident taking for granted that we shall always have allies. I have often pointed out that this is probably but not necessarily so. It depends on ourselves; and I am bound to say that H.M.G. [His Majesty's Government] have done nothing of late years to warrant the certainty of that assumption.[46]

The British believed that France was an inevitable ally in a future war, if only because Germany would have such a hard time getting at Britain if she did not first deal with France. This certainty gave Britain a good deal of leeway in terms of what she would have to do to make herself an attractive alliance partner. Britain could heavily influence the terms under which she would fight in alliance with France. The British also knew, if only from the persistent French courtship, that the French badly needed British aid in a future war. Britain's bargaining position was thus further improved. In short, the French had very little choice about whether or not to defend British interests in Europe, since Britain's principal interest was simply the survival of an autonomous France with a sizeable army. Britain's secondary interest, and one that not all British decision-makers agreed upon, was the continued autonomy of Belgium to keep that country from becoming a base for aggression against Britain. Since the French preference for engaging Germany in Belgium was fairly clear to all, British decision-makers were usually confident that France would ultimately have to defend British interests there as well. Britain had considerably more choice as to which French interests it would defend. Britain was particularly averse to defending France's eastern European allies.

Because of the overall British interest in peace, British security interests on the continent were more narrowly interpreted than were French security interests. To pursue her interests, Britain would put France at risk; it could do so without substantially diminishing French utility as a defensive buffer. These were the conditions under which the British made their various military and diplomatic decisions of the 1930s. British strategy at the time may not have been as clearly articulated as it is here. Nonetheless, British behavior conformed to the strategy outlined here with remarkable fidelity.

The major British military decisions of the 1930s are all consistent with the hypothesis that Britain was "passing the buck" to other states—particularly, though not exclusively, to France. The most notable evidence is the weakness—sometimes complete lack—of a British commitment to send an expeditionary force to Europe to aid the French, Belgians, and Dutch against a German ground invasion.[47] This was not reversed until the spring of 1939. Britain would, as Chamberlain suggested, make its "contribution" in the air and at sea. The spirit of this type of thinking ("limited liability," as it was then called) is perhaps best captured by the observer-participant-critic Lt. Col. Henry Pownall, of the Committee of Imperial Defense. Writing in his diary of the Cabinet's ideas, particularly those of Chamberlain, he worried that:

> They cannot or will not realize that if war with Germany comes . . . we shall again be fighting for our lives. Our efforts must be the maximum, by land, sea, and air. We cannot say our contribution is "so and so"— and no more. . . . The idea of the "half-hearted" war is the most pernicious and dangerous in the world.[48]

Brian Bond's summary of British policy minces no words: "Britain never completely and categorically denied her strategic interests in north-west Europe . . . , but in 1937 and 1938 she went about as far as any power in her vulnerable situation could to shuffle off military responsibilities to potential allies."[49]

Except for some brief and attenuated instances, the British persistently avoided joint military conversations and planning with the French until March 1939, when war seemed all but inevitable.[50] The British knew that there were circumstances under which they would intervene on the continent—and that such intervention would be a vital British interest if it occurred.[51] Yet, they were avoiding the careful advance preparation and planning that would be required to make that intervention a success. They did this out of fear that the advance planning and cooperation with the French might dictate the fact and the *form* of such intervention. It was more attractive to pursue the "wait and see" attitude. France could carry the initial burdens while Britain made up her mind as to what *had* to be done. The dividend of this policy was the confused, poorly coordinated Allied military effort of May 1940, as well as Britain's less than competent contribution to that effort.

Various rationalizations were found for not building a continental-capable army, one of the most interesting being the notion that British spending on air power was somehow more "efficient" than spending on a land army.[52] Indeed, air spending was the number one British priority in the 1930s, directed first at bombers and later at air defense. While it is seldom admitted, one motivation for this was that spending on the Royal Air Force and the Royal Navy gave Britain more control over her own fate than equivalent spending on a land army would have done.

As proved to be the case in 1940, air power, even if ineffective, was highly fungible. It could be used against Britain's enemies even in the worst of eventualities—the fall of the Low Countries and France. A land army would be useful in the defense of the Low Countries and France, but of less direct utility in defending Britain should the worst occur. Indeed, one of the reasons the last vestige of a continental field force was abandoned in May 1937 may have been the belief that the security of the Low Countries was of less immediate concern to Britain than it had been.[53] Both heavy bombers and radar were under development, allowing operations in offense and defense without the aid of Belgium. Strategic bombing was an unproven military technique, but because British territory was invulnerable to overland conquest, substantial resources could be allocated to the bombing experiment in lieu of the land army Britain did not want.[54]

Finally, British naval policy suggests "buck-passing." Although the British Government and the Royal Navy were committed to the dispatch of a sizeable battleship fleet to the Far East in the event of trouble there, the government declined throughout the 1930s to fund the construction of a fleet large enough to handle Atlantic, Mediterranean, and Pacific contingencies.[55] Sufficient naval power would always be held at home to deal with Germany. What was left could go to the Pacific, leaving the French to cope with Italy if they were so inclined, or else the Pacific could be written off.[56] Until 1939 neither of these possibilities was actually admitted. Without having studied the problem, the navy had assumed that the Mediterranean could be temporarily abandoned and a naval war fought in the Pacific with supplies and ships brought around the Cape of Good Hope.[57] A reexamination of this hypothesis prompted by the Far East crisis of 1937–1938, the beginning of open warfare between Japan and China, proved the near impossibility of such a task.[58] Thus, the 1937 promise to Australia and New Zealand that a fleet would be sent would have to be broken. The seeds of this betrayal were sown in the mid-1930s, when the British declined to build a genuine two-ocean navy. Nobody wanted to see the implications of that decision. In "fairness," the British Dominions should have been warned at the time that they had better fend for themselves. The warning was not given, perhaps due to the desire to keep the image of empire alive for deterrent purposes.

To preserve her own naval defenses against Germany, Britain entered into the Anglo-German naval agreement of 1935, another case of buck-passing. This guaranteed that the German Navy's strength would not exceed 35 percent of the Royal Navy's. The agreement ensured Britain's own interests at the expense of legitimating *new* German violations of the old Versailles disarmament clauses. This quite deliberately flew in the face of French policy and French security.[59]

Britain, like France, was somewhat overly committed to "buck-passing." The military doctrines of both states took calculated risks in regard to the Low Countries. The British, however, buffered themselves against continental disaster with their air defense system. The French really had no buffer against failure in Belgium. It is this difference that moves me to call British strategy integrated and French strategy disintegrated. Yet, the integration of British strategy was late in coming. It was held up by the behavior of British military organizations during the interwar period.

Organizational Influences: Disintegration

According to a hypothesis from organization theory (chapter 2), due to their parochial interests, a group of services cannot create a military doctrine on their own. The behavior of the three British services throughout the rearmament period bears this out. Service parochialism was a major cause of the disintegration of British military doctrine from her grand strategy.

Historians agree that the services did not present British civilians with an "agreed strategic doctrine."[60] Each service planned for its favorite war, in a different part of the world, with little attention to the plans of its fellows.[61] The Royal Navy wanted to go to the Pacific and fight the Japanese. The RAF wanted to bomb Germany. The army was interested in various "imperial police" duties, and in 1933 worried about a Soviet attack on the North West Frontier of India.[62] Neville Chamberlain would frequently complain that the chiefs of staff "tended to submit aggregate plans rather than joint plans."[63] The services refused to set any priorities among missions or threats.[64] In general it can be said that each service argued for the military doctrine that most contributed to its autonomy, size, and wealth.

Organizational factors determined both the character of each service's preferred doctrine and the disintegration of overall grand strategy in the 1920s and early 1930s. Civilian inattention to military doctrine provided the condition for this outcome. British leaders, with good reason, did not perceive any serious threats to national security in the immediate aftermath of World War I. This attitude was reflected in the ten-year-no-war planning assumption adopted in 1919 and sustained until 1932. During this period British civilians occupied themselves with treaties and disarmament schemes aimed at controlling international conflict.

In keeping with the no-war assumption and naval arms control, British defense spending plummeted. British civilians were committed to such reductions to facilitate recovery from World War I. Financial stringency in its turn shrunk the pie to be divided by the three services, increasing competition. Each service had an interest in selling its distinctive mission and under-playing military cooperation with the others. This produced organizationally self-serving doctrinal preferences, and prevented any agreement on an overall military doctrine. Because the civilians felt secure, they paid little attention to military matters, and imposed no military doctrine.[65] Thus, the money spent was probably misspent.

The specific long-term effects of this situation can only be suggested, because most histories of the period do not get down to the details of civilian knowledge of military doctrine and capabilities. First, the doctrinal preferences of the services built up a certain momentum. By the time of the establishment of the Defense Requirements Committee in 1933–1934 (responsible for the first serious civil-military look at Britain's interwar military position and capabilities), the services had been left on their own for over a dozen years. Even if the civilians could have quickly developed a coherent strategy, and settled on the forces it required, they would still have had a difficult time imposing their will on the services.

Second, the civilians were so out of contact with military developments that it is not clear how much they understood about British capabilities. One comes away from histories of the rearmament period with the impression that it took some time for the civilians to reaccustom themselves to making strategic decisions. Thus, it was only with difficulty that the civilians could determine what they wanted; what they needed; and what was operationally feasible. They were ultimately driven by pressures in the international environment to impose a military doctrine, to intervene in operational aspects of their forces, and to allocate much greater funds for defense. As Germany, Italy, and Japan became more bellicose, the British set about the difficult task of reversing a dozen years of strategic slovenliness.

The foremost culprit for most of the interwar period was the RAF. Drawing on organization theory, I argued in chapter 2 that military organizations will generally prefer offensive doctrines because such doctrines make the greatest contribution to organizational autonomy and wealth. The RAF, with its radical strategic bombing theory, is an excellent example of such behavior. The RAF made the most wildly optimistic claims for airpower, including its ability to eclipse the role of navies and do away with the need for armies. It promised swift and, by comparison to World War I, cheap victories—if only it were endowed with superiority over its opponents. It would deliver these blessings by means of rapid, early, and intense offensives. The RAF was never too clear on exactly how long it would take to achieve victory, but the implication was that victory would not be very long in coming.

The RAF made the bomber offensive into a religion in the 1920s and 1930s. As noted earlier, the Air Staff had conjured up frightful statistics on the probable effects of aerial bombardment of England, and, by implication, great expectations for British aerial bombardment of

[160]

her enemies. It is clear that the strategy and all the numbers that were produced to support it went without any kind of testing until 1937.[66] When the Air Staff sat down to figure out how to attack Germany, they discovered they had no idea where to begin. They did not know *which* targets to strike. They knew nothing of finding or hitting the target, or of weapons effectiveness against different targets.[67] Yet, in large measure the RAF's dogma was the source of a good deal of the horror of air warfare that so paralyzed British interwar foreign policy.

The RAF's offensive operational preference drove out consideration of other uses of aircraft. This explains the dearth of RAF close support bombing in the Battle of France.[68] Moreover, but for the intervention of a number of civilians (to be discussed below) the RAF would never have invested sufficient resources in Fighter Command to support the performance turned in during the Battle of Britain. The RAF leadership viewed air defense as a waste of money.[69] The Air Staff appears to have made an effort in May 1940 to shut down the production of Spitfires and Hurricanes.[70]

The ritual assertion of both the value and the devastation of bombing offensives, and the denigration of air defense, produced a major disintegration in Britain's overall grand strategy. If offensive bombing was so effective, would Britain have time to mobilize her long-war resources? If the RAF was right, then there was a good chance that the adversary's bombing offensive would "knock out" Britain, before Britain could "knock out" the adversary. This consideration was paramount in the shift of civilian support from bombers to fighters. Early civilian support for the RAF's offensive bombing doctrine stemmed from a diffuse hope that it would deter German aggression. Civilians became more concerned in 1937 about the implications of the doctrine for Britain's real safety in a real war. By these criteria they found it wanting.

While the Royal Air Force was the outstanding culprit of the interwar period, the Royal Navy was not far behind. The sailors are perhaps less to be blamed, since they pursued military operations that were at least in keeping with the imperial fantasies of their civilian masters—although they made precious little effort to dispel those fantasies.[71] Of the three services, the navy suffered least from the drastic post–World War I cuts in defense expenditure.[72] It still suffered, however. For most of the postwar period, indeed up to spring of 1939, the navy had its heart set on what was without doubt the most difficult mission it could choose—combat in the Pacific. The construction of the huge naval base at Singapore was the major item of proposed naval expenditure during the period of the Ten-Year

Rule.[73] One would not want to blame the obsession with the Pacific solely on the admiralty. As argued above, the civilians had their own interest in the empire. But the Navy's attitude reinforced that of the civilians. Moreover, once the civilians had declined to fund a genuine two-ocean navy (one capable of defending British interests in the Atlantic and the Mediterranean, and in the Pacific), the admiralty was loath to forfeit the Far East mission, and continued to plan for it.

The sources of the navy's interest in the Pacific, particularly just after World War I, are not hard to imagine. In home waters, and in the Mediterranean, Britain faced either friends (France, the United States, and Italy) or a disarmed former adversary (Germany). It was only in Japan that the navy could find a genuine "threat" to plan against, and to justify the existence of its prized battleships. Moreover, the Pacific mission was a real challenge—10,000 miles from home. In terms of setting resource requirements it was a sure winner. It was the source of the navy's claims for a "two-power" standard.

To sustain this fiction the navy was willing, regardless of the vagaries of Italian behavior, to assume that the Mediterranean could be safely evacuated in the event of war with Japan.[74] Britain would be able to dispatch roughly half her fleet to the Far East and provision it by way of the Cape of Good Hope. The civilians appear to have agreed with this hypothesis. This particular assumption was only subjected to testing under the pressure of the Far East crisis of 1937–1938, which "confronted the services with the implications of an actual naval evacuation of the Mediterranean, and convinced them that 'the greater the tension in the Far East, the more important becomes the necessity for security in the Mediterranean.'"[75]

Neither in the course of the activities of the Defense Requirements Committee (DRC) in 1934 nor after the expiration of the various Washington and London naval treaty limits in 1936 does it appear that the navy war-gamed the Pacific-War, Mediterranean-abandonment hypothesis. Instead, the so-called "DRC-Standard Navy" was recommended. Although this recommendation favored an increase in the size of the Royal Navy, it allowed for only a small contingent to counter the nascent German fleet, and a large contingent to go to the Pacific. The Mediterranean was still left uncovered. It was hoped that somehow the French would secure the Mediterranean, but there was no joint naval staff planning to ensure this. By late 1935, the Committee itself recognized that German rearmament was proceeding at a pace that would demand a genuine two-power navy. This would require a doubling of the existing fleet[76]—still without any special provision for the Mediterranean. The government would agree to the "DRC-standard," but (owing to financial stringency) not the two-power standard.

Why did sailors not play up the Mediterranean problem to better their chances of getting a two-power fleet? Perhaps the navy feared the consequences of too pessimistic an evaluation of its Pacific capabilities. Had it been shown that the Pacific expedition was a dangerous adventure if the Mediterranean could not be secured, and that the latter could not be achieved without a $2\frac{1}{2}$–3 power navy, the government might simply have written off the Pacific once and for all. Had the civilians simply decided to plan for a war against Germany and Italy, the size of the British Navy might have been stabilized or even reduced—freeing military resources for other tasks.

In sum, the Royal Navy, like the RAF, did not test those strategic hypotheses that best served its organizational interests. This tendency contributed in both cases to the disintegration of British grand strategy. In March 1939, this particular cause of disintegration was largely (though not entirely, due to its accompanying force posture) reversed by the stroke of a pen. The Royal Navy would not be taking any Far Eastern cruises in strength.

Defense and Disintegration: Summary

British military doctrine was broadly defensive, with a strong dissuasive component. British civilians groped for, but did not achieve, what I have called a deterrence strategy. The doctrine was disintegrated for much of the interwar period.

The defensive/dissuasive aspects of the strategy were determined by a combination of technological, geographic, and power political causes. Hard experience with modern military technology had taught Britain the high cost of continental warfare. Experience with air technology suggested that offensive bombing in any future war might mean a disaster of unprecedented proportions. These technological lessons caused British decision-makers to seek to "deter" a future war, and to avoid its costs should that war occur. To "deter," Britain had to convince others that she could mobilize great military power. Her mobilization base would have to appear secure. The goal of dissuasion produced a defensive/denial military doctrine. Similarly, to control the costs of waging war, Britain would have to allocate her military resources to the defense of Britain proper.

At the same time, however, systemic constraints operated. A future war would not merely cost a great deal to fight, it would probably mean the loss of some part of the empire. Britain simply had insufficient power to defend her global interests, even if she could successfully defend herself. This was another powerful reason for avoiding a future war—another cause of the dissuasive component of British strategy. As noted above, the goal of dissuasion demanded a military doctrine of defense.

The availability of France as a continental shield was a critical systemic opportunity. It would allow the British to shift the costs of future land warfare to the French. The French were perceived to have no choice but to fight a future land battle. French soldiers would have to defend British interests on the continent. To ensure that the French would not be able to drag Britain into the land battle, Britain needed to secure her own territory against a German "knock-out blow." This again implied an emphasis on defensive/denial operations.

Here is where British grand strategy "disintegrated" in the interwar period. Neither the Royal Air Force nor the Royal Navy was organizing properly to avoid the "knock-out blow." They got away with this largely because of the long post–World War I period of comparative civilian inattention to grand strategy. The emergence of threats in the international system prompted greater civilian attention to strategic issues, but reasserting strategic control took time. The RAF was allowed to maintain an offensive bombing concept and the navy a Pacific war plan both of which put Britain's overall strategy in jeopardy. The RAF bombing strategy did make a contribution to dissuading Germany. To do so it put the economic sources of British power in jeopardy. These resources were required to dissuade Britain's other adversaries, and to defend if deterrence failed. British civilians were gradually to become aware of this problem.

The doctrine that emerged in the 1920s and early 1930s does not provide a good comparative test of the theories advanced in chapter 2. Each explains some element of the strategy. From the mid-1930s to the outbreak of the war external pressures on Britain increased. British decision-makers responded with quantitative and qualitative, internal and external balancing behavior. (They also responded with appeasement.) The evolution of British grand strategy and military doctrine during these years shows a general tendency toward integration and innovation. Moreover, it suggests the great explanatory power of balance of power theory—since British strategy moves to a defensive/denial military doctrine, more appropriate for the political goals of dissuasion and "buck-passing".

[164]

INTEGRATION AND INNOVATION

In the late 1930s innovation within British military doctrine, and the integration of that doctrine with British grand strategy, were mainly a function of developments within the Royal Air Force. By the outbreak of the war the most substantial, important, and successful changes had occurred in this service. These changes made possible the British victory in the Battle of Britain.

Changes in the roles and capabilities of the other services were less marked, less successful, and came much later. It was not until the spring of 1939 that the government and the Royal Navy admitted the impossibility of major Pacific operations. This change of mind had little effect on the structure of the Royal Navy or its preparedness for war against Germany and Italy. Similarly, the ideas that had determined the army's small size and comparative unpreparedness for continental land warfare were not abandoned until early in 1939. It was only then that the British government awoke to the possibility that the French Army might not secure the Low Countries, and that the Low Countries could still matter a great deal to British security—even in the context of long-range aviation and modern air defenses.[77] Politically the British came to believe that the extent and enthusiasm of the French war effort might depend on the perceived extent of the British contribution to that war effort.[78]

Similarly, in the spring of 1939, Britain came to believe that German aggression in the east might ultimately have the effect of upsetting the overall European balance of power. This was certainly seen to be true in a symbolic, political sense.[79] A continuation of unopposed German expansion in the east might set off a series of capitulations. Small states might bandwagon. The ultimate effect on French political attitudes could be disastrous. More than perceptions were involved. The elimination of Czechoslovakia removed 34–38 divisions from the French wartime coalition.[80] France demanded that Britain replace them. If other eastern European countries were to fall, Germany's position would improve and the French position would erode. Germany would be able to concentrate more and more troops against France.[81] Finally, the British may have begun to worry that German successes in the east (particularly against Romania) would substantially improve the Nazi resource base—circumventing the British blockade strategy.[82]

As with the increasing British investment in air defense, these changes came about as a result of the increasing threats to imperial security. British decision-makers responded to increases in adversary capability and evidence of malign intent with "balancing" behavior. Attention to the air balance and air defense began as early as 1934. The other changes came later because although they involved critical contingencies, the immediate survival of the United Kingdom hinged on none of them.

In some areas Britain could afford to try a "buck-passing" strategy; she could afford to wait. The United States might ultimately carry the British burden in the Pacific. If not, and Britain were to suffer imperial reverses, such reverses would not mean the defeat of Britain. Similarly, there were many countries in eastern Europe, and Britain could afford to see a few of them go down before having to choose to intervene. Finally, France would fight whatever land campaigns were necessary on the continent.[83] It was in her own interests to do so. Britain could afford to wait to see if her own assistance would prove necessary. On the other hand, as the chiefs of staff frequently worried, a premature British commitment to France might cause the latter to engage in the sort of adventurism that could provoke the very war that Britain was seeking to avoid. Britain had "security" slack in all of these contingencies.

British leaders perceived no slack in terms of their vulnerability to German air attack. The World War I experience with air attack and the horrific predictions of the Air Staff combined to make British leaders and the British public extremely wary of modern air power. Germany was the one adversary within aircraft range. Moreover, of the three potential adversaries that they faced, British leaders were never in doubt about the primacy of the German threat.[84] The marriage of air power to overall German technical, industrial, and military capabilities created a British vulnerability to direct attack of an order that had not been perceived for several hundred years.

British leaders were not merely struck by the new air threat; they were dissatisfied with the RAF's remedies. Just as the RAF predicted a massive German air offensive aimed at a "knock-out blow," it wished to counter the Germans with a similar offensive. This was out of step both with the missions assigned to the other services and with the higher-level objectives of British grand strategy. The view of air warfare purveyed by the RAF put a stress on offensive capabilities and operations. If the RAF's theories of air war proved wrong, Britain's classical mobilization strategy would be endangered. First, the Germans might not be deterred; they demonstrated a high propensity for risk-taking. Second, the RAF counteroffensive might not be able to hurt the Germans quickly enough or badly enough to stop a German air offensive before it ate into British industrial capability or national morale.[85] Third, the offensive bombing doctrine did not contribute very well to "buck-passing." If RAF bombing capability appeared sufficiently frightening, Germany might be deterred from any attack on Britain, regardless of her attacks elsewhere. On the other hand, if Germany did attack, Britain would be left in a serious predicament. Even if counteroffensives could somehow stop the German air attacks, Britain would be forced to fight such a campaign at a feverish pace. Moreover, she could be forced to make large contributions to allies such as France, who might offer other ways to end the German bombing offensive. If the RAF counter-blow were to fail, then Britain would be further dependent on a French ground contribution to end the German attacks. Thus, she might be forced into a great ground commitment herself. An effective air defense, on the other hand, would buy some "dissuasion" and some defensive-denial insurance if dissuasion failed, allowing Britain control over the pattern of her participation in a future war.

Whatever the reasons, explicit or implicit, British civilians were not happy with the offensive preferences of the RAF and set about pushing that organization in the direction of a greater emphasis on air defense. Without such civilian intervention it is unlikely that Britain would have fared quite so well in the summer of 1940. The character of civilian intervention into RAF doctrine was influenced by those same systemic factors that determined the general defensive character of British grand strategy—the inadequacy of her own power and the availability of potential allies.

Technological Change, Organizational Biases, and the Evolution of Air Defense

The principal "technological imperatives" and organizational interests associated with air warfare in the middle and late 1930s have already been discussed. Offensive bombers were believed to have awesome capabilities. They could penetrate adversary airspace and wreak terrible destruction. This belief was widely and deeply held. As late as the Munich agreement in fall of 1938, Germany was credited by British soldiers and statesmen with a home-based offensive bombing capability that she was barely to achieve later from Belgian and French bases. By fall of 1938 the British had become much more skeptical about their own offensive bombing capability, but this skepticism had only recently emerged. Poorly analyzed accounts of bombing in the Far East, in Abyssinia, and in Spain contributed to the survival of belief in the efficacy of bombing. The British Air Staff did not dispatch an observer to the Spanish Civil War to study the effects of bombing at first hand.[86] Until 1937, the RAF conducted no systematic tests of its strategic bombing assumptions.[87] Even the tests that were finally made only persuaded the British that their own bombers would not work. It is difficult to view the inflation of German bombing capabilities, unsupported by any serious analysis, and the corresponding denigration of British capabilities, as anything other than organizationally determined myopia. The RAF had every incentive to exaggerate the effects of strategic bombing to justify its preferred doctrine, and to inflate the German bomber threat to buttress the case for more bombers.

While there were few events in the 1930s that might disconfirm offensive bombing theories, there were at the same time few that demonstrated the efficacy of air defense. The origins of radar can be traced to the formation of the Committee for Scientific Study of Air Defense in 1934. Until primitive operational tests could be run (in August 1937), it cannot be said that a new technological "fact" had emerged. Even these tests cannot be said to have been earthshaking. Originally, the government had hoped to have more extensive operational tests before making the final decision to fund a full twenty-station system. In spite of the limited nature of the tests conducted, in 1937 the government decided to authorize production of equipment for the entire system. It looks very much as if the government decided to bet on defense because it wanted defense. Moreover, the preceding development of radar had not been an accident, but rather the result of pressure from a number of British civilian officials. This process will be discussed at greater length below.

On balance, the "technological" reality of the 1930s favored a widespread belief in the efficacy of offensive bombing—not air defense. At the same time, the RAF clung religiously to the doctrine of offensive bombing. We have already seen how the doctrine of the offensive was evolved in the 1920s to aid the RAF in its struggle to set itself operationally apart from the other two services. We have already seen how the offensive doctrine improved the prestige of the RAF, and aided its fight for scarce British defense resources during the lean years from 1918 to 1934. The RAF suppressed every single possible mission for aircraft other than strategic bombing.[88] The Air Staff did not submit its strategic bombing theories to serious testing. It is hard to avoid the conclusion that the bombing doctrine owes its origin and longevity to its organizational-political functions.

Given both the apparent "technological" fact of offensive bombing's efficacy and the intense commitment of the RAF to offensive bombing as a doctrine, how did the integrated air defense system which performed so well in the Battle of Britain ever emerge? This was a defensive military innovation of the first magnitude, achieved in the face of adverse organizational and technological pressures. If there were such a thing as technological determinism, or if organization theory had the explanatory power claimed by some of its proponents, then this innovation should not have occurred. There were two forces working in the direction of offense. Working in the direction of defense was the overall defensive grand strategy of the state. This doctrine owed its origin in part to the simple fact that Britain was a status quo power. At the same time, however, Britain preferred defense because it supported the crude deterrence strategy that was her only answer to the imbalance of power she faced, and because it would help her "pass the buck" should deterrence fail.

Insofar as this defensive innovation owes its origins to civilian pressure, inspired by the constraints and incentives of the international system, balance of power theory achieves greater credibility. Below, I will show that British civilian decision-makers did indeed help "cause" the technological innovation called Radio Direction Finding (radar), and were largely responsible for its integration into an *effective* air defense *system*. They were partners in this endeavor with the RAF insurgent, Air Chief Marshall Hugh Dowding. Demand created supply, and it did so as a response to emerging threats, and in the hope of exploiting political opportunities.

Balancing Behavior

The popular mythology of appeasement has it that the British did not "balance" during the 1930s. Although the picture of British statesmen striving almost too assiduously for peace is largely correct, these same statesmen did engage in both external and internal balancing behavior. Externally, the British relied largely on the French in Europe. It is difficult to call the British relationship to the French in this period "balancing," since the British were so hesitant and restrained in solidifying their nascent alliance. The British were of course concerned that excessive support for France might cause a war. Hence, Britain only rarely engaged in visible manipulation of alliance with France as a deterrent to Germany. The joint military staff talks of 1936 were only agreed to as a sop to the French. The same was more or less true of the 1938 talks. It was only in early 1939 that the British became serious about firming up their alliance with France and engaging in joint staff talks aimed at real planning for a real war.[89] Even these talks were marked by a reticence that disappeared only under the impact of events. In general, it must be said that the British counted on the French alliance, and on the dissuasive effect of that alliance, without doing much to nurture it.

Similarly, British "appeasement" of Italy must be viewed in strategic terms. British policy toward Italy aimed at minimum to neutralize Italy in a future war with Germany and at maximum to gain her cooperation.[90] The Stresa conference of April 1935 aimed to send the message to Germany that British-French-Italian solidarity would preclude piecemeal revision of the European status-quo.[91] Italy was one of the original guarantors of the Locarno Pact, and as such was on record as opposing any alterations in the western European status quo. If she could be persuaded to sustain her commitment to this policy, then her weight would have to be considered by Germany in contemplating any future aggression. The Stresa conference was of course not terribly successful, and the "solidarity" among the three was shattered by Italy's subsequent invasion of Abyssinia.

While Britain's external balancing behavior was weak in the 1930s, and was for the most part subordinated to and restrained by the task of appeasement, it was nonetheless real. At the same time, Britain engaged in measures for quantitative and qualitative internal balancing. In addition to improving Britain's defensive capability, these measures aimed to improve British ability to dissuade potential adversaries and to support British diplomacy.[92] As such, British rearmament was meant to perform some of the essential power-measurement functions discussed in chapter 2. Britain did enter the arms race. The measures taken may not have been adequate to all the contingencies identified by British strategy. In some cases, notably the creation of a continental expeditionary force, the measures came too late. But in those areas most critical to the basic national security of the United Kingdom proper, the measures were for the most part adequate, if only barely.

Changes in the world environment stimulated increases in British defense spending. Japanese aggression in the Far East in 1931 brought the cancellation of the Ten-Year Rule. Nineteen thirty-four brought the appointment of the Defense Requirements Committee, and its reports and advice on remedying deficiencies in British military capability. In February of that year, after some debate, it rightly identified Germany as Britain's most dangerous long-term adversary.

Italian aggression against Abyssinia in 1935, and the subsequent British military demonstrations in the Mediterranean, increased British perceptions of a growing threat and provided stark evidence of inadequate British military capability. This further stimulated increases in defense spending.[93]

Reacting to the remilitarization of the Rhineland, the Spanish Civil War, and the increase in German defense spending, the Defense White Paper of 1937 called for a 1,500 million pound, five-year defense plan—an average annual rate of defense spending 2.2 times that of the average for the preceding four years.[94] Overall, the defense spending of the United Kingdom rose 250 percent from 1933 to 1938.[95] Admittedly, she spent less than Germany—1,200 million pounds to Germany's 2,868 million pounds—but her efforts were not negligible.[96] Moreover, the rate of spending approved in 1939 would have brought the five-year total to nearly 3,000 million pounds.[97] The direction of British defense spending was consistent with her overall grand strategy and the identification of Germany as the principal adversary. While army and navy spending roughly doubled from 1933 to 1939, air force spending roughly quintupled.[98] As we have already seen, spending on the RAF was believed to increase British capability both autonomously to deter a German attack on Britain and to deal with that attack should deterrence fail.

Evolution of Air Defense

The Royal Air Force was not merely the beneficiary of financial largesse during the period of British rearmament. It was the focus of much civilian political attention—some of it resisted by that service. Historians agree that the effectiveness of British air defenses in the Battle of Britain was a result of civilian intervention into the doctrine of the Royal Air Force. While offensive strategic bombing was never eliminated as the RAF's preferred operation, it was suppressed for a time in favor of air defense.

Historians disagree on which civilians should receive credit for the evolution of Fighter Command. It is apparent that there is enough credit to go around. For the reasons outlined earlier in this chapter, there were many civilians in responsible positions with an interest in reducing British vulnerability to air attack.

Radar, the critical building block of the system, owes its origins and development to the high degree of political support it received. In late 1934 (the year of the first report of the Defense Requirements Committee), at the instigation of Lord Londonderry, the secretary of state for air, the Committee for Scientific Study of Air Defense was set up under Mr. Henry Tizard.[99] Almost nothing of any use had been done before to detect the approach of bombers. Within three months Mr. Watson-Watt of the National Radio Laboratory had persuaded the committee that radio waves might be used to detect aircraft, and had conducted a primitive test as a proof of principle.[100] By May 1935 a full-fledged research establishment had been set up. Funding seems to have been readily obtained.

Three civilians stand out in this period. Prime Minister Stanley Baldwin was an early supporter of radar and took the political and organizational steps to protect those responsible for its development from external interference. Baldwin may have been responsible for the first grant of funds for Research and Development.[101] A special subcommittee of the Committee for Imperial Defense was set up under Sir Percival Cuncliffe-Lister (who was later to become Lord Swinton) to watch over radar developments. On June 1, 1935, Cuncliffe-Lister was made secretary of state for air.[102] Finally, the notoriously stingy Treasury was from the first easily persuaded to fund radar research and development. Credit here is usually given to Sir Warren Fisher, permanent undersecretary of the Treasury.[103]

In spite of the difficulties encountered in developing radar itself and the delays in construction of the first five "experimental" stations, the government and the Air Ministry decided to go ahead with construction of the entire twenty-station radar chain. This decision was made in the context of mixed evidence concerning the system's efficacy and was supported by the normally "anti-defense" Air Staff, which argued as late as 1937 that defense was impossible.[104] The reasons for their sudden support remain obscure, but possibly the airmen were insuring themselves against the inadequacy of their own bombers, an inadequacy which may already have been becoming evident. In any event, nearly the entire system was complete by the fall of 1939.[105]

Equally as important as the development of radar was the acquisition of sufficient fighter strength to sustain an extended defensive campaign. While it cannot be shown that the RAF opposed the development of radar, it can be shown that it obstructed the acquisition of large numbers of fighter aircraft. Predictably, its preference was for bombers. In this case, perhaps even more than in the development of radar, civilian pressure tipped the scales.

Until 1937, the civilians supported RAF expansion, and they did so in the Air Staff's own terms—that is, they supported the bomber deterrent.[106] From late 1937 to the outbreak of war, however, the government threw progressively more resources into the production of fighters.[107] In November 1937 the government also gave priority to air defense equipment in army rearmament.[108] These decisions were without doubt principally the work of British civilian leaders—the Chamberlain government and Prime Minister Neville Chamberlain himself.[109]

The impetus for the shift to fighter production came formally from Thomas Inskip, the minister of coordination of defense. He was assisted and perhaps prompted by Warren Fisher, the permanent undersecretary of the Treasury.[110] The Air Staff strenuously opposed the government's view, favoring a continued emphasis on bombers.[111] "The emphasis on defense was imposed on the Air Staff from outside."[112] On November 7, 1938, in the aftermath of the Munich Pact, the British government made what may have been the decision that guaranteed adequate fighter strength for the Battle of Britain. The Cabinet approved ultimate production of 3,700 fighters, immediate orders for 1,850 fighters, and maximum possible fighter production through March 1940.[113] Inskip had explained the strategic reasoning for the emphasis on air defense in his rejection of the bomber oriented "Scheme J" of air force expansion proposed in July 1937. In his memo to Lord Swinton, secretary of state for air, he stated:

> The point I want to put to you, therefore, is as to whether you can devise a revised programme based on the conception that at the outset of a war our first task is *to repulse a knock-out blow within the first few weeks, trusting thereafter to defeat the enemy by a process of exhaustion, resulting from our command at sea,* in the later stages.[114]

Organizational Factors and the Evolution of Air Defense

It would be misleading to conclude a discussion of the evolution of Fighter Command without reference to the part played by its first and most famous commander, Air Chief Marshall Sir Hugh Dowding. He performed a role in the evolution of British air defense analogous to that performed by Heinz Guderian in the evolution of the German Blitzkrieg.

Dowding began his military career in the army, but fought through World War I as an officer in the Royal Flying Corps. His early career had little to do with bombing, but his close connection with air defense began with an appointment in 1930 as commander of the inland area—the Fighter Group of the RAF's combined Bomber-Fighter operational command, Air Defense of Great Britain. A year later he was appointed air member for supply and research of the Air Council. In that role he was deeply involved with the development both of radar and of the Hurricane and Spitfire fighters.[115]

Dowding was also a key actor in the division of the RAF into specialized commands—particularly the elimination of Air Defense of Great Britain and its replacement by Fighter and Bomber commands under independent commanding officers. Different authors give different reasons for this decision, a decision advocated by Dowding. Most believe that one factor was the sheer growth in the size of the RAF after 1934.[116] Air Defense of Great Britain was too much for one operational commander to control. It also appears that both bomber and fighter advocates felt that the co-location of both forces under one commander would mean that inevitably one or the other would be shortchanged. Those favoring the offensive use of bombers were particularly concerned.[117]

Given that Dowding was not a "bomber" man, one suspects that he was trying to prevent any retardation of defensive developments. He had managed to achieve high rank in the RAF without having spent much time in bombers. Moreover, for some reason, he was not well liked. In A. J. P. Taylor's words, "he was pushed off to become head of Fighter Command, then regarded by the other air marshalls as a second-rate post."[118] But Dowding's broad professional background made him uniquely qualified among the RAF high command to turn his "second-rate" organization into something to be reckoned with. Indeed, having seen the original progress of radar as air member for research, he immediately set to work organizing the elaborate Fighter Command ground control system that would ultimately exploit radar warning. He began this task even before the technology was perfected.[119]

Thus, the civilian leaders who favored greater efforts in the field of air defense found a ready instrument in Dowding. At Inskip's request, Dowding worked up the first "ideal scheme" of air defense—specifying overall requirements for fighters, heavy and light anti-aircraft guns, searchlights, and balloons.[120] Dowding seldom needed much prompting to lobby for additional fighter assets for his command. Viscount Tempelwood, formerly Sir Samuel Hoare, had the Home Office at the time of the Munich Pact. He gives Dowding much of the credit for the subsequent increase in fighter production.[121]

It is clear that Dowding and the civilians worked in a kind of partnership. The pattern approximates that suggested in chapter 2. Civilians do not necessarily have the expertise to directly change military doctrine in order to bring it into conformity with an overall grand strategic design. They must rely upon mavericks within military organizations for the details of doctrinal and operational innovation. This appears to have been the pattern in the evolution of Fighter Command.

Summary: The Development of Air Defense

The British air defense system of 1940 was one of the most remarkable and successful military innovations of the pre-atomic machine age. It set a new pattern for civil-military, scientific-industrial cooperation—a pattern which was to serve the allies well throughout the war. The development of this air defense system was fundamental to the integration of Britain's military doctrine with her grand strategy, and provided the underpinning for that strategy's success in defending Britain during World War II. It was obviously less successful at dissuading adversaries from attacking Britain.

Increasing threats by Germany, Italy, and Japan brought intensive civilian attention to military matters. Prompted by systemic pressures, constraints, and incentives, civilians refashioned the doctrine of the RAF, elevating air defense to a temporary position of primacy.

The persistent beliefs in the dominance of the aerial offensive became a factor to be overcome. The RAF's claims for the utility of offensive bombing and the inutility of air defense were ignored. The civilians knew what they wanted and set about getting it. The process unfolded in fits and starts, but the development of an all-new military system in four years was no accident. The development of air defense is more consistent with the predictions of balance of power theory than with either the predictions of organization theory or any crude notion of technological determinism.

The civilians received a great deal of help from Air Marshall Dowding. He was the professional they needed to turn their wishes, resources, and raw radar technology into a functioning military system. Had it not been for Dowding, one wonders if the innovation would have unfolded as quickly or as successfully as it did. To say this is not to undercut the argument for the dominance of systemic forces with a "great man" theory. Organizations frequently harbor people like Dowding; the question is whether such people will find a source of support. But for the attitude of British civilians, the RAF would have suppressed Dowding and air defense. This is not to say that in such a case there would have been no air defense in 1940, but simply that it would have been weak. One doubts if it would have survived the Luftwaffe onslaught. The outcome of the Battle of Britain would then have hung on whether the Luftwaffe could take out the Royal Navy's battleships. The success of air attacks against surface vessels, anchored or underway (at Taranto and Pearl Harbor, and off Norway and Singapore), in the early years of the war suggests that the Royal Navy would have faced difficult odds.

Which theory better explains the character of British interwar military doctrine? Both have an important role to play, but as in the French case, balance of power theory seems to have greater explanatory power. Organization theory plays a subsidiary role.

British military doctrine was defensive, stagnant, and relatively disintegrated from the political aspects of British grand strategy for much of the interwar period. From 1934 on, however, it became more integrated and innovative. Throughout the period the doctrine had a very strong dissuasive component, stronger than that of French military doctrine.

The defensiveness of British grand strategy is of course largely explained by the simple fact that Britain had a lion's share of the world's real estate and would have been hard put to absorb much more. Nevertheless, the important details of the strategy, particularly its stress on dissuasion and on defensive/denial military operations, are best explained by systemic factors. Britain's military and economic power were not equal to her political goals. This drove her to a policy of dissuasion based on the threat of mobilizing her imperial resources for an attrition war. For such a threat to be credible, these resources, particularly the industrial resources of the home island, would have to be defended against a "knock-out blow." At the same time, Britain saw potential allies who might be induced to absorb some of the expected high costs of a future war. This could only be achieved if Britain were not dependent on these allies for her basic national survival. Thus, both dissuasion and "buck-passing" encouraged a stress on ensuring the security of the homeland proper with a defensive military doctrine.

Geographical factors provided an added impetus to the evolution of British military doctrine. The sheer geographic scope of the empire made it difficult to defend militarily, given the limits on British resources. Neither could Britain rely on the rapid transfer of military forces from one theater to another for either offense or defense. Thus, geography increased the impact of the empire's weak power position, and encouraged the British to seek a military formula for dissuasion.

[176]

Paradoxically, although geography weakened the British Empire, it strengthened the British Isles. Given the channel moat, Britain was not very vulnerable to an enemy army, and could concentrate resources on neutralizing the sea and air threats that affected her more directly. Germany had to invest most of her resources in her army—both for offensive and defensive reasons. This restrained her naval investment and, to a lesser extent, her investment in air power, thus reducing the threat to Britain (see chapter 6). France had to build a land army if she were to be secure against German power. Given the limits on both German sea and air power, Germany would have a difficult time getting at Britain if she did not first deal with France. France would defend herself, and would thus defend Britain. British decision-makers perceived that they could afford to pass some of the high costs of land war to France, so long as Britain had ensured herself against French failure. The geography of Europe encouraged and facilitated the buck-passing elements of British grand strategy and the defensive aspects of British military doctrine.

Organizational interests were at variance with these goals. The RAF and the Royal Navy each had an interest in a more expansive strategy—the first in the sky over Germany, the second in the Pacific. If each service had ultimately had its way, Britain's position in the summer of 1940 might not have been a happy one.

Technology made a mixed contribution to the defensiveness of British strategy. Experience with modern firepower had driven the British to pull their army back from the continent. It enhanced the benefits of "buck-passing" and put a premium on finding measures that would secure the island without the help of continental allies. Air technology, on the other hand, suggested that this second task would be difficult. Britain might be vulnerable to a "knock-out blow." The RAF's preferred solution was more bombers, more offense. No evidence suggested that they were wrong; mixed evidence suggested that they were right. If they were right, Britain would be hard put to accomplish her other goals—world-wide dissuasion and wartime "buck-passing." This second "technological imperative" would be turned on its head. In the end, systemic constraints and incentives were to triumph over organizational and technological imperatives, and produce an integrated defensive doctrine.

Balance of power theory best explains both the early disintegration of British grand strategy and its later reintegration. A peaceful world encouraged little civilian attention to Britain's military organizations, and allowed organizational factors to determine military doctrine. Without civilian control the services could not produce a coherent military doctrine—one integrated with the state's grand strategy—would not set priorities among missions, and would not cooperate with one another.

The build-up of German, Japanese, and Italian military power brought a surge of British balancing behavior. Included in this effort was a renewed attention to grand strategy and the role of each service within that grand strategy. The heating up of the international system encouraged civilians to intervene in the operational preparations of the RAF and, against its will, press it in the direction of greater air defense efforts. Historians agree that civilians were largely though not exclusively responsible for the air defense innovation. Pressures from the external environment did more than cause civilian intervention; they determined its defensive/denial character and did so in the face of substantial opposing organizational preferences. Moreover, the civilians reversed almost twenty years of RAF bombing mumbo-jumbo that they themselves had deeply believed.

The creation of the air defense system in the short space of four years provides a critical experiment for testing against each other the theories advanced in chapter 2. Organization theory and the family of hypotheses concerned with technology strongly suggest that this innovation should not have occurred. Both point to offense. Organization theory points to doctrinal stagnation. British civilians, consistent with the predictions of balance of power theory, had other ideas. Their world-wide dissuasive strategy demanded a secure British industrial base. Their "buck-passing" strategy demanded that Britain be secure so that the pressures of war would not drive her to an open-ended continental commitment. They needed air defense.

The desire and opportunity to pass the buck to France also explains why so little effort was expended for so many years to prepare either the RAF or the British Army for a continental land battle. This poor preparation helped pave the way to defeat in the Low Countries, a defeat which put Britain in great jeopardy. But unlike the French, who had neither prepared their army for mobile armored warfare nor strongly fortified their border with Belgium, the British had buffered themselves against a possible disaster in the Low Countries. The French, we recall, did not believe that they could either have an offensively capable army or fortify the Belgian frontier without jeopardizing British entry into the war. Here is where the British were more clever than the French. Each tried to pass the costs of a future war to the other. Each took risks to do so. The British, however, ensured themselves against the worst; the French did not.

[178]

[6]

Germany

German grand strategy and military doctrine in the interwar period were largely, though not exclusively, Hitler's creations. Nevertheless, because Hitler did not like to use formal documents, German strategy must be reconstructed in the same fashion as are French and British strategy. Unfortunately, students of German strategy under Hitler have had to rely on less direct documentary evidence than have students of French and British strategy.

German military doctrine in the late 1930s was offensive, innovative, and integrated with the political aspects of German grand strategy. Few would quarrel with the first two characterizations, but some would question the third. In the end, Germany did fail, perhaps because no military doctrine could support a grand strategy that apparently aimed at total hegemony. T. W. Mason has captured the political dimension of Hitler's strategy: "The Foreign Policy of the Third Reich was dynamic in character, limitless in its aims to achieve domination and entirely lacking a conception of an 'ultimate status quo.'"[1] Could German means, qualitatively or quantitatively, ever be reconciled with such grandiose ends? To such a question one is forced to answer no. Yet, Hitler went a long way on his road to conquest. On close inspection, German military doctrine under Hitler appears to be well designed for a campaign of limitless, if *opportunistic*, aggression. Given Hitler's ends, and given the political circumstances under which he pursued those ends, the rest of German strategy was remarkably coherent. That the war ended with Germany prostrate before her former victims and Hitler a suicide proves both the failure of German grand strategy and Hitler's faulty understanding of international politics. At the same time, we are obliged to try to explain Germany's extraordinary, if brief, success as a European hegemon.

The different outcomes of the Battle of France and the Battle of

[179]

Britain reflect the strengths and weaknesses of German military doctrine. By the spring and summer of 1940 the Wehrmacht (the term meaning all German armed forces—army, navy, and air) was well prepared for a continental land campaign, ill prepared for any other. This state of affairs was no mere oversight. The inadequacy of German military power for the defeat of Britain was, if unintendedly, the price of Germany's preceding success.

What was Hitler's strategy? Hitler aimed first to restore German military power. He intended to use that restored power to regain Germany's lost territory; acquire new German-speaking populations; and seize "living space" in the east (especially the Soviet Union) for the expected growth of his newly unified German nation. These four goals were shared in some measure by the German statesmen and soldiers who preceded Hitler.[2] It was the intensity of Hitler's commitment, particularly to the fourth goal, that set Hitler apart from other German interwar leaders and earlier German statesmen. Careless pursuit of the first three goals could have gotten any German statesmen into trouble. Hitler was not careless but he did get into trouble. Pursuit of the fourth goal brought disaster.

Germany was militarily weak and surrounded by strong neighbors when Hitler initiated his plans. He had to avoid precipitating an overwhelming enemy coalition even as he pursued a course of action that normally would have had just such an effect. Hitler's remedy was to organize his military forces, his economy, and his diplomacy in ways that would allow him to exploit sudden political opportunities, coerce his adversaries, create peacetime schisms among the potential members of a coalition against him, and, finally, defeat such coalitions piecemeal should war actually break out.

How was this achieved? First, Hitler did everything possible to project a fierce and martial German image abroad. At the same time, however, he was careful to make his aims appear limited. While he strove for German rearmament, he was careful to structure that rearmament in ways that would not bring France and Britain together. He deferred naval rearmament for as long as possible. He publicly extolled the virtues of the British Empire.

German rearmament on the ground and in the air was aimed at producing a military instrument that would appear as awesome as possible, as quickly as possible, to Germany's intended victims. Moreover, this military instrument had to be prepared to defend Germany should the other powers of Europe suddenly decide to cut her down. This provided a further incentive to channel rearmament toward land campaigns. Finally, all of the prizes sought by Hitler were on the European land mass.

Beyond the land war orientation, Hitler sought the capability for short wars. He supported elements within his military apparatus who could promise quick results in the event of war. The new apostles of armor and air power found a ready ear even though the old apostles of infantry and Schlieffen-like envelopments were retained. Hitler's personal pressure to achieve his strategic aims was the motive force behind the development of the doctrine ultimately called Blitzkrieg.

When Hitler's diplomacy and drive finally brought about the Battle of France, the German Army was a tried and tested machine specialized in rapid continental aggression. Hitler faced a coalition still rent by the mistrust that he himself had helped to sow. Moreover, due in part to Hitler's prior behavior, Britain, a key member of the opposition, was ill prepared for a continental land battle. The German Army fought the battle for which it had prepared; the French and British fought a battle that to the last they had hoped to avoid.

At the English Channel's edge, however, Hitler finally confronted a battle for which the Wehrmacht had not prepared. Had Germany tried to build a mighty navy and a genuine strategic air force to prepare for engagement with Britain, one wonders what British behavior in the 1930s would have been. If Hitler had behaved more like the pre–World War I kaiser, how long would it have taken for the French and British to firm up their coalition? Moreover, where would Germany have gotten the resources to prepare for modern conflict on land and sea? Success in France was in some measure paid for with failure at the channel's edge.

I will argue that systemic forces account for the pattern of German military doctrine better than do organizational forces or the sheer intensity of Hitler's will-to-conquest. Of course, the intensity of Hitler's ambitions strongly influenced German military developments in the 1930s. But admitting this, I argue that most of the details of the doctrine that emerged by World War II can be explained by balance of power theory. Organizational forces played an important but subsidiary role. The direct influence of technological factors on German doctrine appears to have been weak. As in the case of RAF Fighter Command, technology was pressed into the service of a doctrine that arose from other causes.

German Interwar Strategy before Hitler

German grand strategy after World War I was strongly influenced by the special political and military conditions imposed on Germany at Versailles and by the peculiarities of German domestic politics arising from her defeat and the collapse of the Hohenzollern monarchy. The Versailles Treaty took territory and population away from Germany and gave it to old and new European states. In the west, Germany's defensive capacity was thus reduced. In the east, Poland re-emerged—an almost inevitable adversary. Germany was tightly constrained militarily. She was denied the right to fortify critical areas of her frontier. Her army was reduced to 100,000 men and denied all but the lightest weaponry. Her navy and air force were virtually eliminated. The German arms industry was drastically reduced in size, and severely restricted as to the types of weapons it could produce. In short, Germany was put in a position of maximum vulnerability.

At the same time, the Weimar democracy faced tough opposition from both radical right-wing and left-wing groups. German politicans of the center-right and the center-left found it expedient to avoid conflict with the conservative and traditional army. Rather, a pact was made that allowed the army considerable instrumental autonomy in exchange for its political neutrality and occasional support. Interwar Germany is, consequently, an exceptional laboratory for examining a military organization that has almost totally escaped civilian control. Moreover, this long out-of-control military organization provided the raw material for Hitler's policies. By the logic of organization theory, such an extended period of autonomy should have made the German Army very difficult for Hitler to control. Thus, developments in the 1920s increase the value of the 1930s as a test of organization theory.

The German Army and the Offensive

We have already seen how France and Britain were affected by the technological lessons of World War I and by their postwar international political positions. French civilians so constrained their soldiers as to drive them in the direction of a defensive military doctrine. The soldiers themselves seem to have drawn the lesson from the war that modern military technology favored the defender. In Britain, the effect of civilian reaction on the army was even simpler: The army was pulled off the continent and encouraged to think about other things. Neither its size nor its budget allowed much hope for a continental role. The question of offense or defense became moot. Promising early developments in mechanized warfare were starved for want of funds, political support, and a mission.[3]

The German case gives us a clearer insight into the relative power of technological and systemic versus organizational causes, because civilian control over the military was quite weak during the early postwar years. The peculiar domestic politics of Weimar allow us to filter out civilian interpretations of military technology and international politics. The German Army was highly committed to the offensive before World War I. Its experience with modern technology during the war was similar, though not identical, to that of the Allied armies. The postwar balance of military power between Germany and her allies was certainly not favorable to offensive military action. The German Army's behavior under these circumstances is most suggestive. It returned to its prewar offensive doctrine with scarcely any hesitation. The doctrine was only barely amended to reflect the experience of the Great War, or Germany's postwar military weakness. Left to itself, the German military returned to its offensive roots, as organization theory would predict.

What were the origins of the strategy to which the German Army's postwar chief, General Hans von Seeckt, would so definitely return in 1920? What was its nature? Since the reign of Frederick the Great, the Prussian and later German officer corps had dedicated themselves to a particular style of warfare. The famous German General Staff stressed mobility above all else. It strove for flank attacks, envelopments, and encirclement battles of annihilation. The general staff attempted to exploit the advantage of interior lines of communication, and more especially the improvement of this advantage provided by new railroad technology. Finally, speed of mobilization and concentration were to be exploited in an attempt to dictate the time and place of battle to the adversary. The strategy was offensive in every sense.[4]

Systemic causes, both political and geographic, played an important role in the evolution of this doctrine. Germany faced enemies on several fronts whose total military power exceeded her own. The idea of reducing total adversary strength with powerful sequential offensives, first against one enemy, then another, before the entire coalition could coordinate its military plans, was very attractive. Historians agree that a primary determinant of the character of German doctrine was the two-front war problem.[5] Both the elder Moltke and Schlieffen feared a simultaneous attack by Russia and France. During the Wars of Unification Moltke had to worry about the entry of additional European powers into Prussia's wars, should those wars last too long. German strategists came to believe that superior adversary coalitions could be reduced by "decisive" sequential attacks against Germany's enemies.[6]

Organizational factors also contributed to the offensiveness of German military doctrine. Particularly as embodied in the Schlieffen Plan, offensive doctrine contributed to size, wealth, and autonomy, and to the reduction of operational uncertainty. First, the Schlieffen Plan actually required more forces than Germany had during Schlieffen's tenure as chief of staff.[7] Thus a permanent justification for increases in the army's size and/or capability was generated. Second, in contrast to Moltke's earlier plan, which had called for limited offensives against Russia and France and included the assumption that war termination would require diplomatic action, Schlieffen planned for decisive victory against France and Russia.[8] The army would take care of everything, without the aid or interference of diplomats. Finally, the choice of a decisive offensive operation reduced battlefield uncertainty. As Schlieffen himself said, "To win, we must endeavour to be the stronger of the two at the point of impact. Our only hope of this lies in making *our own choice* of operations, not in waiting *passively* for whatever the *enemy chooses* for us."[9] The German Army, it was believed, could determine the outcome of the battle by setting the conditions under which it would be fought. One must also reckon that reliance on railroads contributed to the uncertainty-reducing advantages of an offensive strategy. The mustering of millions of men by rail was a complicated task of organization and timing. One suspects that settling upon a particular offensive plan and troop concentration made the task of those responsible for mobilization a good deal easier.

The German Army remained committed to this offensive military doctrine for over forty years. During World War I conditions in the eastern theater of operations allowed the army to wage war according to this tradition. In the west the army confronted the same firepower lessons as did the French and British. Yet, in many ways these only confirmed the German General Staff's belief that mobility had to be reintroduced to the battlefield to avoid the effects of firepower. This had been their prewar doctrine, and throughout World War I they strove to return to a mobile strategy. Erich Ludendorff's 1918 offensive was moderately successful in this regard. In the end it failed, however, and it must be said that from the perspective of "technological lessons" this was a weak reed upon which to build a postwar offensive doctrine. The Germans returned to the offensive after World War I nevertheless, and one suspects that organizational pressures were the principal determinants.

The main organizational factor driving the postwar German Army was the need for stability and certainty in order to rebuild the organi-

[184]

zation. It had been defeated on the battlefield, eroded by revolutionary ideologies of the right and the left, and radically diminished both quantitatively and qualitatively by the terms of Versailles. Is it such a surprise that in its efforts to save itself, the organization turned back to the doctrine that had given it its greatest successes—even during the war just ended? Opinion was by no means unanimous. Some did believe that World War I revealed the preeminence of the defensive.[10] Others felt that a slow and ponderous offensive model, similar to that used by the French in the last stages of World War I, should be adopted.[11] Von Seeckt, who commanded the army from 1920 to 1926, would have none of this, and the majority of German officers appear to have agreed with him.[12] Faced with the task of organizational reconstruction, and unrestrained by civilian intervention of the kind we saw in France and Britain, German officers returned to their offensive and mobile tradition. It provided stability and certainty in an unstable and uncertain world.

There is also reason to believe that the kind of army imposed on Germany, in contrast to those of her adversaries, may have provided an incentive for an offensive doctrine. The German Army was legally constrained to a total of 100,000 long-service professionals, augmented by perhaps 150,000 illegal reserves.[13] Germany's enemies retained large conscript armies, capable of mobilizing, with time, hundreds of thousands, if not millions.[14] To avoid a war against such odds von Seeckt elaborated his theory of the attaque brusquée. He proposed in his published writings to hurl his small but highly trained and always-ready Reichswehr against his adversaries before they could complete their mobilization. While this would not give Germany victory, it might buy her time to mobilize at least part of her own manpower for a successful defense.[15] An offensive doctrine would be essential for the initiation of such a preventive attack. It is difficult to tell if von Seeckt actually believed this theory, or was simply making a virtue out of necessity. The notion of an attaque brusquée may have been the only *plausible* offensive strategy for the tiny Reichswehr. Given von Seeckt's desire to restore the spirit of the offensive, it is entirely possible that his advocacy of the attaque brusquée was more for argument than from sincere belief. Certainly, von Seeckt's very cautious behavior during the French Ruhr occupation would seem to confirm this.

Systemic forces, particularly the two-front war problem, may have had some influence on the army's return to an offensive doctrine. After World War I, Germany found herself in an international political position very different from France's or Britain's. It was at the same time similar to, but worse than, Germany's prewar position.[16] Germany was not merely surrounded by hostile states, she was weaker militarily than she had been since unification. It is clear that Germany's geographical and power position before the war had been viewed by German officers as necessitating an offensive military doctrine. Some felt that since these conditions had been aggravated by the Versailles settlement, the need for an offensive doctrine was, if anything, even more acute.

Von Seeckt was convinced of a "fundamental antagonism" between Germany and France, and prepared in 1923 for an imminent resumption of war between the two countries.[17] This attitude may have been reinforced by French treaties with Belgium, Poland, Czechoslovakia, Romania, and Yugoslavia—all signed within three years after the end of the war.[18] France had ringed Germany with alliances. Moreover, one of these allies, Poland, was a recipient of much German territory and thus an inevitable foe of German resurgence.[19] There were factions within Poland who wanted still more German territory. Finally, Poland must have appeared not only hostile but dangerous, as it was freshly rearmed by France and governed by Marshal Józef Piłsudski—a military dictator and a soldier of some accomplishment.[20] Although von Seeckt and the German officer corps looked forward to a day when they might eliminate Poland, they were at the time fearful of combined French and Polish military power since the disarmament provisions of Versailles made Germany weak and vulnerable. Given these security concerns, it is possible that von Seeckt's offensive doctrine was designed in part to cope with Germany's classical security problem—an extreme imbalance of forces between Germany and the French coalition.

If such was the case, the rationale for Germany's post–World War I doctrine was valid in only the most superficial sense. An offensive doctrine, for sequential preventive attacks against the members of an adversary coalition, is justified only if these attacks can achieve something. For Germany, it would be justified if, at minimum, the attacks could deliver a blow capable of delaying one enemy or another in such a way as to avoid having to fight the whole coalition at once. Was it possible for the 100,000-man Reichswehr to achieve this against a French-Polish coalition? One suspects not.

The German Army was probably too weak to achieve even limited victories against either the French or the Poles. The French Army disposed of some 460,000 effectives in France in 1921–1922, organized into 45 divisions, not all at full strength.[21] Many more units could be mobilized. In 1920, at the high point of their struggle against Russia, the Polish Army was 600,000 strong, with 21 divisions and 7 brigades of cavalry.[22] While the army was poorly provisioned, and its strength diminished after Poland's victory, the figure does give an idea of the possible size of the Polish threat to a militarily constrained Germany. Moreover, military relations with France gave Poland access to plentiful, if dated, French World War I armaments. Given such odds, an offensive doctrine made little sense for Germany.

Rather, an improvised, necessarily illegal, guerrilla resistance–style defense, aiming at deterrence through the threat of punishment, would seem to have been more appropriate. As noted in chapter 2, this solution had often been favored by weak states. Indeed, when war appeared imminent during the French occupation of the Ruhr in 1923, von Seeckt found himself driven by necessity to improvise a defensive/delaying war plan and posture very different from the offensive doctrine that he advocated both before and after the crisis.

The French occupation of the Ruhr forced von Seeckt to make a realistic appraisal of the Reichswehr's military capabilities. In January 1923, when the French first marched into the Ruhr, the general apparently toyed with the idea of direct military action to eject the French, should the conflict escalate.[23] On reflection, however, von Seeckt became much less optimistic and even expressed doubts about the army's capability to hold off the Poles in the east, should they attempt to exploit Germany's trouble in the west.

Von Seeckt immediately set about the task of organizing defenses in case the French pressed beyond the Ruhr in an attempt to dismember Germany. Although the Germans would not risk a quixotic defense of the Ruhr, they were willing to fight if the very existence of the state were threatened. Illegal reservists and formations were trained and organized to augment the fighting power of the 100,000-man Reichswehr. Guerrillas were also trained.[24] Contacts were made with the right-wing party militias, the veterans' organizations, and the freikorps (independent armed bands of ultranationalist veterans), who could all help in these endeavors. The large illegal stocks of arms already held in Germany were augmented by purchases abroad.[25] Finally, prepared defensive positions were organized along the Weser River line.

None of these actions suggests any illusions on von Seeckt's part regarding the quantitative adequacy of Germany's Reichswehr or the feasibility of an attaque brusquée. Instead, von Seeckt was preparing for a dogged defensive and delaying action, waged by the combined forces of an illegally expanded army and armed gangs of right-wing nationalist fanatics—the sort of deterrence posture one would expect from a state in Germany's straitened circumstances. In January 1923, von Seeckt made his views clear to the American ambassador: "The distance from Dortmund to Berlin is indeed not great, but it leads through streams of blood."[26]

In spite of Germany's geographic position, balance of power theory would seem to predict a defensive/deterrent doctrine different from that adopted by the German Army. However, unconstrained by civilian supervision, the army opted for an offensive doctrine, consistent with organization theory predictions. This suggests that soldiers are not better equipped than civilians to interpret the international political system and come to reasonable doctrinal conclusions. At the same time, however, von Seeckt's cautious behavior during the Ruhr crisis suggests the limits beyond which organizational biases cannot overwhelm the harsh realities of a state's power position in international politics.

Integration under Weimar

The integration question is difficult to address in the case of Weimar Germany. On the one hand, it can be argued that German strategy was disintegrated. Gustav Stresemann, German chancellor (1923) and minister of foreign affairs (1923–1929), pursued revision of Versailles through negotiation with France and Britain. Von Seeckt sought revision directly, through various subtle and not so subtle violations of the treaty. The more blatant violations hampered Stresemann's negotiations.[27] On the other hand, some historians, such as Gordon Craig, argue that German strategy was rather well integrated even before von Seeckt's retirement in 1926.[28]

How are these two positions to be reconciled? The extent of cooperation between civil and military authorities seems best explained by agreement upon ends; both von Seeckt and Stresemann agreed on the need for treaty revision, for the restoration of German military power, and ultimately for a much closer relationship with Austria. This agreement was a function of Germany's weak power position and the terms of Versailles. The severity of the treaty to some extent predetermined civil-military agreement on the primary German political objective—revision of that treaty. Because the treaty's terms had created such a high level of insecurity for Germany, soldiers and statesmen alike were doubly moved to seek revision.[29] Additionally, it can be argued that the level of integration went beyond mere agreement on ends. It is now known that Stresemann and other members of the German government were not merely aware of Reichswehr treaty violations, but in some measure hid them and defended them from the Allies.[30]

If von Seeckt's machinations made trouble for Stresemann's foreign policy, how is it that Stresemann not merely tolerated them, but defended them? His toleration is explained by the strong domestic power position of the Reichswehr. Von Seeckt had deliberately cultivated this autonomous position, partly due to the normal organizational incentives discussed in chapter 2, partly because he shared in the ultra-conservative nationalism of the German military. It appears, however, that Stresemann went beyond toleration to a kind of grudging support. It may be that the Reichswehr's visible military strength was an asset to Stresemann in his negotiations with the Western powers.

Stresemann had a healthy respect for the role of military power in international politics and wanted to see German military power restored.[31] He could always point a finger over his shoulder at a strong German military and say, "things could be worse; you might have to deal with them." As such, the army may have performed some of the diplomatic "power measurement" functions outlined in chapter 2. Indeed there is evidence to suggest that von Seeckt himself had conceptualized this role as early as 1920.[32] Thus, shared goals and a certain interdependence provided a modicum of strategic integration. At the same time, however, von Seeckt was loath to subordinate the Reichswehr to external control, and continued to pursue policies that gave Stresemann trouble. The degree of actual civil control over the instrumental aspects of the German Army—its doctrine, its recruitment, its armaments, and its cooperation with foreign armed forces— remained low. Things improved a good deal after von Seeckt's retirement in 1926, but German military doctrine remained only partially integrated with the overall grand strategy of the state.[33]

Innovation

How innovative was the postwar Reichswehr? D. C. Watt argues that the German armed forces were, due to their defeat, open "to any military development which promised a return to the war of movement and an end to trench warfare, especially the avoidance of a multi-fronted war."[34] This is not quite true.

The postwar Reichswehr did not pioneer either the weapons or the principles of Blitzkrieg.[35] Rather, to the extent that new weapons such as tanks and tactical bombing aircraft were considered—and admittedly they could not be much considered, due to their proscription by Versailles—German planners saw them as adjuncts to their classical arms and strategy. There was, however, considerable deliberate effort to rectify some of the mistakes of the previous war. Thus, we have some confirmation for two organization theory propositions. First, defeat can be a cause of innovation, if only to a limited extent. Second, there is a tendency to adapt new technology to old doctrines rather than to generate an entirely new doctrine to suit new technology. The latter was to be achieved only later, under Hitler's more or less direct pressure.

It has already been argued that the Reichswehr returned after the war to the offensive doctrine with which it had begun the war. Nevertheless, some changes were made. One set of changes seems to have been a response to new technology. The other set was an attempt to circumvent the problems created for the offense by modern firepower.

Von Seeckt was quick to realize that motorized transport (not armored fighting vehicles) offered a solution to some of the problems encountered during the previous war. In 1914 the German Army had failed to interfere with French mobilization, failed to prevent the redeployment of French reserves, and failed to foresee that foot soldiers and horses lacked the stamina for the great encirclement operations envisioned by the general staff.[36] Von Seeckt increased the use of motor transport to rectify these problems.[37] In 1921 the German Army was already conducting exercises with motorized infantry in rough country.[38] The army maintained illegal motor pools in the guise of civilian transport companies.[39] Motor transport was to be put in the service of mobility, a central requirement for the grand maneuvers aimed at the encirclement and annihilation of the enemy. Later, tanks were given a mission in such conceptions. However, this formulation should be distinguished from "Blitzkrieg."

Von Seeckt's second contribution was the institutionalization of the tactical system evolved during World War I for assaults on prepared positions. These tactics were first used on the Eastern Front, later at Caporetto, and reached their apotheosis in Ludendorff's western offensive in the spring of 1918. These are occasionally called "Hutier" tactics, after their supposed inventor (Oskar von Hutier), but are more often simply called "infiltration" tactics.

These tactics dispensed with the long preliminary artillery bombardments that had typified assaults on the Western Front. A short and intense artillery concentration was substituted, followed immediately by the attack of specially trained infantry "storm troopers." These troops were brought into position at the last possible moment to assure surprise. Gas and smoke shells were concentrated on enemy strong points, which were bypassed by infiltrating storm troopers armed with light assault guns, mortars, light machine guns, and flame throwers. Artillery coordination was much improved, as was the "flexibility" of the division. Cooperation among all arms involved in the assault was critical. This tactical system produced breakthroughs as much as forty miles wide and deep.[40] The system foundered in 1918 on account of insufficient mobility. In the absence of mechanical transport, the infiltrating storm troops could neither be reinforced nor resupplied. Von Seeckt appears to have hoped that motorization would somehow cope with this problem.

The development of these tactics is a revealing case of inventiveness. As an organization, the German Army was committed to the offensive. For some four years, modern firepower technology prohibited it from going on the offensive. Doggedly (even stupidly) it attempted to get around the new technology. In the end, although only partially, it succeeded, and it did so with a new tactical system, not a new technology. (The Allies used the tank instead of new tactics to more successfully accomplish the same end.)

These tactics were improved and expanded after the war. Reichswehr troops were subjected to the most intensive technical training. Extensive field exercises and elaborate instruction of small units were standard. Efficiency and precision in the handling of weapons were stressed. "This was particularly the case in respect to the *coordination* between the various arms, which prior to 1914 had not received the full attention due it in the old army."[41] The stress was on teamwork. Special attention was paid to the means of communication required for the coordination and cooperation essential to the new tactical system. In short, von Seeckt used the lessons of the war to help rectify the prewar failings of the German Army.[42]

Were these changes an innovation? In my view they were not, although the German Army was willing to repair perceived deficiencies in its basic military means. This effort is best explained by the organization's failure in World War I, and its desire to avoid a repetition of that failure. At the same time, however, change was limited by the organizational pressures discussed in chapter 2. The fundamental aim of German doctrine remained the annihilation of enemy forces; the preferred maneuver remained the single or double envelopment. In contrast to the Blitzkrieg doctrine that emerged as a competitor within the German Army by the late 1930s, the doctrine of the von Seeckt army was only an incremental change from that which preceded it.

[191]

Technology had a mixed influence on the doctrine of the von Seeckt army. On the one hand, motor transport was perceived to have reduced some of the logistics problems that had plagued wide envelopment maneuvers. On the other hand, it was hoped that the defensive value of modern weaponry could be circumvented by a careful refinement of World War I infiltration tactics, including vigorous combined arms training for infantry, artillery, and assault engineers. These tactics, however, had only proven partially successful during the war.

Von Seeckt put motor vehicles to work in service of envelopment and tactical innovations to work to overcome firepower. Overall military doctrine, basic military ends and means, changed but little. Organizational factors determined both the extent and the limits of innovation in postwar Germany.

Summary

German military doctrine was offensive, weakly integrated with the state's foreign policy, and only moderately innovative in the immediate postwar period. Organizational factors best explain the offensiveness of the army's doctrine. They also explain both the extent and the limits of doctrinal innovation. Finally, German military doctrine and grand strategy were integrated in the sense that both looked forward to the same goals—rearmament, recovering lost territories, and acquiring new territory. This accord was in part merely a function of the Versailles affront to German nationalism. But it was also a reaction to the real security problems created for Germany by her defeat in World War I and the way that defeat was registered at Versailles. Hence, systemic factors, especially the grave imbalance of power between Germany and her adversaries, do help explain the degree of integration in German grand strategy.

At the same time, however, the German Army violently disagreed with civilian tactics for achieving the overthrow of the Versailles Treaty. German civilian leaders, best exemplified by Gustav Stresemann, preferred a gradual diplomatic approach to revision. He would "teach" to the Allies the lack of political realism inherent in Versailles. The soldiers were less patient, and ceaselessly schemed to evade the disarmament provisions of the treaty and maintain the military power to aggressively exploit or cope with any sudden shift in the European political system. They talked a hostile and violent game. Von Seeckt's writings identifying German military doctrine with the offensive attaque brusquée were widely read and believed in France. To some extent, not easy to measure, the soldiers set back a civilian policy that ultimately proved its utility in achieving the goals shared by soldiers and civilians.

GERMAN STRATEGY UNDER HITLER

Hitler's military doctrine was offensive, integrated with his foreign policy, and innovative. Hitler's grand strategy had much in common with that of Weimar, under Stresemann and von Seeckt. It differed, however, in its geographical and temporal dimensions. Hitler wanted a good deal more than those who preceded him had wanted. The pace of political and military events dictated by Hitler leaves little room for doubt that he also wanted things faster. His commitment to a generally offensive political and military strategy can be explained by many of the same elements that explain Weimar strategy. His commitment to greater breadth of conquest and haste in achieving it can only be explained by his personal psychological make-up. Once he had committed himself to such a course of action, he needed a military doctrine very different in detail from that of his predecessors. These differences are best explained by the ambitiousness of Hitler's designs and by the international political conditions under which he pursued them. Political, economic, and military innovations would be necessary to integrate German military doctrine with German grand strategy for the tasks ahead. The constraints and incentives of the European political system influenced the pattern of these changes. In the case of the all-important German Army, these changes were made in the face of contrary organizational preferences.

Systemic Constraints and Hitler's Diplomacy

What were the political conditions under which Hitler would labor to restore German military power, recover lost territories, absorb new German-speaking populations, and acquire "living space" in the Soviet Union? First, and most obvious, Hitler initiated his plans with no allies. Second, because of the Versailles settlement and Germany's geographical position, Germany faced many potential adversaries; the potential coalition against her could be overwhelming. These were constraints; but there was also an opportunity.

The Europe of the 1930s was a multipolar international political system with five main players: Britain, France, Germany, Italy, and the Soviet Union. Smaller states, such as Spain, Czechoslovakia, Poland, and Romania, all had important assets that made them more important players than their size, population, or GNPs would suggest. The distinction between great and middle powers was not as great as it is today. The differences between the two categories were not so vast as to prevent the middle powers from making trouble for the great. Such a situation might provide *opportunities* for Hitler, as his principal opponents might temporarily be forced to turn their attention elsewhere.

According to balance of power arguments (chapter 2), Hitler's diplomacy and military organization should have been affected by his diplomatic isolation. His policy could be expected to bring him into conflict with other powers. In such conflicts statesmen require mechanisms for the competitive display of power and will. Both the manipulation of alliances and the manipulation of one's own military power have customarily served this function. Hitler was without powerful allies, particularly during the early phases of his campaign. It was not until late in the game that he succeeded in winning Italian acquiescence to the Anschluss (the occupation of Austria, March 11, 1938) that Mussolini had long opposed. Hitler was thus forced into a perhaps greater than normal reliance upon military power for the conduct of his diplomacy. This may not be the only reason Hitler moved to a policy of coercive diplomacy. His domestic political experience had led him to believe that opponents could be dragooned into giving him his way. Percy Schramm, German historian and OKW (Wehrmacht headquarters) war diarist, calls this Hitler's "avalanche" theory and argues that Hitler believed that an initial belligerent display of power would overwhelm any opposition. Capitulations by early victims would set an example that would be followed by subsequent victims. Small victories would lead to large victories; opponents would bandwagon.[43] Although this explanation must be given some credit, one must also note that states bereft of powerful allies frequently show a strong tendency to rely on military demonstrations for diplomatic purposes. Such demonstrations have become an important adjunct of postwar U.S. diplomacy and are so frequent in Israeli behavior as to constitute a way of life.

The political/diplomatic use of military force became an important element in Hitler's strategy. The character of German rearmament, the actual use of German military power, and changes in the organization of German military forces all confirm the hypothesis that Hitler was organizing for armed diplomacy.

The character of Germany's rearmament program in the 1930s suggests an obsession with the image of power.[44] Although the German economy was widely perceived to be fully mobilized for war, by 1938 the country was spending only 18 percent of GNP on defense, up from 9.6 percent the previous year.[45] This misperception of Germany's readiness for war was partly a function of deliberate German decisions about the pattern of defense spending. German military preparations have been characterized as rearmament in "width," not "depth," by General George Thomas, then head of the Economics and Armaments Office of the German High Command, a key participant in Germany's military build-up.[46] This meant that Hitler stressed the acquisition of large stocks of ready armaments rather than the construction of new arms manufacturing capacity.[47] Not until the 1936 Four-Year Plan got under way in 1937 were any serious attempts made to meet shortages of critical materials or increase overall industrial capability for war.[48]

The Four-Year Plan was the first of the famous German programs to find substitutes for certain imported raw materials—to produce synthetic oil and rubber, and to exploit low-grade coal and iron deposits that had previously been commercially unviable. These programs would not show much of a payoff for several years. Until then, the stockpiling of scarce raw materials would have been a prudent hedge against the possibility that Germany might not be able to win a quick victory in the event of war. But as late as August 1939, only three to six months of stocks were available. Hitler did not believe in maintaining large stocks. He preferred to turn imported raw materials into finished armaments as quickly as possible.[49]

Similarly, one gets no sense that a particularly large portion of German defense spending in the 1930s was specifically aimed at preparing the civilian industrial plant for military production. For instance, nothing like the British "shadow factories"-plans and tooling for the rapid conversion of certain automobile firms to aircraft production—seems to have existed.[50] It appears, therefore, that within the funds allocated for military purposes, the German emphasis was on visible military power. This emphasis provided an impressive martial display to back up a campaign of intimidation over an extended period of time.

Hitler personally did his best to exaggerate the appearance of war readiness. He constantly made bellicose claims about the extent of German war preparations.[51] The pattern of rearmament shows an obsession with numbers, to the exclusion of other military considerations. Hitler forced the pace of German Army expansion in the face of resistance from the army. As Hitler demanded more and more divisions, the army was forced to rapidly dilute the professional cadre of each formation. Quality suffered.[52] Hitler's mind turned always to images and appearances. While the generals sought the "horse-shoe nails" of rearmament—heavy artillery, engineers, railroad troops, and communications—Hitler wanted tanks and planes.[53]

German aerial rearmament reveals a concern for appearances. Werner von Blomberg, the German defense minister in 1935, instructed his subordinates, "We must feign as much armed strength as we can, in order to look as powerful as possible to the Western powers."[54] This became air force policy. As late as 1939, when told that ammunition stocks were painfully low, Hitler retorted, "Nobody inquires whether I have any bombs or ammo, it is the number of aircraft and guns that counts."[55]

The obsession with numbers was one of the reasons the Germans did not have an effective four-engine bomber in World War II. When queried about diverting resources to the production of four-engine bombers, a more difficult and resource-intensive task than the production of twin-engine craft, Hermann Goering responded, "The Fuhrer does not ask me what kind of bombers I have, he simply wants to know how many."[56] This obsession with appearances was also reflected in the German practice of devoting most aircraft production capability to finished machines and very little to spare parts. This diminished the Luftwaffe's ability to maintain full combat effectiveness for any length of time.[57] In short, Hitler seems to have believed that the image of armed might was as much of an asset as the armed might itself, and ignored important military details for the sake of a maximally intimidating appearance.

The pattern of Hitler's diplomacy prior to the Anschluss and during the Sudeten episode (see below) supports the hypothesis that he relied upon the manipulation of military power for coercive purposes—to demonstrate both German capability and will.

By early February 1938, confusion among his potential adversaries abroad, consolidation of power at home, the growing size and influence of the Austrian Nazi party, and the discovery by the Austrian police of a plot for open Nazi revolt convinced Hitler that the time had come for aggressive action against Austrian independence.[58] On February 11, at a personal meeting with Kurt von Schuschnigg, the Austrian chancellor, Hitler proposed terms that put Austria under Germany's total control. The intimidation campaign had already begun; Hitler deliberately had his "two most brutal-looking generals" present.[59] Schuschnigg managed to stall Hitler with the legal point that the Austrian president would have to sign such an agreement. Hitler relented, and gave the Austrian four days.[60]

On February 13, General Wilhelm Keitel informed General Jodl and

Admiral Canaris "that the Fuhrer's order is to the effect that military pressure by shamming military action should be kept up until the 15th."[61] Proposals for such maneuvers had been submitted to Hitler and approved the previous day. They did not involve much genuine preparation for war, although maneuvers and training flights were conducted near the frontier.[62] Phoney radio communication was arranged, and deliberate misinformation about military preparations was spread by agents within Austria and by customs agents at the border. Jodl's diary shows that these maneuvers were effective enough to convince the Austrians that Germany was "undertaking serious military preparations."[63]

President Wilhelm Miklas of Austria gave in on February 15, and Hitler's demands for unrestricted political activity for Austria's Nazis were met by February 18. As the full implications of the accord became clear, Schuschnigg began to fight back, ordering a plebiscite on Austrian independence for March 13. Hitler then opted for military action.

Hitler's orders went out on March 11. When first informed of the requirement for military action, General Heinrich von Brauchitsch, commander in chief of the army, argued that the army was not prepared to undertake an immediate invasion of Austria.[64] Yet, by 6:30 P.M. on the evening of March 10, plans had been improvised around the outdated "Case Otto" plan. (This was an old general staff contingency plan for action against Austria in the event of an attempted restoration of the Habsburgs.) As the German invasion preparations unfolded, Schuschnigg succumbed to German pressure, gave up the plebiscite, and resigned in favor of the Austrian Nazi, Artur von Seyss-Inquart. The Germans then occupied the country.

Three important facts emerge from the Austrian case. First, Hitler clearly did manipulate military force for diplomatic purposes. Second, he does not seem to have believed until late in the game that a real invasion would be necessary, because there were no plans for such an invasion. Third, the army itself had not thought about such action, and was unprepared for sudden improvisation to suit Hitler's political needs.

Hitler's efforts to absorb the Sudetenland are another example of his use of military force to back up his diplomacy. Unlike the Austrian case, there is also evidence that Hitler intended to invade Czechoslovakia if intimidation failed. In May 1938, in the face of rumors of German mobilization, the Czechs mobilized and received substantial diplomatic support from France and Britain.[65] Germany, which in fact had not mobilized, reduced her diplomatic pressure against Czechoslovakia, but Hitler ordered revision of the army's existing plans for war against the Czechs. The old plan had called for an opportunistic attack in the event of Czechoslovakian domestic strife or trouble elsewhere in Europe that tied down the forces of Czechoslovakia's guarantors. The new plan was based on Hitler's declaration of his "unalterable decision to smash Czechoslovakia by military action in the near future."[66] According to a covering letter signed by Keitel, the near future meant by October 1, 1938.[67]

We cannot tell whether or not Hitler would actually have gone to war over Czechoslovakia by October. We do know that he got his way, and that the coercive manipulation of his military capability helped him to do so. Two pieces of documentary evidence support the proposition that this was Hitler's intention. A subsection of "Fall Green," the invasion plan, discusses the advance preparations for the invasion: "b.) *Propaganda Warfare* must on the one hand intimidate the Czechs by means of threats and wear down their power of resistance."[68] The document implies that Hitler hoped to bully the Czechs in some way. A letter written by General Manstein to General Ludwig Beck during the Czech crisis indicates that the generals understood Hitler's coercive strategy: "As I see it, in our situation we can be successful only through *either* political pressure or military surprise. If one mixes both, the military surprise will be sacrificed to the political pressure."[69] In short, if the sabre were rattled too hard, the Czechs and their allies might draw their own, and thus eliminate Germany's hopes for a surprise attack. The Fall Green plan counted on such surprise for its success. The movement of troops and other military preparations would thus have to be carefully orchestrated to demonstrate German will but, at the same time, not precipitate adversary mobilization. For the most part, the Germans succeeded.

What was done? At the end of May a general speedup in previously ordered military expansion was begun. Orders were issued to complete the fortification of the western border immediately. Troop maneuvers scheduled for fall were moved forward to the summer.[70] British observers picked up evidence of this unusual activity as early as July, but were not alarmed. The banning of the frontier areas to all military attachés on July 30 was viewed as more ominous.[71] While this action was of course necessary to mask the particulars of German preparations, it did send a signal to Germany's adversaries.

On August 3, Colonel Mason MacFarlane, the British military attaché in Berlin, reported that Germany had scheduled a trial mobilization for September 8. Moreover, it had been announced that many soldiers due for discharge on October 1 would be held in the military

[198]

for an extra month. The attaché viewed these decisions as "most dangerous and provocative."[72] In the view of the British ambassador, Sir Nevile Henderson, the Germans could have made greater efforts at concealment had they been aiming exclusively at military surprise. Instead, he viewed the move as "bluff destined to achieve Germany's objective without war . . . a warning both to His Majesty's Government to put pressure on Benes [the president of Czechoslovakia] and to the latter to mind his step."[73] By the following day, however, Ambassador Henderson began to take Hitler's actions more seriously.[74]

By August 17, MacFarlane informed the Foreign Office that the German "test" mobilization involved troop movements in excess of the large maneuvers already reported. Moreover, he noted "that work on defenses in the West is preceding at almost hectic speed."[75] On August 15, Hitler had described the hoped-for effects of these actions on the Czechs: "Imagine how it must feel to watch your neighbor sharpening up his knife for three months."[76] By the end of August these various maneuvers had had a similar effect in France and Britain. In a dispatch from the embassy in Paris, dated August 30, Halifax (the foreign secretary) was informed that the head of French Army Intelligence was completely convinced that Germany was in a state of total mobilization.[77]

This pattern continued for another month. By September 27 the British ambassador to Germany was certain that if the Czechs did not capitulate immediately, the Germans would invade.[78] The British had good reason to draw this conclusion, since Hitler, at 1:00 P.M. on September 27, had ordered twenty-one regiments (seven divisions) of assault troops to move from their training areas to their jumping-off positions. They were to be so deployed "for action that operations against 'Green' are possible from September 30, the decision having been taken at twelve noon one day previously."[79] The word "possible" is noteworthy. It is logical to assume that Hitler still hoped that his goal could be attained without war.

This background of military mobilization and threat cast a shadow over the negotiations at Munich that began on September 15. They have been chronicled before. The important point is that they were conducted in an environment of visible and credible evidence of the German commitment to undertake an invasion of Czechoslovakia and, if necessary, precipitate another general European conflagration.

Finally, two structural changes in German military organization, one a direct result of Hitler's action and the second an indirect result of his action, support the hypothesis that Hitler was conducting "armed diplomacy" as much as he was preparing for outright military aggression.

The first occurred on February 4, 1938—perhaps not coincidentally, shortly before the events discussed above. On that day Hitler replaced the old German War Ministry with the Oberkommando der Wehrmacht (OKW). OKW was a real military headquarters, with a real staff of officers capable of planning military operations. In theory, it was an overarching planning and command organization that would coordinate the efforts of the army, navy, and air force. From that day forward, Hitler would take direct command of the three services, not as a civilian minister but as a military commander.[80] Direct command and a personal operational staff would provide the maximum personal control for the style of political-military operations he had adopted.[81]

The second structural change came in the army's mobilization system. This was a response to Hitler's Austrian and Czech operations. In both cases the army had been forced into difficult improvisations to produce the forces required by Hitler for his extended coercion campaigns. These campaigns had to be taken seriously, since they could end in war. The German Army commanders could never tell how long the armed diplomacy might last, or when a war might begin. The army's chief of staff, General Franz Halder, spent all of 1938 working on a new organizational scheme more appropriate to Hitler's policy. In December 1938 the new plan was adopted.[82]

This system organized the German Army into four waves or *Welle*. Fifty-one divisions of the first and second waves, all consisting of soldiers on or just released from active duty, could be made available in four days. The other two waves would not be ready for service for four to eight weeks.[83] This system gave Germany something of an advantage over the rest of the European powers. While Germany's total mobilization would require about as long as the total mobilization of other states, partial mobilization of some fifty crack divisions could occur almost immediately.[84] The army could now cope better with Hitler's eccentric diplomacy without having to improvise for either coercive demonstration or sudden attacks. Moreover, "the Army became an instrument uniquely well designed for a policy of quick territorial aggression."[85] In short, Germany now had something of a built-in preventive-war advantage.

In summary, the organization of the German war economy, the character of Hitler's diplomatic actions, and the structure of his armed forces all suggest a more or less deliberate attempt to tailor his military forces for diplomatic utility. This is not to say that actual warfare was ruled out. Nevertheless, he clearly was quite happy to attain his goals without war. While Hitler's expansionist policy and his home-grown "avalanche" theory may explain part of this "armed diplomacy," it is my judgment that his isolated diplomatic position also helps explain his behavior.[86]

The peculiar character of Hitler's military doctrine provides a test of organization theory. Hitler's style of rearmament, his diplomacy, and his "reorganization" of the Wehrmacht were not especially well-received by his military advisors. General Thomas, the army expert on mobilization, preferred rearmament in depth. Army commanders preferred to stress the traditional horse-shoe nails of military power. Military organizations strive to reduce uncertainty by accumulating large stocks of all kinds of their favorite materiel.

Army leaders were uncomfortable with coercive diplomacy, and were in the main opposed to the creation of OKW. Organization theory predicts such resistance. Coercive diplomacy risks the loss of the element of surprise, and gives an enemy the time to prepare his defenses. It raises the level of uncertainty for military organizations. OKW trod heavily on the army's operational autonomy, allowing Hitler to meddle intensively into the army's business—another source of uncertainty. Hitler won on all these issues, notwithstanding organizational preferences.

In explaining these changes it is difficult to unravel Hitler's tyranny from systemic constraints and incentives. Both were stronger influences than were organizational dynamics. Only in comparative perspective can one hope to strain out some of the influence of Hitler's tyranny. For instance, other democracies have both practiced coercive diplomacy and intervened in military operational matters in spite of resistance from professional military men. The introduction of "flexible options" for nuclear targeting by Secretary of Defense James Schlesinger was not welcomed by the U.S. Air Force. In a confrontation these small packets of weapons would figuratively be waved at the Soviet Union, and perhaps even used. Soldiers resisted such options, preferring instead very large counterforce attacks. Similarly, the U.S. Air Force tenaciously opposed President Lyndon Johnson's coercive bombing strategy and close political control of operations during the "Rolling Thunder" campaign against North Vietnam. In both cases civilians got much, although not all, of what they wanted.[87]

Systemic Constraints and Offense

Hitler was constrained by the potential size of the coalition against him. The nations on Germany's borders all had something to fear and they knew it. Hitler had few potential allies. If he were not careful, he could end up outnumbered and outgunned. Two aspects of German military capabilities can be explained by his perception of this constraint. First, as we have already noted, he was forced ultimately to face England with a remarkably inadequate navy. Second, the doctrine of his army came to be focused on a style of warfare that offered the hope of speedy victories. The first characteristic was a function of Hitler's aim to reduce the peacetime cohesion of the potential coalition against him. The second was a function of the desire to defeat the members of this coalition serially, should war come.

Students of Hitler's foreign policy agree that he hoped, until the Polish guarantee, to reconcile Britain to his eastern policy without war.[88] Hitler may actually have hoped that somehow Britain could be brought to abandon her classical balance of power policy on the continent. He did more than hope, however. F. H. Hinsley argues quite persuasively, based on German documents and testimony at the War Crimes Trials, that Hitler offered Britain the Naval Treaty of 1935 in the hope of winning Britain's good will. Admiral Erich Raeder was not in accord with this policy, but Hitler imposed his views. Hitler remained commited to the treaty until the surge of British resistance to his plans after the Munich Pact.[89]

Hinsley fails to point out that, although Hitler did not achieve all of his goals, the British were rather tardy about firming up their alliance with France and preparing for continental war. By avoiding an all-out naval arms race with Britain, Hitler helped secure his "rear" for his eastern plans. As was noted in a preceding chapter, the Anglo-German naval agreement had the immediate effect of driving a wedge between France and Britain. Britain might feel a little more safe than France and thus less willingly commit herself to an anti-German policy. Hitler had bought himself a "window of opportunity" even if he had not achieved Britain's long-term friendship. Hitler may not have sought the lesser goal, but its achievement was to some extent inherent in the pursuit of the greater goal.

The emphasis on speed in military operations was Hitler's second response to the constraints of the European political system; it was to result in that style of military operations called Blitzkrieg. We see this emphasis on speed in documentary evidence from the period. Moreover, the reasoning is quite explicit. Operations must be completed quickly to forestall the intervention of other powers, or meet that intervention should it occur. Germany would have to avoid a repetition of the World War I, multifront, attrition experience.[90]

The Hossbach Memorandum, reporting on a conference held by

Hitler on November 5, 1937, includes many references to the speed requirement and the reasons for it.

> Germany's problem could only be solved by means of force and this was never without attendant risk. The campaigns of Frederick the Great for Silesia and Bismarck's wars against Austria and France had involved unheard of risk, and the *swiftness of the Prussian action in 1870 had kept Austria from entering the war.*[91] [my emphasis]

Hitler went on to argue that the speed of military operations against Austria and Czechoslovakia would determine the attitudes of other powers.

> The degree of *surprise and swiftness* of our action were [sic] decisive factors for Poland's attitude. Poland—with Russia at her rear—will have little inclination to engage in war against a victorious Germany. Military intervention by Russia must be countered by the swiftness of our operations . . .[92]

Hitler's foreign minister, Joachim von Ribbentrop, shared Hitler's views and extended them to the Western Powers.

> In such a case France would hardly have the nerve to storm the German fortifications in the West alone without England. In this connection it appears to me that the *speed* with which such a conflict . . . would be victoriously ended would be decisive. In case of a quick success, I am firmly convinced that the West would not intervene. A longer duration, however, might cause the enemy countries to believe that Germany's forces had really been over-estimated and thus bring intervention by the western powers closer.[93]

The foreign minister reiterated these views in another memo some three months later, on March 10, 1938.[94]

The orders Hitler issued for "Fall Green," the invasion of Czechoslovakia, stressed the importance of speed for demonstrating the "hopelessness" of the Czech position.[95] Hitler apparently hoped that this quick victory would dissuade the Western allies from entering the war. The von Manstein letter shows his understanding of Hitler's purposes. He worried about the possible sacrifice of German surprise by Hitler's coercive diplomacy, and reminded Beck that "a quick success appears necessary because of the political risk."[96] He went on to detail Germany's military weakness on all fronts. We shall see how

[203]

Hitler's obsession with speed was ultimately translated into Wehrmacht doctrine.

Opportunities and Offense

While the international political system placed constraints on Hitler's actions, it also provided opportunities. Hitler recognized that his erstwhile opponents faced security problems other than those posed by Germany. He believed that these problems could produce opportunities for German aggression. Many of the characteristics of German grand strategy already described contributed to a policy of opportunistic aggression.

Armament in width, the long-term, partial mobilization of the German economy for war, would be consistent with a policy of opportunism. On the one hand, it gave Hitler a substantial amount of ready military power at all times. On the other hand, partial as opposed to total economic mobilization might be sustained indefinitely. If Hitler knew exactly when he was going to move, then he probably would have been wise to mobilize his entire economy for war. If he believed that his aggression was contingent on unpredictable events elsewhere, then he needed a military capability that could be sustained until the proper opportunity arose.

The changes in military command relationships (particularly, the formation of OKW) and the emergence of the Wellen mobilization system are also consistent with a policy of opportunistic aggression. These structural changes gave Hitler the necessary flexibility to exploit sudden, and possibly evanescent, political opportunities. Finally, the emphasis on speed in military operations is consistent with the hypothesis that Hitler aimed to exploit political opportunities. If Britain, France, or the Soviet Union should become tied down in a conflict elsewhere, the duration of the conflict could not be predicted. Hitler would have to exploit such situations quickly in order to forestall a return of adversary attention to Germany.

The Hossbach Memorandum illustrates Hitler's belief that opportunities would emerge. Hitler argued that Germany could afford to take action against Austria and Czechoslovakia if France became "embroiled by a war with another state." He noted that Poland would probably not intervene because she had "Russia at her rear." He discounted the possibility of Russian intervention because of "Japan's attitude." Hitler saw a French war elsewhere as "coming definitely nearer; it might emerge from the present tensions in the Mediterranean, and he [Hitler] was resolved to take advantage of it whenever it happened, even as early as 1938."[97] Hitler stressed the value of a long Spanish Civil War, suggesting that it might draw France and Britain into war with Italy. It is to be remembered that Hitler did all he could to keep this war going. He declared that Germany could support Italy's war effort, if Britain and France were to attack her; this would tie down their forces. Hitler wanted "to exploit this favorable situation which would not occur again, to begin and carry through the campaign against the Czechs. This descent upon the Czechs would have to be carried out with 'lightning speed.'"[98]

This was no mere rhetoric. It was Hitler's modus operandi. Norman Rich notes that the Italian action in Ethiopia, and the Allied reaction thus precipitated, provided the spur to Hitler's remilitarization of the Rhineland.[99] Indeed, Rich's history of Hitler's aggression points to a general sensitivity to strategic opportunities in German strategy. The sort of opportunism discussed thus far is an example of the more abstract category of "preventive behavior"—the exploitation of an apparently temporary superiority in military power before it disappears. We find Hitler constantly talking about the exploitation of temporary advantages in German military power produced by either the diversion of enemy power to other contingencies, the temporary neutralization of a particular adversary, or Germany's real but fading lead in arms production. We also find Hitler continually engaging in "preemptive" invasions of countries on the grounds that the resources thus acquired would substantially increase Allied military power if the Allies got there first, and would substantially increase his power if he got there first.[100] One might add that such calculations were frequent and in many cases accurate in the prenuclear age.

An Innovation in Military Doctrine: Blitzkrieg and Its Origins

Thus far I have discussed the systemic constraints and incentives surrounding Germany, and their general effects on Hitler's military doctrine. To what extent were these systemic factors actually reflected in the details of Wehrmacht doctrine, and by what mechanism of influence?

Hitler sought speed above all else in military operations. He also sought to exaggerate German military power in others' perceptions. In the form of "Blitzkrieg" he succeeded in doing both. In Poland, the Low Countries, and France Hitler achieved victory with astonishing speed. Those who did not understand his method tended to attribute these victories to a quantitative superiority that he in fact did not have.

What was Blitzkrieg? How did it differ from the strategy developed by the German Army during the Weimar period? Where did it come from? The first two questions will be discussed in brief; the third at greater length.

The Blitzkrieg doctrine was summarized in chapter 3.[101] The focus of a Blitzkrieg attack is its distinguishing characteristic. Such operations aim directly at the adversary's command, control, communications, and intelligence functions (C^3I). Today, when strategists talk about C^3I, they generally talk about communications and surveillance hardware. Attacks on C^3I in the 1930s, however, were attacks on particular parts of an adversary military organization—figuratively, its brains and circulatory system.

Operationally, the Blitzkrieg was aimed at breaking through an enemy's front line and penetrating its rear area as quickly as possible. The speed of mechanized formations would produce the illusion of attacks in many places, overwhelming an enemy intelligence system with reports. The attacker's forces would, by their very presence, disrupt the movement of information, people, and machines in the enemy rear. Air power would concentrate on the destruction of critical command and transportation nodes deeper in the enemy rear. The combination was designed to bring about the confusion and collapse of the enemy combat organization, avoiding the necessity for its defeat in detail. At the same time, the attacking Blitzkrieg force would be designed to function effectively in a chaotic environment. Decision-making authority would be decentralized to the commanders of the advancing spearheads. These spearheads would possess dense and redundant signals capability. The spearheads were richly endowed with organic reconnaissance elements. Thus, as the enemy's C^3I were driven down, one's own efficient C^3I in a fluid and confused environment would provide an increasing military advantage. This description is, I believe, as accurate for modern Israeli armor doctrine as it is for German doctrine in 1939 in 1940.

Theorists might see the mode of attack described above as actually supplanting the need for the encirclement battles of annihilation long favored in German military strategy. In practice, this was not the case. Rather, the attack on the enemy's C^3I, the Blitzkrieg, provided a highly levered, low-cost, high-speed way to achieve the encirclement battle of annihilation. It is worth noting that the pure attack on the enemy's command organization was originally a British idea, most probably the invention of General J. F. C. Fuller.[102] It is not clear that

Blitzkrieg's German father, Heinz Guderian, although a student of all the early British armored theorists, actually conceived the armored attack as directed mainly at C³I. As a signals officer, he surely realized the value of disrupting the adversary's ability to control its organization. One doubts, however, that Guderian believed he could altogether avoid the requirement for an encirclement battle. For example, the campaign in the Low Countries, perhaps the most successful Blitzkrieg operation, ended with the Allied armies partially encircled, their backs to the channel and subjected to a terrific air and artillery bombardment. Nevertheless, one must conclude that the emphasis on attacking the enemy's brain, his C³I, is the characteristic that fundamentally distinguishes the Blitzkrieg from earlier German military strategy.

While the description above best describes the expert's image of Blitzkrieg, the term conjures up for the layman the image of a torrent of tanks and aircraft. The layman's image is partially correct. Aircraft and armor did provide the mobile and protected firepower essential for the penetration and disruption of the enemy's rear. Less well understood are the key roles of infantry—using a much-polished version of the World War I infiltration tactics—and of high-velocity, flat-trajectory, anti-tank and anti-aircraft guns, deployed at the very forefront of the battle. The infiltrating infantry played a vital role in the initial breakthrough into the enemy rear area. High-velocity, direct-fire anti-tank and anti-aircraft guns provided the crucial support for these attacks—suppressing the fire of enemy strong points. Anti-aircraft guns also provided a modicum of air defense for the ground formations, freeing fighters for concentration on critical targets. The infantry, anti-tank, and flak combination would also follow up the tanks to protect their lines of communication, and deal with strong points that either had been bypassed by the tanks or were stalling the advance of the tanks. One can see that the Blitzkrieg placed a heavy emphasis on combined-arms operations. As in the infiltration (Hutier) tactics evolved during World War I, and von Seeckt's subsequent embellishment of those tactics, cooperation and mutual support among all arms, ground and air, played a key role in the Blitzkrieg.

It has been observed by students of Blitzkrieg that the whole method of attack appears to be Hutier—infiltration tactics elevated to the level of the military campaign (the operational level) and executed by tanks, aircraft, and mechanized infantry. The motorization of logistics would solve the supply problem that had plagued Hutier tactics during World War I. Given this similarity, and given Blitzkrieg's stress on decisive offensive operations, one is tempted to portray the strategy as a logical, evolutionary development of traditional German military strategy. If any army "should" have arrived at this innovative doctrine, the German Army should have done so. To a certain extent this is true. Even the British, who had pioneered armored tactics during and immediately after World War I, did not have the "feel" ultimately developed by the Germans. It would be a mistake, however, to assume that Blitzkrieg evolved naturally in the interwar German armed forces. Blitzkrieg demanded some substantial changes in the German Army. These changes were not greeted enthusiastically by professional soldiers. Although one cannot say that Hitler "invented" Blitzkrieg, nor that the entire German Army ever completely adopted it, Hitler's intervention does appear to have been instrumental to the substantial progress that was made.

Early Development of, and Opposition to, Blitzkrieg

The first extensive thinking about tanks and mechanized warfare began in the early 1920s in the person of then Captain, later General, Heinz Guderian. In 1922 Guderian became chief of staff to the Inspectorate of the Motorized Transport Corps. Three facts are relevant: Guderian came from a Jaeger (light infantry) regiment; he had been a communications specialist; he knew nothing about motor transport, which at the time was considered to be merely a logistics device.[103] The first fact is relevant because as far back as the eighteenth century the "light infantry" specialized in rapid movement. Liddell-Hart (see below) reminds us that "the three earliest prophets of fast-moving armored warfare, in Britain, came from Light Infantry or Rifle regiments."[104] The second fact is important because of the key role of communications as both a means and an end in Blitzkrieg. The third fact is important because Guderian came to this "service" arm with a clean mental slate. Moreover, the Motorized Transport Corps was a new branch, and like most fledgling branches was eager to expand its role. Guderian's unique background would allow him to see the military possibilities of this new arm. He was the right man, in the right place, at the right time.

Guderian made careful observations of the British armored experiments of the 1920s. The British had set up an independent "Royal Tank Corps" after the war to experiment with tanks. Guderian studied the conceptual writings of the first British armored theorists, Captain B. H. Liddell-Hart and General J. F. C. Fuller. He also studied their reports of the early British experiments.[105] By 1924 he was already lecturing on mobile warfare.

Guderian received command of a motorized battalion (700 or 800 men) in 1929. It consisted of a reconnaissance company, a motorcycle company, a "dummy" tank company, and a "dummy" anti-tank company.[106] At the same time, a quiet and limited development of the tank got underway: the Krupp armaments firm was invited to deliver some experimental models. (It is to be remembered that these were still proscribed by the Versailles Treaty.) The Red Army provided some secret testing facilities as part of the special relationship evolved by von Seeckt. Because the disarmament provisions of the peace prohibited tanks, a great deal of work within Germany was done on armored cars and other cross-country wheeled vehicles.[107]

One would have thought this was an auspicious beginning. Guderian had succeeded in forming motorized combat units under the protection of a sub-organization with an interest in innovation.[108] He developed these units according to a tactical doctrine that had achieved widespread acceptance throughout the German Army.[109] The next steps were to be more difficult, as Guderian began to come into conflict with other elements of the German Army.

There had even been trouble within the Motorized Transport Corps. Guderian tells of his 1929 experiments:

> The Inspector of Transport Troops, indeed, had so little faith in this new unit that he forbade us to carry out combined exercises with other battalions stationed in the area. When the third division, of which we formed a part, went on maneuvers, we were not allowed to be employed in units of over platoon strength.[110]

Guderian complains that nobody believed that "the motorized troops, who were only service troops, after all, were capable of producing new and fruitful ideas in the tactical and even the operational field."[111] As one would expect, the cavalry became a major opponent, first relinquishing the light reconnaissance role to the motorized troops, then grabbing it back.[112]

Many of Germany's World War II armor specialists are on record concerning the extent of prewar resistance to Guderian's ideas. General Wilhelm von Thoma, who commanded German tanks in Spain in 1936, told Liddell-Hart after the war about the "resistance from the higher generals of the German Army. . . . The older ones were afraid of developing such forces fast—because they themselves did not understand the technique of armored warfare, and were uncomfortable with such new instruments."[113] General Erwin Rommel, the "Desert Fox," had written before his suicide in 1944 that "there was a particular clique that still fought bitterly against any drastic modernization of methods and clung fast to the axiom that the infantry must be regarded as the most important constituent of any army."[114] (It is to be remembered that Rommel made his prewar reputation as an infantry theorist.) Hasso von Manteuffel, one of the best German armor tacticians of the later part of the war, declared that in the 1930s Guderian was almost alone in advancing the cause of the tank and the special tactics that were to become Blitzkrieg.[115]

In *The German Army, 1933–1945*, Matthew Cooper chronicles the different ways in which the plans of the armor proponents were subverted by the High Command. The officers of the older arms, infantry, artillery, and cavalry tended to form mutual protection societies—promoting their brethren to higher rank. The army's official manuals were closed to the armor theorists. Scarce tanks, half-tracks, and trucks were diverted from Guderian's preferred, combined-arms Panzer divisions to the cavalry and infantry. Finally, the High Command indulged in Byzantine maneuvers designed to divert Guderian and other armor proponents into meaningless jobs without authority. Guderian was at one point slated for command of a reserve infantry corps in 1939.[116] Cooper concludes, in my view *incorrectly*, that "Guderian and his supporters failed; the military establishment triumphed."[117]

The resistance to innovation outlined above is exactly the sort of thing that organization theory would predict (see chapter 2). We know, however, that something rather remarkable happened on European battlefields in 1939–1941. Germany went into the Low Countries in 1940 with ten of Guderian's combined-arms Panzer divisions, the biggest and best-organized units of concentrated mechanized fighting power to be found anywhere at the time. In comparison to the other armies of Europe, the German Army was quite innovative. How did the development of Blitzkrieg proceed as far as it did?

Hitler's Role in the Evolution of Blitzkrieg

Historians agree that Hitler played an important role in helping the advocates of Blitzkrieg to overcome organizational resistance. (It is worth noting that the term *Blitzkrieg* only came into use late in 1939 and does not seem to have been a German creation. The Germans adopted the term for propaganda purposes.)[118] There is little direct evidence to support the proposition that Hitler had a detailed understanding of Guderian's ideas, or that he *wholeheartedly* embraced them and imposed them on the German army. However, it does appear from the little evidence available that Hitler provided the essential political support for armor in the face of traditionalist resistance.

Guderian's memoirs include an account of his first opportunity to introduce Hitler to armor. Although Guderian claims that this occurred in 1933, others reckon that Hitler got his first glimpse of tanks in action in February 1935.[119] Guderian remarks that "Hitler was much impressed by the speed and precision of movement of our units, and said repeatedly: 'That's what I need! That's what I want to have!'"[120] While we have little specific evidence regarding what Hitler did to support Guderian after this demonstration, it is widely believed that he became a convert.[121]

How were Hitler's interest and support translated into military decisions? First, we know that Hitler liked the machinery of Blitzkrieg—tanks, aircraft, and other tracked vehicles. In part, as argued earlier, this was a result of his desire to create a fierce impression abroad. But, it may also have been true that Hitler actually came to believe in the military efficacy of these arms. Hitler pressed for the adoption of these weapons in spite of resistance from the Army High Command.[122] General George Thomas, the Wehrmacht's expert on war production, has said that "Hitler attached much importance to the possession of much heavy artillery, many mechanical weapons, and anti-tank weapons. The great importance of the tanks was not recognized until the success in the Polish campaign."[123] This supports the hypothesis that the dictator was favorably taken with modern weaponry, but does not suggest that he extended any special support to armor. (Thomas is wrong on the question of Hitler and heavy artillery. The German Army had very little heavy artillery, even though its commanders wanted it.) Thus, it is difficult to conclude that Hitler was a convert to Guderian's ideas per se. We can conclude, however, that he was responsible for making available the mechanical parts for the Blitzkrieg. He may have seen in modern weaponry the means to speedy victories, even if he did not quite understand the "how" of their use. On balance, Hitler's intervention in the matter of military production was extremely important to the ultimate success of German operations during the first three years of the war.

What about Hitler's understanding of armored operations? Again, the evidence is scanty. In late 1938 Hitler is reported to have said to Guderian, "Together, we'll see that the necessary modernization is carried through." Historian Matthew Cooper argues that Hitler did not actually provide the promised help.[124] On the other hand, the circumstantial evidence that Hitler came under the spell of the armor theorists is strong. Hitler seems to have taken a personal interest in Guderian's career.[125] Indeed, Hitler and Guderian frequently saw each other socially. It is unlikely that Guderian failed to exploit these opportunies to advance his ideas. Moreover, Guderian somehow always got a leading role in Hitler's early adventures—in Austria, Czechoslovakia, and even Poland.[126] In short, it is hard to believe that Guderian's ideas were not known to Hitler, or that they did not meet with a favorable response. While it is true that the attack on Poland was not a Blitzkrieg in the pure sense, it is at the same time remarkable that the armored and air forces played as large a role as they did. With Hitler's support, these arms had fought their way to a respected, though not dominant, position in the German military. Although the Polish campaign was a classical German double envelopment, the air and armored forces that were engaged did, in many cases, successfully direct their attention at the adversary's C^{3}I—the brain and circulatory system of the Polish Army.

In the aftermath of Poland, one piece of explicit evidence of Hitler's understanding of Blitzkrieg emerged. On October 10, 1939, Hitler directed his military leaders to begin preparing for an offensive in the west. As part of "Directive No. 6" he discussed new tactics derived from the Polish experience for the use of tanks and aircraft. Hitler discussed the necessity to avoid towns and military strong points, to concentrate forces at decisive points, to maintain momentum, and to improvise.[127] One doubts that Hitler could have developed such "lessons" so quickly in the absence of Guderian's previous tutoring.

What are we to make of this evidence? We know that Hitler favored speed above all else in military operations. We know that Guderian promised speed. We know that the ideas of the armor theorists were opposed from within the German Army. We know that the German Army adopted these ideas to a greater extent than did any other army in the world at the time. Hitler's intervention on the matter of the necessary equipment—ground and air—for Blitzkrieg is clear. His personal support for Guderian's career is clear. He is on record stating ideas that are similar to, if simpler than, Guderian's. Finally, as remarked in chapter 3, Hitler was one of the earliest boosters, if not one of the originators, of the Campaign Plan ultimately used in May 1940, generally agreed to be the apotheosis of Blitzkrieg.[128] In my judgment, to the extent that the German Wehrmacht achieved a doctrinal innovation that can be called Blitzkrieg, Hitler's intervention was decisive. In the absence of his intervention, it seems likely that normal organizational dynamics would have been determinative. Guderian might well have ended up commanding that infantry corps in 1939. His ideas would have been suppressed and the German Army would have entered World War II with a much more traditional doctrine. While one can hardly doubt that the Wehrmacht would have beaten the Poles under any circumstances, events in the Low Countries might have turned out very differently indeed had Guderian and the other pioneers of mechanized warfare in the German Army not received Hitler's support.

The Luftwaffe and Blitzkrieg

I have only briefly addressed the role of the Luftwaffe in Blitzkrieg. That role was very important, but not in the way that is normally believed. It is often supposed that the Luftwaffe provided "close air support" for the advancing armored columns, laying down a curtain of aerial firepower just in front of the advancing tanks. Indeed, it is often thought that the ground forces could literally "call in" air strikes. While this occurred from time to time in the German campaigns, it is not an accurate picture of the role of air power in the Blitzkrieg.

As noted earlier, the primary role of air power was the disruption of the enemy's rear area. The highest priority was the neutralization of enemy air power by attack of its airfields.[129] After that, German medium bombers—twin-engine machines—would range along the enemy lines of communications, attempting to destroy key nodes and interdict the movement of enemy reserves.[130] The vaunted "Stukas"—dive bombers—were generally held under a central command. They were concentrated against critical targets to facilitate particular phases of the ground operation. They would be used as highly mobile reserves to reinforce critical areas of the front. Stukas might even be used in close support tasks. The Stuka was the "precision guided munition" of its day. Fighters would be used in a similar way—sanitizing the air space over particularly crucial areas such as bridgeheads and troop concentrations. The Luftwaffe was thus a key element in the disruption of C^3I deep in the enemy army's rear area, as well as a source of immediate support to key armored spearheads.

Based on organization theory arguments (chapter 2) as well as the examples of the British and French air forces (chapters 4 and 5), the Luftwaffe should have fought against this role. The Luftwaffe's role in Blitzkrieg, although an offensive one, tied that organization closely to the ground forces. It did little to promote organizational size, wealth, or autonomy. Why was the Luftwaffe so cooperative?

First, the provisions of the Versailles Treaty had proscribed an independent German Air Force. This did not stop the ever-resourceful von Seeckt, who did everything possible to assure that the Reichs-wehr would maintain a reservoir of air power expertise.[131] From 1924 to 1933 the German Army kept the German hand in at an illegal air station at Lipezk, in the Soviet Union. The Luftwaffe did not achieve formal autonomy from the army until February 26, 1935.[132] Thus, the German air arm spent much of the interwar period under army tu-telage. It was not independent, large, or legal, and needed all the help from the army that it could get.

Although the Luftwaffe achieved its independence rather late, it was nevertheless immediately secure in that independence. This is because Hermann Goering, Hitler's right-hand man and a veteran fighter pilot of Richtofen's Flying Circus of World War I fame,[133] immediately got control of the Luftwaffe. He defined that organiza-tion's role and spirit in highly colored, National Socialist, ideological terms. Goering's political power, and his identification of the Luft-waffe with the Nazi movement, secured the organization in its new autonomy and guaranteed it a fat share of the financial resources allocated for rearmament.[134] Thus, the organization did not require any doctrinal gymnastics to protect its position or assure its growth.

The Luftwaffe had done more than spend an extended adolescence as ward of the German Army. It was of necessity formed by a huge infusion of army talent, some representatives of which, such as Gen-eral Albert Kesselring, were products of the German Army's general staff.[135] Many of these new transfers had never flown aircraft before. Like Kesselring, these officers remained sympathetic to the concerns of their brothers still serving on the ground. Thus, there was a gener-al tendency to relate the new air arm to the traditional ground arm.[136]

Finally, some rather fortuitous learning took place during the Span-ish Civil War. This may be one of the rare occasions in the evolution of German strategy in which experience with a technology was ex-plicitly translated into a doctrinal tenet. The Germans found that counter-population, terror bombing had much less effect on civilian morale than was widely supposed.[137] Moreover, they learned that level bombing was not terribly accurate, so attacks on industrial tar-gets would not be easy.[138] They also discovered that support of ground operations was well within the limits of their technology and provided a substantial payoff.[139] These lessons were not missed be-cause they were not filtered through any prior doctrinal preferences. The air force probably had a bias toward cooperation with the ground forces, if it had any bias at all. Thus, the conditions of the Luftwaffe's adolescence and early adulthood were ideal for what I judge to have been a correct interpretation of the lessons of Spain.

For all of the reasons outlined above, the Luftwaffe was willing to take on a role that tied it to ground operations. This, combined with Hitler's obsession with numbers rather than types of aircraft, drove Goering to give the development of four-engine strategic bombers a low priority.[140] Some historians say that a shortage of sufficiently powerful aircraft engines also limited development of a strategic bomber.[141]

In summary, the provisions of the Versailles Treaty, the appointment of Goering as the Luftwaffe's chief, the large infusion of army officers at its birth, technological experience in Spain, and Hitler's own preferences all drove the Luftwaffe toward close cooperation with the army. The organizational dynamics that we would ordinarily expect to see were short-circuited. The Luftwaffe had all the political support it needed. It could concentrate on finding a sensible and feasible military task for itself. The organization concentrated on missions that made sense from an army perspective but could not be accomplished by ground weaponry. The Luftwaffe thus, logically, aimed directly at the rear of the enemy army—and provided the Panzer divisions with exactly the help they needed.

SUMMARY AND CONCLUSIONS

The behavior of the German Army after World War I offers a good test of organization theory. The German Army had escaped civil control after the war, and retained its autonomy on instrumental questions up to Hitler's takeover. It had experienced the devastating effects of modern firepower technology on the Western Front; indeed, one might argue that German commanders had become masters of the defensive utilization of modern firepower. Yet, true to its traditions, and to its interests, the army returned to its prewar offensive doctrine. Drawing on organization theory, I argued in chapter 2 that military organizations like offensive doctrines, and that they do not like to innovate. The behavior of the German Army conforms with these predictions.

To some extent, German military doctrine after World War I offers a test of balance of power theory against organization theory. Germany's strategic situation superficially resembled that of the prewar period—a difficult two-front war problem. At the same time, however, Germany was so weak militarily that the traditional offensive solution to this problem did not make much sense. The army advocated such a solution nevertheless. In the absence of civilian intervention, organizational dynamics prevailed. But in spite of the formal adoption of an offensive doctrine, when the Ruhr occupation created a real threat to German security, von Seeckt quickly improvised a more appropriate and feasible defensive military response. In short, when the threat became immediate, even a politically uncontrolled military organization could respond sensibly to the realities of the state's power position in international politics.

One must draw mixed theoretical conclusions from this episode. Certainly the commitment to an offensive doctrine predicted by organization theory was sustained in the face of contrary signals from the international system. Yet, as events increased the threat to Germany, the army—apparently on its own—improvised a defensive plan very different from what was implied by its doctrine. Organization theory is a quite powerful predictor of the behavioral tendencies of military organizations. Yet, even without civilian guidance, balance of power considerations can overcome organizational biases when threats are sufficiently great.

The degree of political-military integration in German postwar strategy would seem to be a function of the Versailles Treaty. The Foreign Office and the army were in substantial agreement concerning Germany's strategic position and objectives. All could agree on the necessity to overthrow the Treaty. However, Versailles was merely the paper symbol of the decline in German security brought by the Allied victory. Legitimate civilian authority over the military was relatively weak in this period, particularly regarding operational matters. We would expect to see a good deal of "disintegration." There was some, particularly in the area of army violations of the disarmament provisions of Versailles. Yet, foreign and defense policy were in remarkable accord. This is to be explained by Germany's extremely difficult security situation. That the direct lines of authority were so weak, but policy coincidence so high, provides something of a test for balance of power theory. The constraints and incentives of the European political system were sufficiently stark to drive soldiers and statesmen in similar directions.

Innovation in German doctrine was limited after the war. Experience with modern firepower had encouraged the German Army to search for a tactical method to overcome its effects. Modest success was achieved. After the war, this tactical system was married to new technologies such as motor transport and wireless communication. Nevertheless, there is little evidence to suggest any decisive technological influence on German strategy. To the extent that the army did innovate, we cannot credit civilian pressure, since civilian influence on military doctrine was so weak. Instead we have an organiza-

[216]

tion seeking to repair its classical doctrine after meeting with a co-lossal failure—the loss of the war. I have already discussed why the army remained committed to the offensive. Its problem was to make the offensive possible. This goal, coupled with the army's recent failure, explains the extent and the limits of postwar innovation in the German Army.

Hitler's overall strategy was even more offensive than that of his predecessors. He wanted more, and he wanted it more quickly. Upon seizing power, Hitler inherited the German Army's offensive doc-trine, so he had good raw material to work with. Yet, he needed a doctrine that was more offensive than the one he inherited. His ends were more ambitious, so his political and military means would need adjustment. The extent of adjustment achieved would determine the integration or disintegration of his military doctrine vis-à-vis his grand strategy.

The changes wrought by Hitler were consistent with the interna-tional constraints and incentives that he faced. Germany was politi-cally isolated and surrounded by enemies, but she was also tantalized by the diplomatic opportunities inherent in a multipolar system. These systemic factors loomed large for Hitler because of the intensity of his commitment to his goals. (I do not propose to explain the latter; but once such goals were chosen, the influence of systemic con-straints and incentives would grow.) Developments in German strat-egy were remarkably consistent with these constraints and incen-tives. Moreover, since such developments were in many ways opposed by the German military, they stand as fairly potent evidence in support of balance of power theory.

In chapter 2, I deduced from balance of power theory that diplo-matically isolated states would try to use military power as a direct adjunct to diplomacy. I proposed that states facing multifront wars would stress offensive doctrines in order to defeat their enemies se-rially. Finally, I suggested that states seeking to exploit fleeting op-portunities would prefer offensive military doctrines. All of the fun-damental pieces of Hitler's military doctrine conform to these predic-tions.

Hitler did practice coercive diplomacy. His partial war economy, characterized by armament in "width," was designed to produce the most intimidating military appearance. His obsession with numbers, with mechanized weaponry, and with direct personal control of the military are all consistent with this practice. As noted earlier, Hitler pursued these elements in the face of opposition and foot-dragging from his military organization.

Hitler's careful attention to Britain during Germany's rearmament shows an understanding of the value of keeping his adversaries apart. His obsession with speed in military operations was directly related to Germany's weakness vis-à-vis the possible coalition against her. Hitler wanted to defeat his enemies one at a time, and his whole military system was geared to this.

Both the character of German rearmament and the commitment to speed in military operations were consistent with a policy of opportunism. If Hitler were waiting for the "right time" to move, he could hardly maintain a fully mobilized war economy until then. He needed a high level of ready military capability, preferably higher than the ready military power of the coalition that might oppose him. He needed speed in his military forces if he were to exploit any period during which his enemies were occupied elsewhere. Hitler's concern with speed was ultimately reflected in his military forces.

While the German Army itself had always been committed to speed in military operations, Hitler pressed the organization well beyond the limits it thought feasible. To the extent that an innovation called "Blitzkrieg" happened in interwar Germany, it was a result of Hitler's intervention. This is a good test of balance of power theory against organization theory. It was pointed out earlier that the German High Command strove to suppress Guderian's ideas and opposed the extensive mechanization favored by Hitler. This is consistent with organization theory. Germany's interwar commanders had been trained, socialized, and promoted according to a different doctrine. It would have been strange for them to embrace Guderian's views. Hitler, however, could not afford such foot-dragging. He had problems and he needed solutions. While he could not dream up all the solutions himself, and probably did not fully understand the solutions advanced by Guderian and his like, he did support the people and the programs that seemed to offer him the fierce appearance and the operational speed required for his policy. Both the extent and the character of the Blitzkrieg innovation in Germany are to be explained, in my judgment, by the dominance of systemic over organizational influences.

Hitler was of course a tyrant bent on conquest. This would explain his commitment to an offensive doctrine and his ability to pressure the military. But Hitler went beyond the mere question of offense or defense. He changed matters of nuance in German doctrine in ways that substantially altered Germany's ability to cope with the constraints and incentives of the European political system.

The direct influence of technology on the evolution of Blitzkrieg can only be viewed in comparative perspective. Blitzkrieg exploited new technology; it was not created by that technology. The essence of Blitzkrieg was its elaborate combination of old and new service arms and technologies to attack directly a new military objective—the command, control, communications, and intelligence functions of an enemy army. While this objective was in practice only partially attained, it was nevertheless the distinguishing characteristic of the doctrine. When the technology of the Blitzkrieg is viewed in comparative perspective, technology does not appear to be especially determinative. Tanks and aircraft aplenty were present in the British and French armed forces in the spring of 1940. An innovation in military doctrine for land warfare was not.

In sum, the offensive character, integration, and innovation of German military doctrine in the late 1930s are best explained by the influence of systemic factors. Neither organization theory nor notions of technological determinism can explain the fundamentals of German military doctrine under Hitler. Indeed, on the whole they would seem to predict a very different doctrine. As such, German military doctrine in the late 1930s illustrates the explanatory power of balance of power theory.

Because Hitler was a tyrant, and apparently bent on unlimited aggression, the "test" is not quite as good as we would like. One could argue that everything in German strategy follows from Hitler's insane drives and his unchallenged tyranny. It is worth noting, however, that his predecessors sought many of the same foreign policy goals and sought to achieve them in similar ways, and justified both by balance of power considerations. Finally, Hitler did not change the gross dimensions of German military doctrine; he changed important matters of nuance. All of the peculiarities of German grand strategy and military doctrine discussed in this chapter coincide remarkably well with what one would deduce from balance of power theory. This coincidence persuades me that systemic constraints and incentives—particularly the distribution of power in interwar Europe, Germany's relative political isolation, and Germany's geographic position—exerted a powerful influence on Hitler's strategy.

[7]

Conclusions

I have attempted three tasks in this book: first, to elaborate and refine the concept of military doctrine, paying particular attention to three important dimensions along which doctrines can vary; second, and of greater importance, to systematically employ two important theories of state behavior, as well as some widely held though poorly developed propositions about technology and geography, as tools for the study of doctrine; and third, in the process of using these tools, to test the two theories and the less well-developed propositions against one another for their explanatory power. The case studies of British, French, and German doctrine in the interwar period have served as a vehicle for the accomplishment of these tasks.

Grand strategy has been viewed in this essay as a political-military means-ends chain. It encompasses foreign policy, military doctrine, and even tactics. My discussion of grand strategy has included only those elements of foreign policy that seem directly related to the basic national security of the state; that of military doctrine has included only those aspects of military tactics that seem directly relevant to an understanding of how the state connects its military means to its political ends. Without some boundaries, the concept of grand strategy as a political-military means-ends chain can expand to unmanageable dimensions.

Military doctrines are important because they affect the stability of the international political system and the security of states. I have argued, consistent with the diverse work of Hoag, Jervis, Quester, Schelling, and Waltz, that the offensive, defensive, or deterrent characteristics of military doctrines can affect the probability and intensity of arms races, and the probability and intensity of war. Thus, the offensive, defensive, or deterrent character of a military doctrine is one of its key aspects, and well worth examining. I have argued, in agreement with Clausewitz and, to a lesser extent, Philip Selznick, that the integration of grand strategy—the reconciliation of military doctrine with political ends—can affect the security of states. Thus, integration is also worthy of examination. Finally, I have argued that innovation within military doctrine can affect the security of states. Stagnant doctrines may lead to disintegration. They may also simply lead to defeat on the battlefield. The degree of innovation is the third key aspect of military doctrine examined in this book.

I have used two theories as tools to study military doctrine. Organization theory has become a very popular tool for the study of strategic matters, particularly weapons system development and crisis behavior, over the last ten or fifteen years. Much has been claimed for its explanatory power, although both Robert Art and Stephen Krasner have raised serious questions about just how useful the theory really is.[1] Hence, I decided to use organization theory alongside its longer-lived competitor, balance of power theory.

Balance of power theory has been around in one guise or another since Thucydides' account of the Peloponnesian War. Organization theorists have imputed to it rational, unitary national actor assumptions, and have criticized it on these grounds. This is not entirely fair, particularly regarding the more recent incarnations of balance of power theory. These are more concerned with the *constraints* and *incentives* inherent in an anarchical international system than they are with the accuracy of a unitary rational actor assumption. Balance of power theory suggests that the nature of the international environment will strongly influence the behavior of states, or those who decide for them. Much arms race behavior, coalition behavior, and military action have been explained by historians and social scientists alike with the simple observation that "a balance had to be maintained." Both logically, because one theory stresses causes at the level of the system and the other at the level of the state, and topically, because the proponents of each have directly challenged each other, it seemed worthwhile to pit organization theory against balance of power theory in this study of military doctrine.

I have integrated some discussion of propositions about the influence of technology and geography on military doctrine with my discussion of organization theory and balance of power theory. By the terms of organization theory, technology and geography should have only a weak and erratic influence on military doctrine; balance of power theory suggests greater influence.

Not even balance of power theory predicts that technology will have a decisive direct influence on military doctrine. When political and geographical constraints and incentives converge in favor of a military doctrine that deviates from what technology seems to permit, balance of power theory predicts that efforts will be made to change the technology.

I have integrated geography with the distribution of power as one of the key environmental factors influencing military doctrine. Geography appears to exert a strong influence on military doctrine—a more powerful long-term influence than that of a given military technology. This seems to be true because geographical constraints are simply harder to change than are technological ones. Even insofar as technological and geographical constraints are closely related, it seems easier to alter technologies that influence how military organizations fight than it is to change technologies that influence where they fight, and in what strength. Distance and obstacles remain important factors over the long term. Therefore, although it is not as important as the distribution of power to the military doctrine of individual states, geography can be viewed as an environmental constraint that strongly affects the real-world military implications of that power distribution.

I have thus handled the two theories and the technology and geography propositions in two ways. First, I have used them as lenses—devices for the examination of doctrine. Each reveals something different about the elements of military doctrine selected for study. Second, I have actually made them coequal with doctrine as subjects of *study*. I have tested them in a comparative framework for their overall explanatory power. I hope that by doing so I have helped to sharpen our sense both of their overall relative value and of the strengths and weaknesses of each as an instrument for the study of national strategy.

ORGANIZATION THEORY

Organization theory seems to provide a good explanation for the operational preferences and behavior of military organizations. It does not provide a particularly good explanation for the overall character of the three doctrines selected for study.

In general, organization theory predicts offensive, disintegrated, and stagnant military doctrines. The case studies suggest that this would normally be the result if military organizations were left to their own devices. Organization theory further suggests that military organizations frequently *will* be left to their own devices. The structure of the modern state is characterized by the division of functions among specialist bureaucracies. Different bureaucracies command different types of expertise. According to organization theory, non-soldiers should have difficulty evaluating the state's military needs and should become dependent on professional military organizations for such advice. Organization theory also predicts that these organizations will deliberately try to escape civilian control in the pursuit of their own interests. The militaries of France, Britain, and Germany did behave in ways consistent with the theory. They were not, however, left entirely on their own, and their respective military doctrines depart in important ways from the theory's predictions. Civilians somehow found ways to overcome the limits on their own military knowledge and get around the bureaucratic shenanigans of their military organizations.

It was argued in chapter 2 that military organizations would probably prefer offensive doctrines because such doctrines reduce uncertainty and increase organizational size, wealth, and autonomy. The Royal Navy and the Royal Air Force conform to these predictions. Both preferred offensive doctrines in the early part of the interwar period. The Royal Navy wanted to go all the way to the Pacific with its big battleships. The sailors never made clear what they would do once they got there. The Royal Air Force stressed the role of offensive "strategic" bombing, without ever doing the serious homework necessary to discover how success might be achieved. In both cases the doctrines made an important contribution to the parochial interests of the organizations, even if they had precious little to do with fighting the next war.

The German Army and Air Force also show a remarkable preference for the offensive. The German Army immediately returned to its offensive tradition following World War I. That tradition had evolved, in part, because of Germany's international political and geographical position, but also because of organizational interests. After the war, organizational interests drew the army back to the offensive. The German Air Force was of course proscribed for much of the interwar period. When it emerged under Nazi sponsorship it faced few of the problems faced by the other fledgling air forces of the time. As an outgrowth of the army, it had compatible offensive proclivities. Moreover, Hitler encouraged the air force to take up an offensive role to support his diplomacy.

The French Army and Air Force deviate somewhat from the predictions of organization theory. The air force did flirt with a strategic bombing doctrine for a time, but, constrained as it was by the close supervision of the army, did not get very far. Tactical bombing and air defense were its primary missions, and it did neither very well. Regrettably, historians have not done enough work to allow us to draw any definitive conclusions about the air force's behavior. The army, however, seems to represent a more marked deviation from the rule. Although it evinced some proclivities toward the offensive in the immediate postwar period, even these seem restrained. Constraints imposed by civilians suppressed whatever latent offensive inclinations remained in the army. It must be remembered that although the army stressed defense, it did undertake a moderately offensive mission in the Low Countries. This mission, on which both soldiers and statesmen agreed, may have satisfied the predicted organizational predilection for offensive action. It is not unreasonable to suggest that Gamelin's Plan D and Breda variant were the sort of offensive action that organization theory predicts. Considering the overall constraints imposed on the army by the civilians and the strong defensive component of the French Army's stated doctrine, even the few offensive remnants that survived are remarkable. Still, there is not really sufficient evidence to argue that the army behaved "true to form." In terms of offensiveness, the doctrine of the French Army in the interwar period barely conforms to the predictions of organization theory.

I argued in chapter 2 that military organizations will seldom innovate autonomously, particularly in matters of doctrine. This should be true because organizations abhor uncertainty, and changes in traditional patterns always involve uncertainty. It should also be true because military organizations are very hierarchical, restricting the flow of ideas from the lower levels to the higher levels. Additionally, those at the top of the hierarchy, who have achieved their rank and position by mastering the old doctrine, have no interest in encouraging their own obsolescence by bringing in a new doctrine. Thus, innovation should occur mainly when the organization registers a large failure, or when civilians with legitimate authority intervene to promote innovation.

We see very little internally generated innovation in the three cases examined. The military organizations seem not to like innovation. The German Army, the loser of a great war, is the most notable exception. Even there, I am hard put to call the measures introduced by von Seeckt an innovation. Von Seeckt was a reformer, not an innovator. He took the German Army back to its prewar doctrine. He introduced a variety of new tactics, and some new technology, to restore the army's ability to effectuate its old doctrine. Thus, the German Army represents a mixed case. An organization will change as a result of defeat, but it will attempt repairs rather than major innovations.

One might argue that the Royal Air Force's invention of "strategic bombing" amounts to an innovation in doctrine. It must be remembered, however, that the RAF was created by a civilian order. Because it was a new organization, there was not much traditional doctrine for it to overcome. Moreover, the doctrine that was developed existed only in theory. Little was done to turn it into a real weapon of war—until war was forced upon England. Once the RAF evolved its preference for bombing, all other possible uses of aircraft were suppressed. Hence, the RAF conforms very well to organization theory predictions.

The same must be said of the French Army during the 1930s. Admittedly, the defensive doctrine that evolved after the war was a marked change from the organization's prewar doctrine. The organization itself was in some measure responsible for this change. The French Army's victory in World War I was Pyrrhic at best, and the officer corps was resolved to avoid a repetition of such heavy casualties. Nevertheless, the civilian leaders of France had a great deal to do with the evolution of this defensive doctrine. It cannot be credited solely to the soldiers. Once this doctrine was accepted, the French Army sustained it with a vengeance. Civilians did not intervene to promote anything new, and the soldiers certainly did not encourage innovative thinkers among themselves. Again, organization theory seems vindicated.

The two most noteworthy instances of civilian intervention and innovation in military doctrine occurred in Britain and Germany. In Britain, it is clear that RAF Fighter Command and its air defense system owed their existence and capability to civilian intervention. The bomber advocates who dominated the RAF never would have adequately funded it in the absence of strong civilian pressure. The reasons for the civil intervention will be discussed below. That such intervention was necessary at all is another illustration of the explanatory power of organization theory. It does correctly predict organizational tendencies. Systemic forces constrain statesmen to oppose those tendencies.

The Blitzkrieg doctrine is another innovation that required civilian intervention. Considering the extreme offensive predilections of the German Army, this might seem a surprise. After World War I the army appeared to be quite willing to make reforms that would allow a return to decisive offensive operations. This was not actually the case. The proponents of daring, high-speed, deep armored thrusts were opposed within the German Army. Hitler's emphasis on the newest weaponry was resisted. The German Army preferred to superimpose new technology on its old offensive doctrine, rather than innovate doctrinally to exploit more fully all the offensive potential of the new technology. Hitler was more daring. While one must be careful not to overstate how fully or correctly Hitler conceptualized the Blitzkrieg, his support for its various elements must be credited as the key pressure that brought the doctrine to operational fruition. Again, the reasons for Hitler's intervention can be traced in part to Germany's international political position. That even the offensively inclined German Army required a good kick from the outside to create such an offensive innovation provides still more support for the utility of organization theory in explaining certain tendencies within modern military organizations.

I argued in chapter 2 that organizational factors work against integrated grand strategies. This is partly due to the reluctance to innovate. Statesmen may change the state's foreign policy; soldiers may not be inclined to change their doctrine to stay in step. A second factor working against strategic integration is the multi-service character of most national military capabilities. Each service—army, navy, air force—fights for its own interests. I argued in chapter 1 that the setting of priorities among means and ends is a key aspect of grand strategy. No service willingly accepts second priority, with an inferior claim on resources. Military organizations, like most organizations, will attempt to maintain a "negotiated environment." Sometimes this will manifest itself in equal splits; other times by long-standing treaties about relative shares of national defense spending. Military organizations will oppose the rigorous statement of strategies because such statements provide ammunition for critics to use against them. Because each service is concerned for its autonomy, a group of services is not likely to produce an agreed multi-service strategy or doctrine that does anything more than combine their independent service doctrines. Such a strategy may set priorities among services, but these priorities are likely to reflect traditional agreements on budget shares, not any serious strategic thinking. In general, only civilian intervention can shake loose these inter-service treaties and jealousies to produce an integrated grand strategy.

Britain offers the best example of this problem in the interwar period. The reason is clear. Britain was the first of the three states to move to a genuine three-service system. Each service enjoyed a high degree of autonomy from the others. The results are predictable. English statesmen of the period complained over and over again that the chiefs of staff could not arrive at a strategy. Budget shares did change substantially over this period due to civilian preferences for spending on the Royal Air Force. It is hard to imagine the three services agreeing on such a shift in priorities by themselves.

France also offers a good case of disintegration. The French military was seriously negligent in the development of the French Air Force. The new air force was weak. Poorly endowed with resources, it was ill-equipped to fight for a role of its own. The army was materially and politically very strong, and did its best to dominate the youthful air force. For reasons that are still not clear, French civilians failed to press for more aggressive development of aerial capabilities. Only in the late 1930s, with the stimulus of massive and obvious German aerial rearmament, did the civilians set fighter production and air defense as the primary tasks of the air force. The army and the air force were simply unable to agree between themselves on an "all-arms" strategy for France.

Germany presents the best example of integration *between* services. The German Army and Air Force developed in relative harmony with each other, and cooperated rather well on the battlefield. This was due in part to the extreme youth of the Luftwaffe, in part to its large personnel component of army-officer transfers, and in part to its overwhelming political and budgetary support from the political leadership. While army–air force cooperation was excellent, there was a serious dearth of cooperation between the Luftwaffe and the navy. Cooperation between these two services was poor during the 1930s and poor during the early years of the war. The naval air arm was not given much budgetary support. Indeed, like the Royal Air Force leadership, Goering appears to have opposed an independent naval air arm. Arguably, better cooperation might have improved German effectiveness in the war on British commerce.

In summary, organization theory explains a great deal about general tendencies within military organizations that affect military doctrine and grand strategy. The three case studies do not, however, show military organizations riding roughshod over their civilian superiors. Often, militaries prefer offense, yet defensive strategies emerge. Militaries oppose innovation, but we see some remarkable innovations. Military organizations attempt to go their own way and avoid the setting of priorities. Services avoid cooperation with each other. In spite of such tendencies priorities get set, and military organizations are deflected from their preferred course. Civilians do affect military doctrine. Their intervention is often responsible for the level of innovation and integration achieved in a given military doctrine.

What prompts civilians to intervene in the instrumental aspects of their military organizations? What determines the character of their intervention?

BALANCE OF POWER THEORY

France, Britain, and Germany are most differentiated from one another in the interwar period by their respective international political and geographical positions. They are similar to one another in their dependence on professional military organizations for their security. For part of the period, all had "democratic" governments, although this obviously changed once Hitler took power. One should not underestimate the effects of the Nazi system of government on German foreign policy and military doctrine. Nevertheless, for the entire interwar period Germany was, for the most part, an "isolated" state without important military allies. Britain and France, on the other hand, in spite of periodically bad relations, never ceased viewing each other as probable allies in any future coalition against a resurgence of German expansionism.

Having chosen for herself a path of aggression, Germany had to rely on her own devices, and behaved accordingly. Britain and France, however, each could reasonably expect the other to take on a large share of the responsibility for opposing German expansion. The British were in a somewhat stronger position in this "buck-passing" relationship, but much of the behavior of each state, so criticized by students of the interwar period, is explained by their "structural" positions. Balance of power theory helps explain the tardiness of their internal balancing behavior (i.e., rearmament), its quantitative and qualitative strengths and inadequacies, its peculiarities, the poor coordination of British and French diplomacy, and even the poor war plan of May 1940.

In his recent *Theory of International Politics*, Kenneth Waltz argues that there is an historical association between multipolarity and certain recurrent international problems. The preceding case studies tend to support his argument, and are suggestive of the problems that might arise if the international political system were to return to extreme multipolarity. Aggressors find many opportunities in a multipolar system which tend not to emerge in bipolar systems. Such opportunities allow the expansionist state to improve its capabilities, making such a state harder to check. Collective goods problems among status quo powers not only create opportunities for expansion but tend to dislocate the opposition to expansion. Disputes over costs and risks may continue even after a defensive coalition has formed. Multipolar systems should thus produce lengthy, wide, and destructive wars. That description fits World War II, World War I, and the Napoleonic Wars. It may fit others.

I deduced a number of propositions regarding civilian preferences for offensive, defensive, or deterrent doctrines from balance of power theory. Many of the propositions about offense are confirmed by the German case. Of course (as was noted in the text), statesmen embarking upon conquest will of necessity prefer offensive doctrines. Nevertheless, both before and during Hitler's reign, political and geographical factors played a role in the evolution of Germany's offensive strategy.

First, Hitler's offensive strategy facilitated the passing of war costs to his adversaries. Hitler was committed to keeping war away from German territory. This was partly out of fear for his own legitimacy, and partly out of a somewhat misplaced fear that German industry was vulnerable to attack from neighboring countries. While the purpose of passing war costs on to others was but one cause among many of the offensiveness of *German* strategy, and one that I did not address directly, it appears to be the main cause of the only offensive aspect of *French* interwar strategy—the advance into Belgium. That such a markedly defensive strategy could include offensive elements in order to facilitate the transfer of war costs to an ally is a good test of the proposition. Germany, because it was committed to an offensive doctrine for so many reasons, is a weaker confirming instance.

The desire to wage "preventive" war gives rise to offensive doctrines. Hitler was planning an aggressive campaign in a multipolar world. The potential coalition against him was very strong, yet that coalition might be temporarily weakened or distracted by events elsewhere. "Windows" would open, and for the time that they remained ajar Germany's military power would be adequate to support particular acts of aggression. If Hitler were to exploit these opportunities, he would need an offensive doctrine.

As a variant on the "preventive" war motivation, I argued that states facing multiple enemies will often opt for offensive doctrines in the hope of achieving piecemeal defeat of an adversary coalition. This is of course not entirely a function of the distribution of power. Geography, technology, and the overall balance of forces will affect whether or not a state can actually hope to defeat one adversary and then successfully shift forces to cope with another. Germany has had this option since the construction of an extensive national railway network. Israel has this option today, due to her small size and the great mobility of mechanized ground forces. Even if we assume a purely conventional conflict, the Soviet Union probably does not have this possibility today because of the length and vulnerability of her lines of communication from east to west. Thus, she maintains large forces at both ends of the country. Technological and geographical conditions unfavorable to the success of such an offensive doctrine have not always suppressed it, however. Its seductiveness is borne out by the British contemplation of an offensive strategy against Italy, the weakest of her three interwar adversaries. It is true that she did not contemplate the option for very long; the breadth of her empire and the limits of transportation technology may have made it impossible for her to execute a "knock-out" blow in one theater. Nevertheless, her consideration of the option does lend some support to the proposition that states with inadequate capabilities, facing conflicts on many fronts, will be attracted to offensive doctrines that allow the piecemeal defeat of their enemies.

Finally, I argued that politically isolated states will prefer offensive doctrines as aids to diplomacy. States must competitively measure power and will when their interests collide. An offensive doctrine provides a somewhat more useful tool for diplomatic manipulation of military capabilities than does a defensive doctrine. Isolated states may find themselves driven to rely upon their military organizations as an adjunct to diplomacy.

Germany under Hitler offers some evidence for this proposition. Hitler deliberately manipulated his military power for coercive diplomacy. He directly or indirectly forced changes in his military organization that would facilitate its coercive utility. These changes also made it a better offensive instrument. Hitler was of course bent on aggression, and believed in his "avalanche" theory. These inclinations also explain his use of military force to support his diplomacy. One even finds such practice, albeit more subtle and constrained, in Stresemann's diplomacy.

Other states in positions similar to Germany's have used military force in similar ways. Israel has long had a policy of armed demonstration; indeed Israel frequently embarks on demonstrative air, naval, and ground raids. Israeli military doctrine is highly offensive. The United States and the Soviet Union, though far from being "isolated" states, have both led coalitions of much weaker partners. The threat of alliance has seldom been brought into play in their relations with each other or with other states. Rather, both have frequently resorted to armed demonstrations, both violent and nonviolent, to back their diplomacy. Both include important offensive elements in the doctrine of their nuclear and conventional forces, although the Soviet Union is more offensively inclined than is the United States.

Finally, it is interesting to note that during the interwar period, Britain and France were loath to manipulate military force to support their diplomacy. More often, they manipulated the threat of firming up their coalition with each other or with other states. They saw a world of alliance possibilities and tried to exploit it. One might conclude that this was merely a function of their generally defensive status quo policy. But it should be remembered that neither Israel nor the United States is a non–status quo power. A comparative perspective supports the proposition that states with few or weak allies tend toward military demonstration to support their diplomacy, and that such a tendency itself supports offensive doctrines.

Balance of power theory predicts a tendency toward deterrent doctrines when military capabilities are scarce. Deterrent doctrines stress raising an adversary's risks and costs in war rather than reducing one's own. Such strategies tend to stress *punitive* military operations. They turn wars into competitions in risk taking, punishment, and suffering. They put a premium on the demonstration of national will in advance of a conflict as well as during a conflict. It is also of critical importance that states with deterrent doctrines show in peacetime that their military capabilities can *inevitably* punish an aggressor. Such persuasion was no mean feat before the advent of nuclear explosives.

Britain most nearly fits the theory's predictions. Britain flirted with an offensive strategy, as noted above, but her interests were too far-flung and her capabilities too limited to effectuate such a strategy. For a time the RAF stressed direct attack on enemy cities and industry to deter a war. Unfortunately, the doctrine was not very clear; it could only be employed against one of Britain's three adversaries and proved, upon close examination, to be unworkable in any case. Even during the period when the RAF was allowed to stress long-range bombing, British civilians had a more general "deterrent" strategy in mind. It was far from perfect, and I recognize that the pattern of British interwar grand strategy only loosely fits the deterrence mold.

In simplest terms, Britain tried to convince her adversaries that she had the will, the skill, and the resources to wage a long, grinding, attrition war. Such a war would resemble the preceding world war, with the important exception that Britain would avoid the trenches. Both sides would suffer in such a war, but the British tried to convince others that they would wage it and, somehow, even win it. Britain's punitive capability did not rest in the operations of any one service, but rather in the cooperation of all of them, over an extended period of time, in an attrition campaign. To convince their adversaries that this campaign would be waged, that "punishment" was inevitable, the British had to appear to be, and be in fact, invulnerable to a knock-out blow. This drove the British to stress their military forces' ability to deny an adversary a quick win. Defense became the special concern of British civilians; it was the prerequisite to their "deterrence" strategy.

States preparing to fight in coalition will often prefer defensive strategies. Such strategies will allow time to settle disputes within the coalition about relative shares of the risks and costs of conflict. There will also be disputes over spoils. Some readers might challenge this proposition, noting that although the members of the Triple Entente had long planned to fight in coalition, France and Russia began World War I with wild offensive lunges. It must be remembered, however, that most decision-makers at the time expected a short and cheap war.

As pointed out in chapter 1, and consistent with organization theory, long out-of-control military organizations had promulgated a cult of the offensive prior to World War I. Its effect was to merge the individual and collective "goods." Each state could best defend itself by assuring the immediate annihilation of the aggressor—a goal agreed to be feasible and cheap. The experience of World War I changed such views. War was no longer perceived to be cheap, and victory was not seen to be easy. The individual and collective "goods" were separated. Each state had an interest in passing the costs of its own defense to its allies, because these costs were high. Moreover, there was a widespread belief in a defensive advantage, so states did not believe that their allies might fold. The argument becomes somewhat circular: the apparent dominance of the defense in World War I caused states to see the costs of war as high; high war costs magnified the advantages of buck-passing; buck-passing was best faciliated by defensive doctrines. Moreover, buck-passing was safe because of the perceived advantage of the defense. Leaving one's ally a little bit in the lurch was not seen to represent a high risk to the ally's survival or one's own.

Both Britain and France showed a marked inclination to pass war costs to each other. This inclination manifested itself in the military doctrines of the two states (chapters 4 and 5). France built the Maginot Line, organized her army, and facilitated both her own and German entry into Belgium in order to pass the costs of the war to Britain, Belgium, and other potential allies. Britain avoided the organization of a sizeable land army and stressed the development of air defenses at home, in order to buy herself maximum independence from the outcome of continental warfare and so pass the costs of that warfare to France. Buck-passing was a primary motivation of both countries. Lest this be taken as an argument for *technological* determinism, it is to be remembered that France by planning to enter Belgium violated the Great War's technological lessons, and Britain defied widely perceived technological "realities" of air warfare to build an air defense system.

Balance of power theory can also help explain integration and innovation in military doctrine. I have argued that civilian intervention in military affairs is a key determinant of integration and innovation. Balance of power theory can help explain the causes of such intervention.

Of course, civilian leaders contemplating aggressive campaigns are likely to give their military organizations a quick audit before getting started. Aggressors are not normally bent on getting beaten, so they are likely to look to their capabilities. This is more of a commonsense notion than one derived from balance of power theory. But balance of power theory does suggest a number of important propositions. These propositions all have to do mainly with threats to the state.

First, states without allies are likely to pay a good deal of attention to their military organizations. As noted above, statesmen without allies will find it expedient to use their military forces for diplomacy. In so doing, they come into close contact with the operational characteristics of those forces. Moreover, the absence of allies often correlates highly with an imbalance of power. States may find themselves without allies in a multipolar system for many reasons. Whatever the reasons, internal balancing behavior is a likely response. This may be quantitative or qualitative. One component is likely to be increased political attention to the state's military organization. Thus innovation and integration should tend to correlate highly with political-diplomatic isolation.

Germany's military doctrine was generally more integrated and innovative than those of her competitors in the late interwar period. Israeli military doctrine has also tended to be more innovative and integrated than those of her competitors. This proposition must of course be wielded judiciously because diplomatic isolation is often the result of an ill-considered and bellicose foreign policy. Causing one's own encirclement is certainly no mark of a "good" grand strategy.

Statesmen will intervene in the doctrines of their military organizations as part of an overall pattern of balancing behavior. This is best exemplified by the British case. British statesmen were not unaware of Germany's military build-up, or the build-up of Italian and Japanese military power. They took, within the limits of their "buck-passing" strategy, measures to balance the increase in enemy military power. They correctly identified Germany as their most dangerous adversary, and correctly identified the air balance as the aspect of British defense most needful of attention.

British civilians did more than review their military capabilities. The bombing doctrine of the RAF was inconsistent with both the deterrence and buck-passing aspects of British strategy. It had to change. British civilians' intervention to construct a defensive fighter arm flew in the face of military preferences for offensive bombing. This is a good test of balance of power theory against both organization theory and notions of technological determinism. The constraints and incentives of the international political system had driven British statesmen to a defensive/deterrent doctrine. The build-up of German military power encouraged them to increase their own military capability. Yet, the doctrine offered by the Royal Air Force could not support British grand strategy.

The civilians were prime movers in the development of a defensive military innovation in the face of an offensively inclined and inertial service. This service had, moreover, escaped close civilian supervision for over a decade. It was in an extremely strong organizational position. Civilians had also been propagandized to the effect that aerial bombing could be decisive. They had bought a good deal of the military argument to this effect, and had seen mixed evidence to support it. This case is thus a clear test of both organization theory and notions of technological determinism. They fail. Balance of power theory, on the other hand, goes a long way to explain the peculiarities of British military doctrine and the air defense innovation.

Finally, it was argued that civilians will intervene out of fear of high costs of military action. Such intervention may stem from a recent disaster, or some sudden change in the perceived costs of war. This may not have anything to do with question of victory or defeat. The behavior of French civilian leaders after World War I best exemplifies this proposition. While the French had won the war, the costs had been high. French statesmen were determined to avoid such costs in a future war. They intervened in the doctrine of the French Army and surrounded it with constraints that would bind the army to defensive warfare. There is more to protecting the security of a state that just

[234]

"winning." When war costs appear to be terribly high, avoiding them becomes an important national security goal. French civilians helped build a rather carefully integrated French military doctrine. Moreover, it was somewhat innovative, certainly a far cry from the army's prewar offensive preferences. The Maginot fortifications were probably the most remarkable military construction program ever seen on the European continent to that date. Unfortunately, the doctrine failed to keep pace with political changes elsewhere.

If British civilians paid attention to developing German armaments and intervened in the doctrine of their military organizations to promote innovation and integration in response to the German threat, why didn't the French? The French did increase their expenditure on armaments; they bought a good deal of modern equipment before the war; they organized new formations for the deployment of military equipment. Yet, both the ground and air doctrine stagnated. French military power became less and less adequate to cope with the threat. This was mainly a qualitative problem, not a quantitative one.

The disintegration and stagnation of French military doctrine is difficult to explain. Both France and Britain were interested in buck-passing; both preferred defensive strategies. The British innovated in the last years of peace; the French did not. While it is difficult to prove, it appears that French civilian leaders spent a disproportionate amount of time and energy chasing coalition partners—more than did the British. This was almost certainly a function of France's comparative weakness. For instance, her national income was roughly half that of the United Kingdom and her population was a little smaller. German national income was in the same range as the British and she had half again the population of either Britain or France. If one disaggregates the national income figures to facilitate the comparison of relative industrial potential for modern war, the figures look even worse from the French perspective. By one estimate, in 1937 Germany controlled 14.4 percent of "world war potential," the U.K. 10.2 percent, and France only 4.2 percent.[2] Moreover, Britain had the English Channel and France did not. France was more threatened by Germany and had much less slack to play with. One would have thought that this unhappy situation would have driven French statesmen and soldiers to greater exertions—particularly in the military sphere.

The French, however, saw a world of diplomatic opportunities and were attracted *by their very weakness* to the exploitation of those opportunities. Besides, the defensive doctrine evolved in the 1920s appeared to be well-suited to this task, even if it meant the loss of

France's allies in eastern Europe or risked an encounter battle in Belgium. British standoffishness further encouraged French defensiveness. As argued in chapter 2, states seeking allies must construct their grand strategies and military doctrines to make themselves attractive to preferred partners. Because the French were so weak, they badly wanted British cooperation, and were not inclined to flirt with any offensive doctrine that might scare off the British. French diplomats and statesmen occupied themselves with the search for allies, and had neither the energy nor the incentive to scrutinize military doctrine. In the absence of close civilian supervision, the military organization behaved as predicted.

TECHNOLOGY AND GEOGRAPHY

What conclusions can be drawn about the influence of technology on doctrine? Mainly, we must conclude that the influence of technology is seldom direct, and is usually filtered through organizational biases and statesmen's perceptions of the international political system. Moreover, the British, French, and German cases tend to suggest that technology exerts a diffuse influence. Britain and France reacted to the *high cost* of World War I more than to its particular lessons about particular military technologies. They concluded that future wars would be very costly and should therefore be avoided. If war proved inevitable, then its costs should be carefully controlled by sitting on the defensive and by passing the burden of war costs to one's allies. Germany also drew the lesson that modern war could be very costly. This lesson was translated into a special kind of offensive doctrine that might allow Germany to defeat her enemies piecemeal—avoiding a long attrition war. Similar general conclusions about modern military technology led to highly dissimilar military doctrines. As argued above, the specifics of each strategy seem best explained by a combination of systemic (including geographic) and organizational factors.

When one drops to the level of specific technological lessons and judgments, one finds wide differences among the three powers. French soldiers and statesmen do seem to have drawn the conclusion that modern military technology gave the defender an advantage in land warfare. British soldiers and civilians also seem to have drawn this conclusion. Nevertheless, the British Army's early postwar experiments with armor were some of the most innovative in Europe. At least initially, the British Army appears to have been slightly less doctrinaire than the French Army. The German Army set to work changing the defensive advantage perceived by the Allied armies. Von Seeckt believed that attrition war could never be effective for Germany and set about perfecting new tactics that would restore the dominance of the offensive. Thus, we see in the interwar period no automatic connection between technology and doctrine.

As "new" technology was deployed in the armies and air forces of Europe in the 1930s, we see a diversity of responses and doctrines. In some cases the new technologies were screwed on to old doctrines; in other cases they were integrated into new doctrines. The Germans and the British achieved new doctrines with new technologies. The French did not. Developments in the air are especially suggestive, since aerial warfare in World War I was so primitive and its lessons so obscure.

The Germans were initially forbidden air capabilities by the terms of the Versailles Treaty. Once they returned to aerial warfare, they showed a general preference for cooperation with the army, mainly through offensive operations. The Royal Air Force achieved autonomy early in the postwar period. It interpreted aerial technology to favor the offensive, and suppressed any suggestions that this offensive action should be closely tied to ground operations. Mixed evidence from German bombing experience in World War I, and a few episodes in the interwar period, lent some empirical support to the Royal Air Force's claims. We saw in chapter 5 that this evidence was largely "cooked" for organizational reasons. British civilians grew dissatisfied with this particular technological "reality" and successfully moved to change it. The French never decided what they believed to be the implications of modern aerial technology, and were simply buffeted from position to position. The three cases together suggest that limited experience with a new technology can provide support for any doctrinal conclusion that soldiers or civilians wish to draw—for either organizational or grand strategic reasons.

We may come to somewhat more definitive conclusions regarding the influence of geography on military doctrine. Geographical factors had a direct influence on British and German military doctrine in this period, but a less clear influence on French military doctrine.

On the one hand, the extra margin of security provided by the English Channel reinforced British defensive preferences; British decision-makers perceived that they could forego an early, substantial commitment of ground forces to the continent without unduly affecting the state's chances for survival. On the other hand, for much of the interwar period, the effect of distance on Britain's ability to defend the *empire* was seldom fully admitted. The Royal Navy seems to have been particularly sluggish in this regard. As the power of Britain's adversaries increased, geographic constraints were more explicitly acknowledged, but even so, Britain made one last quixotic effort to hold her Pacific bastions.

Germany offers a similar case of mixed geographic influence on doctrine. Formally, under von Seeckt, the exploitation of interior lines through offensive operations was overemphasized. Germany objectively lacked the power to exploit this geographical potential, and von Seeckt's behavior during the Ruhr crisis shows that he understood this. It appears that the offensive doctrine hung on for organizational reasons. Later, under Hitler, Germany had the power to exploit her interior lines, and used it.

The French were influenced by what they perceived to be geographical constraints and opportunities. As noted earlier, a large part of French industry was close to the Belgian border, so fortification of the border could not protect these assets. Moreover, lacking any major natural obstacles, the terrain was deemed unsuitable for fortifications as great as the Maginot Line. Belgium would provide an excellent battleground to counter the Germans, far from French territory.

While these arguments are credited as plausible by most historians, there is room for suspicion about why the north was not more heavily defended. Industry in Lorraine was also within artillery range of a frontier—the border with Luxembourg—but this did not stop the French from extending the Maginot Line to cover it. It was, admittedly, more naturally defensible than the Belgian frontier, but the differences seem less striking than the French claimed. The French were interested not merely in defending themselves from conquest, but in keeping the collateral effects of battle as far from French territory as possible *and* roping in Belgian, Dutch, and (most of all) British allies to serve the French cause. These purposes were best served by leaving the border unfortified, thus inducing the Germans to invade through Belgium. This strategy was, of course, facilitated by geographical accidents. Belgium lies between France and Germany; and Belgian ports were of potential utility as a base for an amphibious assault against Britain, so Britain might be coaxed to defend them once again. But to exploit these possibilities France would have to take some risks. A poorly fortified Belgian frontier and the dispatch of the best French troops to Belgium would leave little margin for error. The French argue that the location of their industry and the nature of the border terrain left them little choice in the matter, but, as noted above, this is not wholly persuasive. Gross power disparities and political opportunities drove the French to manipulate the geography of Europe to produce a clash in Belgium. They did so because the rectification of the imbalance of overall capabilities between France and Germany was perceived as the paramount national interest.

Generally, then, one can conclude from these cases that statesmen and soldiers do take geography into account in making their military decisions. At the same time, however, they are often willing to understate or overstate its impact to suit organizational interests, policy preferences, or constraints and incentives presented by the distribution of power in the international system.

RELATIVE EXPLANATORY POWER

These three cases have provided a good laboratory for testing the explanatory power of organization theory and balance of power theory, and examining the influence of technology and geography on military doctrine. What can be said about the relative reliability of the two theories and the propositions discussed in this book?

Technology per se is a weak explanation for any of the aspects of military doctrine selected for study. It plays a role, but a very indirect one. World War I had provided stark lessons regarding modern military technology; yet these lessons were translated into a wide range of doctrines.

Geographical factors provide only partial explanations for fundamental aspects of military doctrine. The role of geography does appear to be more powerful, direct, and long-lasting than that of technology, although a detailed examination of the last thirty years would probably show nuclear technology exerting a greater influence than geography on the military doctrine of the two superpowers.

Organization theory and balance of power theory offer more persuasive and comprehensive explanations than either technological or geographical propositions for particular elements of military doctrine. In my judgment, balance of power theory is a slightly more powerful tool than organization theory for the study of doctrine. In the broadest sense, organization theory predicts offensive, disintegrated, and stagnant military doctrines. The three case studies show that these are powerful tendencies. Yet, these tendencies are mitigated in important ways by the intervention of civilians into operational matters. The case studies show that the intervention itself, and its character, can be explained by balance of power theory. The studies even contain some evidence to suggest that when threats become sufficiently grave, soldiers themselves begin to reconsider organizationally self-serving doctrinal preferences, if those preferences do not adequately respond to the state's immediate security problem. Von Seeckt displayed great flexibility during the Ruhr occupation, even without civilian intervention. Royal Air Force bomber advocates became more responsive to civilian interest in fighters and air defense, as war began to appear imminent. Once the RAF examined the immediate utility of its strategic bombers for fighting the Germans and found that it was low, it became more willing to entertain other ideas—at least temporarily.

The peculiarities of German and British military doctrine in the late 1930s are especially suggestive concerning the relative power of organization theory and balance of power theory. The German Army was offensively inclined, but in many ways opposed to the Blitzkrieg strategy required by Hitler. To the extent that there was a Blitzkrieg strategy (and I believe that there was), Hitler's intervention was responsible. The operational, economic, and political aspects of this strategy conformed remarkably well to the environmental constraints surrounding Germany. An innovation was imposed, more or less against the will of the German Army.

In Britain, both organizational interests and technological "lessons" predisposed an offensive bombing strategy. Britain's international position required something else. British civilians imposed a new doctrine in the face of contrary organizational preferences. The civilian intervention and its character are best explained by balance of power theory.

The tests or "critical experiments" offered by the interwar period are of course not perfect. Reality is always more complicated than we would like it to be, and seldom conforms perfectly to the predictions of any theory. Hitler is obviously something of a wild card. French domestic politics played a role in French grand strategy that I have not even attempted to analyze. I have not, however, purported to fully explain all there is to explain about the military doctrines of these three states. Nor do I claim to have *definitively* tested the two theories introduced in chapter 2.

I have used theories for what they are—tools for the apprehension of reality. They are abstractions from reality that identify broad causal forces. I have stretched these theories a good bit to examine the phenomenon of military doctrine. In so doing, I have subjected them to a fairly rigorous test. I believe that the test is very suggestive. It lends a great deal of support to balance of power theory, more so than the current widespread popularity of organization theory would lead one to expect. The test also shows the strengths and the weaknesses of organization theory. That theory is a powerful tool, but in the analysis of strategic matters it should always be employed in combination with its more mature cousin—balance of power theory. Finally, we should always be leary of explanations of military doctrine that include implicit or explicit assumptions of technological determinism or that overstress the causal impact of geography.

SOME GENERAL, POLICY-RELEVANT CONCLUSIONS

While this study has stressed prediction and explanation, it leads to some general, policy-relevant conclusions as well.

First, organization theory predicts that militaries will frequently behave in ways that are inimical to the interests of the state. I argue that military organizations are usually, though not always, closely watched in times of increasing tension. In times of relative calm, they are frequently ignored. Civilians must carefully audit the doctrines of their military organizations to ensure that they stress the appropriate type of military operations, reconcile political ends with military means, and change with political circumstances and technological developments.

Second, the political isolation of a state is dangerous. The creation of international pariahs should be avoided. Such states are thrown back upon their own military resources, with unpredictable consequences. Arab policy toward Israel has probably made the state stronger militarily than it otherwise would have been. It is interesting to note that the Israeli Defense Forces suffered their greatest relative qualitative decline in the period 1967–1973, perhaps the golden age of perceived Israeli security.

Third, both the theoretical and the substantive aspects of this book underline the continued value of the NATO alliance. As this book is being completed, the alliance finds itself in one of its periodic crises of confidence, this one brought on by the controversial decision to modernize its long range theater nuclear forces. A review of the implications of balance of power theory for state behavior under conditions of multipolarity, and an examination of how those implications manifested themselves in the interwar period, provides stark evidence of some of the dangers that could arise if NATO were to dissolve. We should be concerned about these dangers, since Europe remains the greatest prize in range of Soviet conventional military power.

While it is true that, from a theoretical perspective, the world would remain bipolar even in the absence of NATO, and many of the beneficial effects of bipolarity would probably remain, it also seems likely that the dissolution of NATO would spell a major decline in U.S. attention to European affairs. The United States' engagement in Europe could—at least for a time—be as ambivalent and erratic as Britain's during the 1920s and 1930s. Many of the predictions of balance of power theory for state behavior under conditions of multipolarity might therefore hold in the absence of the NATO alliance.

As discussed in chapter 2, expanding hegemons can get an initial advantage under such circumstances. Because states are out for themselves, disputes among status quo powers over the risks and costs of opposing an imperialist are likely to be frequent. This gives an expansionist state a head start, both in building up its internal power and in making foreign conquests. This makes ultimate resistance to the expansionist more difficult. Moreover, as we discovered in the examination of Britain and France, disputes among status quo powers continue even as the defensive coalition begins to form. These disputes quantitatively and qualitatively affect the balancing behavior of the defenders. As they pass the security buck back and forth, the status quo powers may do less militarily than they could or should.

Similarly, the efforts of the defenders may be poorly coordinated and uncomplementary, so that their combined forces are unbalanced and capable of only limited battlefield cooperation. This was true of British, French, and Belgian military cooperation during the 1930s and during the Battle of the Low Countries and the Battle of France. Britain's large air force, both fighters and bombers, could exert little influence on the ground battle in 1940. During the interwar period France probably invested more in her navy (not discussed in the French case study) than she would have had she been confident of British military help; these resources might have contributed to a stronger army. Finally, British, French, and Belgian ground force commanders had a difficult time coordinating their actions on the battlefield. They lacked both good communications facilities and any common doctrine. In the absence of NATO, and after a U.S. withdrawal from continental affairs, it seems likely that these peacetime and wartime problems could reemerge. As they did for Hitler, such problems might provide temptations for a future Soviet leader more daring than those we have seen recently.

The continued existence of NATO presents the would-be aggressor with a difficult situation. The presence of the United States, a leader willing and able to take on a disproportionate share of the risks and costs of maintaining the status quo, ensures speedy reaction to expansionist gambits. The presence of a single great power in the alliance also helps secure and manage the defensive contributions of smaller states, who fear being left in the lurch should their futures be entrusted to the less dynamic middle powers. While the presence of such a leader may, as collective goods theory suggests, encourage middle powers such as France, Britain, and Germany to spend less on defense than they might if they were forced to rely wholly on their own resources, it probably encourages small states to make greater efforts. If forced to try to defend themselves, countries like Belgium, Holland, and Norway might view the task as hopeless and deploy relatively weak forces, as was true for most of the interwar period. Only in collaboration with a great power can their efforts count for something. Indeed, in the absence of assured protection by a great power, small states often find appeasement of expanding hegemons more attractive than the prospect of complete defeat in a total war.

A high level of peacetime coordination of planning and training is assured in an alliance context. This increases the overall complementarity and efficiency of the military efforts of the member states, and may, in some measure, make up for some of the free-riding by the middle powers.

Finally, these peacetime collaborative efforts would almost certainly pay off in enhanced battlefield performance. Military organizations that have planned and trained together in peacetime are better able to deal with the friction of combat, particularly after an extended period of peace.

While many complain about the limited degree of military cooperation achieved by the alliance thus far, particularly in the area of weapons standardization, one need only carefully study the 1930s and the Battle of the Low Countries to appreciate how much worse things could be in the absence of NATO.

A fourth policy-relevant conclusion is that we should not be overly complacent about nuclear weapons technology. The debates on military strategy conducted within and between the Soviet Union and the United States notwithstanding, it is difficult to understand how anyone can fail to see that mutual deterrence is all these states can hope for. If queried about the probable outcome of a general thermonuclear war between the two superpowers on planet Earth, the proverbial man from Mars would surely reply that mutual destruction is assured. We sometimes pretend differently.

This book has suggested some of the organizational and systemic reasons why we do so. Military organizations generally prefer the offensive. I have no doubt that this is true of the Soviet Strategic

Rocket Forces and the Strategic Air Command. Statesmen, locked in conflict with powerful international adversaries, burdened with security dependencies, deprived of politically meaningful allies, unsure of their own military expertise, and simply inclined to try to limit damage to their states should war come, are vulnerable to the soldier's arguments for offensive doctrines. Moreover, both American and Soviet leaders have been able to draw liberally on the copious industrial and technological resources of their respective societies for military purposes. Fortunately, civilians have not fully followed the course of the offensive. Deterrence has been an important component of the nuclear strategies of both sides. Nevertheless, there is a marked ambivalence, and this ambivalence provides the opportunity and sometimes an additional motive force for military organizations to pursue offensive innovations.

Nuclear weapons technology has proved to be remarkably resistant to innovation. The advantage still clearly lies with military forces oriented neither to disarming nor denial operations but to punishment. Unfortunately, this book suggests the existence of strong pressures for change. In the 1930s it was believed that the bomber would always get through. A consortium of statesmen, scientists, and soldiers altered this "reality" just enough for Britain to survive the summer and autumn of 1940. No one can tell how resilient is the technology of nuclear deterrence, but powerful political pressures are at work to change technological realities in favor of the offense. No one can say when or if these pressures will meet with success. If they do, arguments advanced in chapter 1 suggest that the resulting world of nuclear arms and offensive advantages would not be pleasant. The systemic and organizational forces discussed in this book encourage constant vigilance on the part of both superpowers in the context of their military competition. Prudence demands that the United States not let down its guard in this struggle. At the same time, however, knowledge that this vigilance could produce a destabilizing breakthrough should prompt both sides to renew their cooperative efforts to place some controls on the arms competition. The dual policy of vigilance and accommodation has not been easy, but considerations advanced in this book suggest that we cannot afford to leave the arms competition unregulated. The most powerful forces affecting the military doctrine of both sides seem to lead each inevitably in a dangerous direction.

Notes

1. The Importance of Military Doctrine

1. Edward M. Earle, ed., *Makers of Modern Strategy* (Princeton: Princeton University Press, 1971), p. viii.

2. Bernard Brodie, *Strategy in the Missile Age* (Princeton: Princeton University Press, 1959), p. 361; N. H. Gibbs, *Grand Strategy*, vol. 1, *Rearmament Policy*, in *History of the Second World War*, United Kingdom Military Series (London: HMSO, 1976), pp. 772–775; Arnold Horelick, "Perspectives on the Study of Comparative Military Doctrine," in *Comparative Defense Policy*, ed. Frank B. Horton (Baltimore: Johns Hopkins University Press, 1974), p. 195; Paul M. Kennedy, ed., *The War Plans of the Great Powers, 1880–1914* (London: Allen and Unwin, 1979), pp. 1–22, esp. 7; Henry Kissinger, *Problems of National Strategy* (New York: Praeger, 1965), pp. 9–10.

3. Military writers do not agree on definitions of the terms strategy, military doctrine, and tactics. In simplest terms, however, tactics is the study of how fights are fought. In my view, once one begins to ask questions about how battles are fought, one has entered the realm of military doctrine. When one begins to ask *which* wars shall be fought, or *if* war should be fought, one has entered the realm of strategy.

4. Robert Jervis, *Perception and Misperception in International Politics* (Princeton: Princeton University Press, 1976), p. 64.

5. Robert Jervis, "Cooperation under the Security Dilemma," *World Politics* 30 (January 1978): 169.

6. Jervis, *Perception*, p. 76.

7. This is an old proposition that can be traced back to the writing of Thucydides. In the guise of balance of power theory the proposition emerged again in the eighteenth century. In its early incarnation this was a prescriptive theory that enjoined the wise statesman to make alliances in ways that "balanced" the increasing power of an expanding hegemon. The same basic concepts and assumptions are common to Kenneth Waltz's more predictive restatement of balance of power theory and to Robert Jervis's discussion of the security dilemma. States are assumed to be unitary actors proceeding in reasonable ways to ensure their security in a self-help system. If one state should embark upon expansion, it is reasonable within an anarchic context for others, if they enjoy their autonomy, to form a coalition against the expansionist power. The theory predicts that balancing behavior should be a frequent occurrence in interstate or international systems and that a constellation of power that crudely resembles a balance

should be a frequent result. See Thucydides, *History of the Peloponnesian War* trans. Rex Warner (1954; Harmondsworth, England: Penguin, 1972); and Kenneth Waltz, *Theory of International Politics* (Reading, Mass.: Addison-Wesley, 1979), pp. 116–123.

8. Waltz, *Theory*, p. 168.

9. See, for example, A. J. P. Taylor, *The Struggle for Mastery in Europe, 1848–1918* (Oxford: Oxford University Press, 1971).

10. Jervis and Waltz have independently advanced the same simple explanation for why this is so. This explanation does not require that states understand the system that they inhabit, nor that they consciously seek "balances of power." The explanation takes as a given that states wish to remain states, a plausible proposition. It allows that some may want to expand and that others realize this and, in their own self-interest, are likely to respond.

11. Jervis, "Cooperation," pp. 186–190.

12. For one such interpretation and, to a lesser extent, imitation, see Harold Brown, *Department of Defense Annual Report, Fiscal Year 1981* (Washington, D.C.: GPO, January 29, 1980), pp. 65–83.

13. Fritz W. Ermarth, "Contrasts in American and Soviet Strategic Thought," *International Security* 3 (Fall 1978): 152; see also Benjamin Lambeth, "The Political Potential of Soviet Equivalence," *International Security* 4 (Fall 1979); Stanley Sienkiewicz, "SALT and Soviet Nuclear Doctrine," *International Security* 2 (Spring 1978).

14. Desmond Ball, "Counterforce Targeting: How New? How Viable?" *Arms Control Today*, February 1981; Desmond Ball, *Politics and Force Levels—The Strategic Missile Program of the Kennedy Administration* (Berkeley: University of California Press, 1980), pp. 31–34, 195–201; Aaron L. Friedberg, "A History of the U.S. Strategic Doctrine, 1945–1980," *Journal of Strategic Studies* 3 (December 1980): 37–71. The remarks of General David Jones, chairman of the Joint Chiefs of Staff, in U.S. Congress, Senate, Committee on Foreign Relations, *SALT II*, 96th Cong., 1st sess. pt. 1, p. 381; U.S. Congress, Senate, Committee on Armed Services, *Military Implications of the Treaty on the Limitation of Strategic Offensive Arms and Protocol Thereto (Salt II Treaty)*, 96th Cong., 1st sess., pt. 1, pp. 169–170; David Alan Rosenberg, " 'A Smoking Radiating Ruin at the End of Two Hours': Documents on American Plans for Nuclear War with the Soviet Union, 1954–1955," *International Security* 6:3 (Winter 1981–1982): 3–38; and Henry S. Rowen, "Formulating Strategic Doctrine," Appendix K—Commission on the Organization of the Government for the Conduct of Foreign Policy, June 1975 (Washington, D.C.: GPO, 1976), pp. 217–235. A careful reading of these sources shows that U.S. nuclear war plans have always included the option to launch a massive attack on Soviet strategic nuclear forces.

15. "If a general nuclear war is a threat to both sides, what must be done to achieve the necessary aims, to destroy the enemy with the minimum loss and destruction on one's own side? The American imperialists and their Western European allies give the following answers: first, a sharp *increase in the armaments race,* with emphasis on nuclear missiles and space weapons; and second, the element of *surprise.* . . . Surprise assures taking the initiative, *rapidly destroying the armed forces of the enemy* (primarily his strategic forces and weapons), *disrupting the control of troops* and the country as a whole, and undermining the economy and morale of the people. It is believed that *a forceful and sudden attack* will leave the *enemy paralyzed* in all respects, and that his fate will be decided in the very first days of the war" (my emphases). Marshall V. D. Sokolovsky, *Military Strategy: Soviet Doctrine and Concepts* (London: Pall Mall Press, 1963), p. 66.

16. International Institute for Strategic Studies, *The Military Balance, 1983–1984* (Lon-

don: International Institute for Strategic Studies, 1983), pp. 3, 11; and author's estimate.

17. Ibid.; U.S. Congress, House, Permanent Select Committee on Intelligence, Subcommittee on Oversight, "Statement of the C.I.A. Concerning C.I.A. Estimates of Soviet Defense Spending" (mimeographed, September 3, 1980), pp. 13–14.

18. Taylor, *Struggle*, p. xxix.

19. Ibid., p. xxviii.

20. Jervis, "Cooperation," pp. 186–190, 199–200.

21. The effects of nuclear deterrent doctrines are similar to those of conventional defensive or deterrent doctrines. The one notable difference concerns the long-war assumption. Short wars are highly probable with nuclear explosives, though victory is deemed impossible. Nuclear deterrent doctrines do make status quo powers easier to identify. Forces optimized for punishment tend not to make the best counterforce weapons. Such doctrines assume that punishment is easier than offense (disarming first-strike capabilities or area defenses). Finally, they assume that adversary increases in offensive capability can be offset with relative ease.

22. Jervis, "Cooperation," p. 76; Herman Kahn, *On Thermonuclear War* (New York: Free Press, 1960), pp. 357–375; Thomas Schelling, *Arms and Influence* (New Haven: Yale University Press, 1966), pp. 221–248.

23. Alfred Vagts, *Defense and Diplomacy: The Soldier and The Conduct of Foreign Relations* (New York: King's Crown Press, 1950), p. 381.

24. Michael Howard, "The Armed Forces," in *Material Progress and World-Wide Problems, 1870–1898*, vol. 11 of *The New Cambridge Modern History*, ed. F. H. Hinsley (Cambridge: Cambridge University Press, 1962), p. 217; Taylor, *Struggle*, p. xxviii, table 4.

25. Vagts, *Defense and Diplomacy*, p. 380.

26. Ibid., p. 410.

27. Jervis, "Cooperation," p. 19.

28. Ludwig Reiners, *The Lamps Went Out in Europe*, trans. Richard Winston and Clara Winston (New York: Pantheon, 1955), p. 136; L. C. F. Turner, *Origins of the First World War* (London: Edward Arnold, 1970), p. 76.

29. Henri Michel, *The Second World War*, trans. Douglas Parmee, 2 vols. (New York: Praeger, 1975), 1:36.

30. Philip Selznick, *Leadership in Administration* (Evanston, Ill.: Row, Peterson, 1957).

31. Carl Von Clausewitz, *On War*, trans. and ed. Michael Howard and Peter Paret (Princeton: Princeton University Press, 1976), p. 605.

32. F. H. Hinsley, *Power and the Pursuit of Peace* (Cambridge: Cambridge University Press, 1963), p. 245.

33. Taylor, *Struggle*, p. 173.

34. Michael Howard, *The Franco-Prussian War* (London: Granada, 1979), pp. 33–38, provides the basis for my remarks on Prussian and French military doctrine and capabilities.

35. The war was conducted mainly with artillery, fighter aircraft, ground-based air defenses, and commandos. Egypt initiated the fighting in order to convince Israel that the cost of holding Egyptian territory was unbearable. Israel attempted to convince Egypt that the costs were manageable, and that Egypt would have to pay for any attempt to raise Israeli costs.

36. Nadav Safran, *Israel: The Embattled Ally* (Cambridge, Mass.: Belknap Press, 1978), p. 316.

37. Michael Handel, *Israel's Political-Military Doctrine*, Occasional Papers in International Affairs, No. 30 (Cambridge, Mass.: Center for International Affairs, Harvard University, July 1973), pp. 65–66.

38. Safran, *Israel*, p. 285.

39. This brief account relies mainly on Chaim Herzog, *The War of Atonement* (Boston: Little, Brown, 1975); London Sunday Times Insight Team, *The Yom Kippur War* (Garden City, N.Y.: Doubleday, 1974); and Safran, *Israel*.

40. Safran, *Israel*, p. 275.

41. Herzog, *War of Atonement*, p. 271.

42. Insight Team, *Yom Kippur War*, p. 123.

43. William McElwee, *The Art of War: Waterloo to Mons* (Bloomington: Indiana University Press, 1974), p. 314.

44. Along with Captain Auger, Baron von Freytag-Lorinhoven, and Lt. Col. Edmonds, the more widely known civilian commentator, Ivan Bloch, predicted the war of the trenches. Ibid., pp. 319–322.

2. Explaining Military Doctrine

1. Of course, Hans Morgenthau, *Politics among Nations: The Struggle for Power and Peace* (New York: Alfred Knopf, 1978), offers the most comprehensive exposition of the realist perspective.

2. Waltz, *Theory*, pp. 79–81.

3. Among organization theorists who stress the concept of structure are: Chester I. Bernard, *The Functions of the Executive* (Cambridge, Mass.: Harvard University Press, 1968); James March and Herbert Simon, *Organizations* (New York: John Wiley & Sons, 1958); James D. Thompson, *Organizations in Action* (New York: McGraw-Hill, 1967). The concept appears frequently in the work of Max Weber, although it is ill-explicated in translations of the shorter essays. See *From Max Weber: Essays in Sociology*, trans., ed., and intro. H. H. Gerth and C. Wright Mills (New York: Oxford University Press, 1946), pp. 159–179. For a very useful and suggestive discussion of structure and power, see Arthur L. Stinchcombe, *Constructing Social Theories* (New York: Harcourt, Brace, & World, 1968), especially chapter 4, "The Conceptualization of Power Phenomena."

4. Stinchcombe, *Constructing Social Theories*, pp. 16–17. To the extent that this effort has any formal methodological foundation, that foundation has been provided by Arthur Stinchcombe; Waltz, *Theory*, pp. 13–17; and Alexander George, "Case Studies and Theory Development: The Method of Structured, Focused Comparison," in *Diplomacy: New Approaches in History, Theory, and Policy*, ed. Paul Gordon Lauren (New York: Free Press, 1979), pp. 43–68. All three of these theorists would, no doubt, find something with which to quarrel in this effort. I have, however, used the demanding standards that they set as guideposts for my own work. I would be the first to admit that this work does not fully meet those standards. The limits of information and time, the vagaries of history, and the peculiarities of my own interests have conspired to make this a less than perfect test of the theories in question. In my judgment, however, this is the closest thing to a competitive test of the two theories that can be found in the literature of the international relations and foreign policy fields.

5. Stinchcombe, *Constructing Social Theories*, p. 25.

6. Ibid.

7. Graham Allison, *Essence of Decision* (Boston: Little, Brown, 1971); Kenneth Waltz, *Man, the State, and War* (New York: Columbia University Press, 1959).

8. Richard Smoke, "National Security Affairs," in *Handbook of Political Science*, vol. 8, ed. Fred Greenstein and Nelson Polsby (Reading, Mass.: Addison-Wesley, 1975), p. 311; "The Colloquium: Exploring Ideas," *Tech Talk* (News Office, Massachusetts Institute of Technology) 24:37 (May 28, 1980): 6–7.

9. Nicholas Spykman, *America's Strategy in World Politics: The United States and the Balance of Power* (New York: Harcourt, Brace, & World, 1942), pp. 98–113.

10. Jervis, "Cooperation"; George Quester, *Offense and Defense in the International System* (New York: John Wiley, 1977), p. 11.

11. Chester Barnard is first and foremost among organization theorists stressing the importance of purpose. See also Thompson, *Organizations*.

12. Herbert Simon, "Rationality and Administrative Decision Making," in *Models of Man, Social and Rational* (New York: John Wiley, 1957), pp. 196–206.

13. Thompson, *Organizations*, pp. 29–39.

14. March and Simon, *Organizations*, pp. 169–171; Richard Cyert and James March, *A Behavioral Theory of the Firm* (Englewood Cliffs, N.J.: Prentice Hall, 1963), pp. 101–113; and Allison, *Essence of Decision*, p. 68.

15. Allison, *Essence of Decision*, p. 83.

16. Stinchcombe, in *Constructing Social Theories*, p. 109, derives his notion of institutionalization from Selznick, *Leadership*, pp. 130–142. For a more jaundiced view of what would seem to be the same phenomenon, see Michel Crozier, *The Bureaucratic Phenomenon* (Chicago: University of Chicago Press, 1964).

17. Allison, *Essence of Decision*, p. 81.

18. Samuel Finer, *The Man on Horseback: The Role of the Military in Politics*, 2nd ed. (London: Penguin, 1975), p. 6.

19. Thompson, *Organizations*, pp. 19–21, 74–75; Selznick, *Leadership*, pp. 119–133.

20. Thompson, *Organizations*, pp. 14–24.

21. Alfred Vagts, *A History of Militarism, Civilian and Military* (New York: Free Press, 1959), esp. pp. 13–15.

22. *From Max Weber*, pp. 233–235.

23. Finer, *The Man on Horseback*, p. 23.

24. Richard K. Betts, *Soldiers, Statesmen, and Cold War Crises* (Cambridge, Mass.: Harvard University Press, 1977), pp. 5–15.

25. Allison, *Essence of Decision*, p. 84.

26. Ibid.

27. On incremental change, and discussions that suggest it will be the rule, see March and Simon, *Organizations*, pp. 169–171; Anthony Downs, *Inside Bureaucracy* (Boston: Little, Brown, 1967), pp. 167–174; John Steinbruner, *The Cybernetic Theory of Decision* (Princeton: Princeton University Press, 1974), pp. 71–86; Charles Lindblom and David Braybrooke, *A Strategy of Decision* (New York: Free Press of Glencoe, 1963); V. A. Thompson, "Bureaucracy and Innovative Action," in *Bureaucracy and the Modern World* (Morristown, N.J.: General Learning Press, 1976); Martin Landau, "On the Concept of a Self-Correcting Organization," *Public Administration Review* 33 (November/December 1973): 533–537; Aaron Wildavsky, "The Self-Evaluating Organization," *Public Administration Review* 32 (September/October 1972): 509–520.

28. Allison, *Essence of Decision*, p. 85; Crozier, *Bureaucratic Phenomenon*, p. 196; Cyert and March, *Behavioral Theory*, pp. 278–279; Downs, *Inside Bureaucracy*, pp. 191–193, 208.

29. Allison, *Essence of Decision*, p. 85; Downs, *Inside Bureacracy*, p. 200; Albert O. Hirschman, *Exit, Voice, and Loyalty* (Cambridge, Mass.: Harvard University Press, 1970).

30. Downs, *Inside Bureaucracy*, pp. 198–199, 274.

31. For examples of United States Navy views on this matter see U.S. Congress, House, Committee on Armed Services, *Hearings on Department of Defense Appropriations for Fiscal Year 1980* (Washington, D.C.: GPO, 1979), p. 841; and U.S. Congress, Senate, Committee on Armed Services, *Hearings on Department of Defense Appropriations for Fiscal Year 1980* (Washington, D.C.: GPO, 1979), p. 557.

32. Norman Dixon, *On the Psychology of Military Incompetence* (New York: Basic Books, 1976), pp. 71–79.

33. Norman Stone, *The Eastern Front, 1914–1917* (New York: Scribner's 1975), pp. 44–69.

34. Dixon, *Psychology*, p. 96.

35. "Lehman Seeks Superiority," *International Defense Review* 5 (1982): 547–548.

36. Clausewitz, *On War*, p. 87.

37. Ibid., p. 606.

38. Ibid., p. 608.

39. Ibid.

40. Russell F. Weigley, "Military Strategy and Civilian Leadership," in *Historical Dimensions of National Security Problems*, ed. Klaus Knorr (Lawrence: University Press of Kansas, 1976), pp. 38–39.

41. Charles Tilly, ed., *The Formation of National States in Western Europe* (Princeton: Princeton University Press, 1975).

42. Ibid., p. 42. For similar views, see William Graham Sumner, "War," and Robert E. Park, "The Social Function of War," in *War*, ed. Leon Bramson and George W. Goethals (New York: Basic Books, 1964), pp. 205–244.

43. Bernard Brodie, "Technological Change, Strategic Doctrine, and Political Outcomes," in *Historical Dimensions*, ed. Knorr, p. 299.

44. Brodie, "Technological Change," p. 300; and Edward Katzenbach, "The Horse Cavalry in the Twentieth Century: A Study in Policy Response," in *American Defense Policy*, ed. Richard Head and Erwin Rokke (Baltimore: Johns Hopkins, 1973).

45. Katzenbach, "Horse Cavalry," p. 406.

46. For example, see Brodie, "Technological Change," pp. 288–292; Michael Howard, *War in European History* (London: Oxford University Press, 1976), pp. 101–106; Katzenbach, "Horse Cavalry," pp. 408, 412–414; McElwee, *Art of War*, pp. 307–327.

47. Bernard Brodie and Fawn Brodie, *From Crossbow to H-Bomb* (Bloomington: Indiana University Press, 1973), p. 150.

48. Major-General J. F. C. Fuller, *The Conduct of War, 1789–1961* (London: Methuen, 1961), pp. 104–105.

49. Brodie, "Technological Change," p. 284.

50. Katzenbach, "Horse Cavalry," pp. 411–414.

51. Jervis, "Cooperation." In his early work, Kenneth Waltz calls this the "third image." In his recent work, he explores the influence of the system at greater length. Putting aside the attributes of particular states, and focusing on the influence of the international environment on all states, Waltz develops what he terms a structural theory of international politics, a formalization of balance of power theory. See *Man, the State, and War* and *Theory of International Politics*.

52. From a survey of all wars since 1700, the Australian economic historian Geoffrey Blainey has concluded that though wars may find their origins in a variety of particular disputes, they boil down to disputes over relative power. They occur when the relative ability to do violence is unclear. "Wars usually begin when two nations disagree on their relative strengths and wars usually cease when the fighting nations agree on their

relative strength." To some extent the major purpose of war is to measure the strength of the disputants. Regrettably, Blainey leaves out the question of will in his survey.

Will is central to the ideas of modern deterrence theory. Thomas Schelling is perhaps the best known of postwar civilian "strategists." In his work, diplomacy and (by logical extension) war are treated as competitions in risk-taking, punishment, and suffering. Schelling stresses the sheer violence and unpleasantness associated with war as a major element in the settling of disputes among states. In the past, this particular aspect of military capability received less attention than it deserved, since the infliction of pain on the adversary was frequently dependent upon first defeating his forces. With the invention of nuclear weapons, and their rather obvious ability to destroy national values without first destroying military forces, a number of civilian scholars quickly realized that wars would now be tests of will as much as of skill. Technical capabilities for pure violence had reduced the importance of the soldier's art. In disputes among nations, civilians would have more to say about a strategy that had to consider not merely what forces could do, but what the state would pay. Summarizing the effects of nuclear weapons, but also capturing latent aspects of military strategy that are present in conventional wars, Schelling remarks: "Military strategy can no longer be thought of, as it could for some countries in some eras, as the science of military victory. It is now equally, if not more, the art of coercion, of intimidation and deterrence. The instruments of war are more punitive than acquisitive. Military strategy, whether we like it or not, has become the diplomacy of violence." Thus, another function of war is the measurement of relative will. As with power, anything that contributes to understanding of relative will in the context of a particular dispute helps avoid recourse to war. Geoffrey Blainey, *The Causes of War* (New York: Free Press, 1973), p. 246. See also Thomas Schelling, *The Strategy of Conflict* (New York: Oxford University Press, 1963); and *Arms and Influence*, p. 34.

53. John M. Sherwig, *Guineas and Gunpowder* (Cambridge, Mass.: Harvard University Press, 1969), p. 97.

54. Vagts, *Defense and Diplomacy*, p. 232.

55. Barry M. Blechman and Stephen S. Kaplan, *Force without War* (Washington, D.C.: Brookings Institution, 1978), p. ix.

56. Scholars have differed on whether a system of many great powers or few great powers leads to stability. Some analysts believe that a system of many makes it difficult for any two to concentrate their energies on each other. The potential for intense hostility is muted by the presence of many possible enemies. At the same time, fear is muted by the presence of many possible allies. Bipolar systems are taken to be bad because they lead to high levels of mutual attention and hostility. Two superpowers become obsessed with one another. For example, see Karl W. Deutsch and J. David Singer, "Multipolar Systems and International Stability," and Richard N. Rosecrance, "Bipolarity, Multipolarity, and the Future," in *International Politics and Foreign Policy*, ed. James N. Rosenau (New York: Free Press, 1969), pp. 315–324, 325–335. For the argument that bipolarity contributes to stability, see Waltz, *Theory*, ch. 8.

57. Robert Gilpin, *War and Change in World Politics* (Cambridge: Cambridge University Press, 1981), pp. 86, 92; John Herz, *Political Realism and Political Idealism* (Chicago: University of Chicago Press, 1951), ch. 2, sec. 2; and Morgenthau, *Politics*, pp. 215–218.

58. Gilpin, *War and Change*, p. 51.

59. Waltz, *Theory*, pp. 127–128.

60. Spykman, *America's Strategy*, p. 29.

61. Handel, *Israel's Political-Military Doctrine*, p. 66.

62. Colin Gray, "Victory is Possible," *Foreign Policy* 39 (Summer 1980): 14–27; Her-

man Kahn, *On Thermonuclear War* (New York: Free Press, 1960), pp. 523–550; Glenn Synder, *Deterrence and Defense: Toward a Theory of National Security* (Princeton: Princeton University Press, 1961), pp. 79–84, 148.

63. Schelling, *Arms and Influence*, p. 13.

64. C. W. C. Oman, *The Art of War in the Middle Ages* (Ithaca, N.Y.: Cornell University Press, 1953), p. 42.

65. Vagts, *Defense and Diplomacy*, p. 465.

66. Waltz, *Theory*, p. 165.

67. Howard, *War in European History*, pp. 62–63.

68. Lynn Montross, *War through the Ages* (New York: Harper & Brothers, 1960), pp. 318–319.

69. Montross, *War*, pp. 452–455.

70. For a general discussion of the report, see Avi Shlaim, "Failure in National Intelligence Estimates: The Case of the Yom Kippur War," *World Politics* 28:3 (April 1976): 348–380.

71. William O. Shanahan, *Prussia's Military Reforms 1786–1813* (New York: Columbia University Press, 1945), p. 127.

3. The Battles of 1940

1. Walter Ansel, *Hitler Confronts England* (Durham, N.C.: Duke University Press, 1960).

2. Brian Bond, *France and Belgium, 1939–1940* (London: Davis Poynter, 1975), p. 93.

3. Len Deighton, *Blitzkrieg* (London: Jonathan Cape, 1979), inside front cover.

4. D. C. Watt, *Too Serious a Business* (Berkeley: University of California Press, 1975), p. 75.

5. Gunsburg, *Divided*, pp. 173–174.

6. Ibid., p. 108.

7. According to Major L. F. Ellis, *The War in France and Flanders, 1939–1940* (London: HMSO, 1953), p. 310, the British had 544 bombers of all types in May 1940. Parkinson gives the RAF 700 medium and heavy bombers as of "early summer" 1940 (*Dawn*, p. 27). Descriptions of Bomber Command's contribution to the battle found in Ellis, *War in France and Flanders*, pp. 309–313, and in Sir Charles Webster and Noble Frankland, *The Strategic Air Offensive against Germany, 1939–1945*, vol. 1, *Preparation*, pts. 1, 2, and 3, History of the Second World War, United Kingdom Military Series (London: HMSO, 1961), p. 156, indicate that the role of the bombers in supporting the ground battle had been badly planned and was poorly executed. It is clear that the Royal Air Force preferred to attempt its long-planned campaign against German industry and infrastructure, regardless of how little impact that might have on the ground battle. When the weight of effort was shifted to enemy ground forces, Bomber Command was incapable of performing very well because it had refused to give such missions much attention before the war.

8. Although German quantitative superiority in the air cannot be denied, it is difficult to argue that it *decisively* affected the battle's outcome. The campaign histories reveal few critical engagements that appear to have been decided by air power. The major exception was the German crossing of the Meuse near Sedan. Continuous dive bomber attack over a period of several hours demoralized the French defenders of the river crossings, particularly the supporting artillery, causing the gunners to break and run. Many students agree, however, that the real material damage and loss of life was

comparatively small. Well-trained German troops were to withstand far heavier tactical air attacks later in the war. Similarly, German air attacks on allied lines of communication—road and rail—had considerable nuisance value, but do not seem to have been terribly destructive, and did not greatly affect the movement of troops. (The British official history by Ellis, *War in France and Flanders*, offers a different view.) See Marc Bloch, *Strange Defeat* (New York: Octagon Books, 1968), pp. 56–57; Goutard, *Battle of France*, pp. 133, 136, 206–207; Gunsburg, *Divided*, pp. 190, 213; Alistair Horne, *To Lose a Battle* (London: Macmillan, 1969), pp. 261–266; and Ellis, *War in France and Flanders*, pp. 45–46.

9. See Bloch, *Strange Defeat*, esp. ch. 3, "A Frenchman Examines His Conscience"; and Horne, *To Lose a Battle*, pp. 103–115.

10. For perhaps the most comprehensive, if overly sympathetic, discussion of French doctrine, see Gunsburg, *Divided*, pp. 41–45. See also Bond, *France and Belgium*, pp. 31, 54; Deighton, *Blitzkrieg*, pp. 192–200; Goutard, *Battle of France*, pp. 30–31, 40–41; Robert J. Young, *In Command of France* (Cambridge, Mass.: Harvard University Press, 1978), pp. 179–183.

11. For example, when the war began in September 1939, France had only three DLMs, mechanized divisions structurally similar to Germany's Panzer divisions. Unlike the Panzer divisions, they had not evolved a doctrine of their own, but rather were subjugated to classical cavalry doctrine. By May 1940, France also had three new DCRs, armored divisions, but these were undertrained and poorly equipped.

12. British doctrine is less important. The British Army had returned to its imperial police role after World War I. Good infantry, not heavy armor, were required to police the empire. As at the beginning of World War I, a small force of good infantry was what the British committed. This force was supported by designated, though ill-equipped, army cooperation units of the RAF.

13. Because Blitzkrieg was such a striking innovation, a remarkably large number of books have been written about it. A recent and quite comprehensive attempt is Len Deighton's *Blitzkrieg*. See also Larry H. Addington, *The Blitzkrieg Era and the German General Staff* (New Brunswick, N.J.: Rutgers University Press, 1971); and ch. 6, below.

14. This account of the battle relies heavily on the work of Bond, Deighton, Dupuy and Dupuy, Ellis, Goutard, Gunsburg, Horne, and Jacobsen.

15. John J. Mearsheimer, *Conventional Deterrence* (Ithaca: Cornell University Press, 1983), pp. 118–125.

16. Both General Billotte, commander of the First Army Group (the combined British-French force that would enter Belgium), and General Henri Giraud, commander of the Seventh Army (allocated to the Breda mission), made this observation in their planning documents for the campaign. General Georges, commander of the entire northeast front, brought this to Gamelin's attention, with no results. See Bond, *France and Belgium*, p. 77; Gunsburg, *Divided*, pp. 131.

17. Bond, *France and Belgium*, p. 50; Horne, *To Lose a Battle*, p. 205.

18. Neither General Georges nor General Corap (commander of the Ninth Army) seem to have been persuaded of the impenetrability of the Ardennes. General William Ironside, chief of the Imperial General Staff (Britain), apparently thought that the Ardennes might be a good avenue of attack. In October 1939, even General Gamelin had seriously considered the possibility of a German offensive through the Ardennes. He later rejected the idea. See Gunsburg, *Divided*, p. 142; Horne, *To Lose a Battle*, p. 168; Bond, *France and Belgium*, pp. 60–61; and Ellis, *War in France and Flanders*, pp. 317–318.

19. Bond, *France and Belgium*, pp. 78–80; Gunsburg, *Divided*, pp. 147–148.

20. General Georges, commander of the northeast front, worried most about an

encounter battle arising from any advance into Belgium. Nothing about French behavior during the Phoney War suggests any sudden shift away from respect for fortified positions. The French Army was not retrained for mobile warfare outside fortifications. Instead, training during this period seems to have been poor and erratic, particularly for the Series B reservist divisions that needed it most. Much time was spent digging field fortifications. French activity during this period contrasts sharply with what is known about the German Army. German divisions of all types went through intensive retraining. See Bond, *France and Belgium*, p. 77; Gunsburg, *Divided*, pp. 101, 129; Horne, *To Lose a Battle*, pp. 90, 108–109; Goutard, *Battle of France*, pp. 79–80, 135; and Williamson Murray, "The German Response to Victory in Poland: A Case Study in Professionalism," *Armed Forces and Society* 7:2 (Winter 1981): 285–298.

21. Doubts about, if not outright opposition to, the Breda variant were more widespread than opposition to the original Dyle Plan. British and French commanders questioned the move into Holland. Many were concerned about the commitment of the high-quality, motorized and mechanized operational reserve to Breda. With these forces committed, the best insurance against the unexpected was gone. General Georges, who most feared the consequences of this oversight, considered pulling six infantry divisions out of the Maginot Line to reconstitute the reserve. But by May 10, only three had been moved, and Georges claimed at the time that the political influence of other commanders prevented him from moving the rest. See Bond, *France and Belgium*, pp. 54, 76–77; Goutard, *Battle of France*, p. 88; Gunsburg, *Divided*, pp. 131–132, 138, 142; and Horne, *To Lose a Battle*, pp. 108–109.

22. Bond, *France and Belgium*, p. 32.

23. Hans Adolf Jacobsen, "Dunkirk 1940," in *Decisive Battles of World War II: The German View*, ed. Hans Adolf Jacobsen and Jurgen Rohwer, trans. Edward Fitzgerald (London: Andre Deutsch, 1965), pp. 36–37.

24. Ibid., p. 38.

25. Discussions of Luftwaffe doctrine are found in Deighton, *Blitzkrieg*, pp. 185–189; Edward Homze, *Arming the Luftwaffe* (Lincoln: University of Nebraska Press, 1976), pp. 131–132, 146; Kenneth Macksey, *Kesselring: The Making of the Luftwaffe* (London: B. T. Batsford, 1978), pp. 50–52; Richard Suchenwirth, *The Development of the German Air Force, 1919–1939*, ed. Harry R. Fletcher (Maxwell A.F.B., Ala.: Air University, 1968), pp. 167–169; Derek Wood and Derek Dempster, *The Narrow Margin: The Battle of Britain and the Rise of Air Power, 1930–1940* (London: Hutchinson, 1961), pp. 49–64.

26. Goutard, *Battle of France*, p. 38; Macksey, *Kesselring*, p. 73.

27. Parkinson, *Dawn*, pp. 202–208; R. Stanhope-Palmer, *Tank Trap 1940, or No Battle in Britain* (Devon, England: Arthur Stockwell, 1976), pp. 182–188. The latter is a little-known book from an obscure publisher, but is one of the most thorough and persuasive debunking efforts I have ever seen.

28. For the best accounts of RAF Fighter Command doctrine and organization see Len Deighton, *Fighter: The True Story of the Battle of Britain* (London: Jonathan Cape, 1977), pp. 126–130; Wood and Dempster, *Narrow Margin*, pp. 170–181, 197; Robert Wright, *Dowding and the Battle of Britain* (London: Macdonald, 1969), pp. 160–174. In many respects Fighter Command's air defense doctrine and its air defense system were inseparable. However, integral to the use of the system was Inskip's fundamental aim of avoiding the German knock-out blow. The connotation of "knock-out blow" changed, however. At first, people feared a concentrated bombing offensive that would destroy so much, and kill so many, that no government in England could survive. Surrender would be inevitable. As more experience with air warfare was gained, the difficulties of reducing an entire country by air war became clear. From

then on Fighter Command, in the person of Air Chief Marshal Lord Dowding, understood its purpose to be the maximum disruption of offensive German air operations to help combat any German invasion attempt. This purpose dictated the careful, economical tactics that were the hallmark of Fighter Command during the battle.

29. Deighton, *Fighter*, pp. 12–13.

30. Ibid., pp. 197, 263.

31. F. W. Winterbotham, *The Ultra Secret* (New York: Dell, 1974), pp. 67–98.

32. Deighton, *Fighter*, p. 227.

33. Among the best discussions of the Battle of Britain are Deighton, *Fighter;* Parkinson, *Dawn;* and Wood and Dempster, *Narrow Margin.* These accounts provide the basis for my own discussion.

34. Parkinson, *Dawn*, p. 204; Wood and Dempster, *Narrow Margin*, pp. 212–214.

4. France

1. Philip C. F. Bankwitz, *Maxime Weygand and Civil-Military Relations in Modern France* (Cambridge, Mass.: Harvard University Press, 1967), pp. 121–122; Gunsburg, *Divided*, pp. 9–10; Irving Gibson (pseud.), "Maginot and Liddell Hart: The Doctrine of Defense," in *Makers of Modern Strategy*, ed. Edward M. Earle (Princeton: Princeton University Press, 1971), pp. 373–375.

2. Walter McDougall, *France's Rhineland Diplomacy, 1914–1924* (Princeton: Princeton University Press, 1978), pp. 245–247.

3. Judith M. Hughes, *To the Maginot Line: The Politics of French Military Preparation in the 1920's* (Cambridge, Mass.: Harvard University Press, 1971), p. 12.

4. Dupuy and Dupuy, *Encyclopedia of Military History*, p. 990.

5. John Keegan, *The Face of Battle* (New York: Viking Press, 1976), p. 271.

6. Richard D. Challener, *The French Theory of the Nation in Arms, 1866–1939* (New York: Russell & Russell, 1965), pp. 143–146.

7. Robert J. Young, *In Command of France: French Foreign Policy and Military Planning, 1933–1940* (Cambridge, Mass.: Harvard University Press, 1978), pp. 15–21.

8. Challener, *French Theory*, pp. 147–148.

9. Ibid., pp. 172–173.

10. Ibid., pp. 222–224.

11. Gibson, "Maginot and Liddell Hart," p. 373.

12. Ibid.

13. Challener, *French Theory*, pp. 221–222; Young, *In Command*, pp. 18–19.

14. Donald J. Harvey, "French Concepts of Military Strategy, 1919–1939" (Ph.D. diss., Columbia University, 1953), p. 22.

15. Hughes, *To the Maginot Line*, p. 193.

16. Hillmann, "Comparative Strength of the Great Powers," p. 446; Milward, *War, Economy, and Society*, p. 43; McDougall, *France's Rhineland Diplomacy*, p. 7; Young, *In Command*, pp. 16–17.

17. Bankwitz, *Maxime Weygand*, pp. 53–54; Challener, *French Theory*, pp. 187–188; Gunsburg, *Divided*, pp. 4, 13, 266; Young, *In Command*, pp. 16–17.

18. Milan Hauner, "Czechoslovakia as a Military Factor in British Considerations of 1938," *Journal of Strategic Studies* 2 (September 1978): 208–209.

19. Hillman, "Comparative Strength," p. 446.

20. McDougall, *France's Rhineland Diplomacy*, pp. 162, 166, 185, 264, 358, 362.

21. Harvey, "French Concepts," p. 32; Hughes, *To the Maginot Line*, pp. 79, 228.

22. Bankwitz, *Maxime Weygand*, p. 163.

23. Young, *In Command*, p. 96.

24. Ibid., p. 218.

25. Ibid., p. 160.

26. Hughes, *To the Maginot Line*, pp. 94–95.

27. Ibid., pp. 145, 186; Arnold Wolfers, *Britain and France between Two Wars: Conflicting Strategies of Peace since Versailles* (New York: Harcourt, Brace, 1940), pp. 177–180.

28. Watt, *Too Serious a Business*, p. 91.

29. Harvey, "French Concepts," p. 124; Hughes, *To the Maginot Line*, p. 223.

30. On this point see Hughes, *To the Maginot Line*, p. 202; David Kieft, *Belgium's Return to Neutrality* (Oxford: Clarendon Press, 1972), p. 8; Great Britain, Admiralty, Naval Intelligence Division, *France*, vol. 3, *Economic Geography* (Great Britain, 1942), pp. 174, 183, 198, 208; and Young, *In Command*, p. 167. The survey prepared by the Naval Intelligence Division is extremely useful. Maps on the pages cited largely confirm the great vulnerability and relative indefensibility of the northern border. They also show, however, that roughly one-half of the Lorraine coal basin was vulnerable to artillery fire from the area of the Luxembourg border, as was other heavy industry in Lorraine. This did not stop the French from extending the Maginot Line to cover this frontier. The argument is also advanced that the terrain along the Belgian border did not permit the construction of large fortifications. This may be true, although smaller works were constructed at various places along the Belgian border after 1936. These were not comparable to the Maginot Line, but their construction does indicate that more could have been done along the Belgian border had the French made an early and firm decision to look after themselves. That they did not would seem to support the argument advanced in this chapter.

31. This calculation and decision was made by the Conseil Supérieur de la Guerre as early as 1927. Harvey, "French Concepts," p. 98; Hughes, *To the Maginot Line*, pp. 217–218.

32. For the requirements of this operation and the problems that arose between the Belgians and the French see Harvey, "French Concepts," p. 216; Hughes, *To the Maginot Line*, p. 223; and Kieft, *Belgium*, pp. 8 (n. 4), 9, 73–75, 144, 148, 168–169, 171. Kieft details the extent of the planning that occurred before the Belgian withdrawal from Locarno and declaration of neutrality in 1936. There were contacts between the Belgian and French General Staffs through military attachés in 1926, 1927, and 1928. Kieft argues that these were not very important although they were highly valued by the participants. After the German occupation of the Rhineland in March 1936, France, Britain, and Belgium engaged in joint staff talks. The talks between the French and Belgian staffs in the spring and summer were apparently rather detailed. While Belgian soldiers and statesmen tended to minimize the importance of such talks, the French did not. Not until April 1937, when France and Britain formally consented to Belgium's withdrawal from Locarno, did French pressure for regular and detailed talks subside. France acquiesced to forestall a German diplomatic gambit that might have led to improved Belgian-German relations. In any case, all Belgian-French military staff talks ceased until October 1939, and in my judgment those that then occurred appear to have been circumscribed.

In Kieft's estimation the evidence concerning the extent of the Franco-Belgian military relationship is rather scanty, since all French documents on the Military Agreement of 1920 have disappeared, and Belgian General Staff documents are not a part of the official Belgian diplomatic collection.

33. Chauvineau, General Maurice. *Une invasion: Est-elle encore possible?* (Paris: Berger-Leurault, 1934).

34. Harvey, "French Concepts," pp. 73–75.

35. Young, *In Command*, p. 199.

36. Ibid., p. 62; Harvey, "French Concepts," p. 120.

37. Hughes, *To the Maginot Line*, pp. 218–219.

38. McDougall, *France's Rhineland Diplomacy*, pp. 246–247.

39. Harvey, "French Concepts," p. 18.

40. Challener, *French Theory*, p. 162.

41. Hughes, *To the Maginot Line*, p. 192.

42. The term "attaque brusquée" refers to a then well-known stratagem advanced by General Hans Von Seeckt, postwar commander of the German Army. He theorized that the small but highly trained Reichswehr might be rapidly hurled against an unprepared France to disrupt her mobilization. This would buy time for Germany to improvise a larger, mass army.

43. Hughes, *To the Maginot Line*, p. 192.

44. Harvey, "French Concepts," p. 82; Hughes, *To the Maginot Line*, pp. 199–202.

45. Harvey, "French Concepts," pp. 75–79, 103; Hughes, *To the Maginot Line*, pp. 80, 203.

46. Hughes, *To the Maginot Line*, p. 172.

47. Bankwitz, *Maxime Weygand*, pp. 45–47, 94–95.

48. This is the crux of Philip Bankwitz's argument in his biography of General Maxime Weygand, first chief of staff and then commander-in-chief of the French Army from 1930 to 1935. While Bankwitz's discussion grows mainly from a political analysis of civil-military relations in interwar France, both the causal forces he abstracts and the results he ascribes to those forces can easily be translated into organization theory terms. The autonomy of the French Army was threatened and the organization took the measures necessary to preserve that autonomy, even if such measures compromised other preferences of the organization. Bankwitz, *Maxime Weygand*, pp. 377–378.

49. Ibid., p. 123; Challener, *French Theory*, pp. 274–276.

50. Gibson, "Maginot and Liddell Hart," p. 370.

51. Hughes, *To the Maginot Line*, pp. 203–211.

52. Bankwitz, *Maxime Weygand*, p. 158.

53. Hughes, *To the Maginot Line*, p. 122.

54. Ibid., pp. 101–105.

55. Military booty from the bloodless conquest of Czechoslovakia aided a rapid expansion of German infantry and mechanized formations. See Hauner, "Czechoslovakia," p. 207. Infantry equipment, artillery, and medium-gun tank holdings were probably augmented by 50 percent. Ibid., p. 209; Deighton, *Blitzkrieg*, pp. 196–197.

56. Watt, *Too Serious a Business*, p. 90; Young, *In Command*, p. 58.

57. Young, *In Command*, p. 91.

58. Ibid., p. 160.

59. Ibid., p. 212.

60. Wolfers, *Britain and France*, p. 75.

61. Young, *In Command*, p. 150.

62. Watt, *Too Serious a Business*, p. 120.

63. Young, *In Command*, p. 55.

64. Ibid., p. 63.

65. Gibson, "Maginot and Liddell Hart," p. 372.

66. Hughes, *To the Maginot Line*, p. 211.
67. Challener, *French Theory*, p. 264.
68. J. W. Wheeler-Bennett, *Munich: Prologue to Tragedy* (London: MacMillan, 1948), p. 253.
69. Gibson, "Maginot and Liddell Hart," p. 372.
70. Harvey, "French Concepts," p. 198.
71. Ibid., p. 212.
72. Young, *In Command*, p. 166.
73. Ibid., ch. 7.
74. Ibid., p. 233.
75. Challener, *French Theory*, p. 265.
76. Brodie, "Technological Change," p. 299.
77. Gibson, "Maginot and Liddell Hart," p. 373.
78. Harvey, "French Concepts," p. 29.
79. Hughes, *To the Maginot Line*, p. 73.
80. Ibid., p. 79.
81. Harvey, "French Concepts," p. 137.
82. Ibid., p. 144.
83. Gunsburg, *Divided*, p. 43.
84. Harvey, "French Concepts," p. 147.
85. Ibid., pp. 155–156.
86. Watt, *Too Serious a Business*, p. 94.
87. Gunsburg, *Divided*, pp. 41–43.
88. Bankwitz, *Maxime Weygand*, pp. 131–132.
89. Ibid., p. 153.
90. Goutard, *Battle of France*, p. 39.
91. Robert Young, "The Strategic Dream: French Air Doctrine in the Interwar Period," *Journal of Contemporary History* 9 (October 1974): 57–76.
92. Gunsburg, *Divided*, p. 51.

5. Britain

1. Gibbs, *Grand Strategy*, vol. 1, Rearmament Policy, p. 796.
2. Brian Bond, *British Military Policy between the Two World Wars* (Oxford: Clarendon Press, 1980), pp. 8, 338.
3. Ibid., p. 10; David Dilks, " 'The Unnecessary War?' Military Advice and Foreign Policy in Great Britain, 1931–1939," in *General Staffs and Diplomacy before the Second World War*, ed. Adrian Preston (London: Croom Helm, 1978), p. 103; Michael Howard, *The Continental Commitment* (London: Temple Smith, 1972), p. 99; Stephen Pelz, *Race to Pearl Harbor* (Cambridge, Mass.: Harvard University Press, 1974), p. 97. Lord Kitchener, the British Minister of War, improvised a mass army of a million volunteers in 1914. Initial casualties were high among these enthusiastic but ill-trained formations. B. H. Liddell-Hart, *History of the First World War* (London: Pan, 1972), pp. 64, 231; see also Keegan, *The Face of Battle*, pp. 215–225.
4. Phillip Knightly, *The First Casualty* (London: Quartet, 1978), p. 109.
5. Gibbs, *Grand Strategy*, vol. 1, *Rearmament Policy*, p. 795. Perhaps the greatest practitioner of this strategy was William Pitt, the Younger, against Napoleonic France. See Sherwig, *Guineas and Gunpowder*.

6. Telford Taylor, *Munich: The Price of Peace* (Garden City, N.Y.: Doubleday, 1979), pp. 592–593.

7. Ibid., p. xv. See also Keith Middlemas, *Diplomacy of Illusion* (London: Weidenfeld and Nicolson, 1972), p. 294; Sir Charles Webster and Noble Frankland, *The Strategic Air Offensive against Germany, 1939–1945*, vol. 1, *Preparation*, pts. 1, 2, and 3, in *History of the Second World War*, United Kingdom Military Series (London: HMSO, 1961), pp. 78–80; Barry D. Powers, *Strategy without Slide Rule* (London: Croom Helm, 1976), p. 207.

8. Powers, *Strategy*, pp. 126, 166, 174–175.

9. Paul Bracken, "Unintended Consequences of Strategic Gaming," *Simulation and Games* 8:3 (September 1977): 302–304; George Quester, *Deterrence before Hiroshima* (New York: John Wiley and Sons, 1966), pp. 60–61.

10. Bracken, "Unintended Consequences," pp. 304–305; Powers, *Strategy*, pp. 122–123.

11. Bracken, "Unintended Consequences," p. 310.

12. This estimate is derived from casualty figures in Parkinson, *Dawn*, p. 212. Powers suggests a wartime average of 15–20 casualties per ton (p. 123).

13. Winston S. Churchill, *The Gathering Storm*, vol. 1 of *The Second World War* (New York: Bantam, 1977), pp. 186–187.

14. Dilks, "Unnecessary War?" pp. 101–102; Lawrence R. Pratt, *East of Malta, West of Suez: Britain's Mediterranean Crisis, 1936–1939* (Cambridge: Cambridge University Press, 1975), p. 3; Howard, *Continental Commitment*, p. 138.

15. Pelz, *Race*, pp. 104–110.

16. Pratt, *East of Malta*, p. 3.

17. Dilks, "Unnecessary War?" p. 119; Pratt, *East of Malta*, pp. 95–96.

18. Gibbs, *Grand Strategy*, vol. 1, *Rearmament Policy*, p. 293.

19. Wolfers, *Britain and France*, pp. 205–206.

20. Dilks, "Unnecessary War?" p. 102.

21. See the remarks of Sir Thomas Inskip, minister for coordination of defense, in *Grand Strategy*, vol. 1, *Rearmament Policy*, pp. 283–285; see also Pratt, *East of Malta*, p. 102.

22. Charles Kindleberger, *The World in Depression, 1929–1939* (Berkeley: University of California Press, 1973), p. 282.

23. Gibbs, *Grand Strategy*, vol. 1, *Rearmament Policy*, pp. 283–284.

24. Ibid., p. 284.

25. Ibid.

26. Dilks, "Unnecessary War?" p. 125; Gibbs, *Grand Strategy*, vol. 1, *Rearmament Policy*, p. 277.

27. Pelz, *Race*, p. 117.

28. Howard, *Continental Commitment*, pp. 135–136.

29. Dilks, "Unnecessary War?" p. 126.

30. Bond, *Military Policy*, p. 239.

31. Gibbs, *Grand Strategy*, vol. 1, *Rearmament Policy*, pp. 284–285.

32. Ibid., p. 106.

33. Keith Middlemas and John Barnes, *Baldwin: A Biography* (London: Weidenfeld and Nicolson, 1972), p. 735. See also Chamberlain's remarks quoted in Pelz, *Race*, p. 183; and Powers, *Strategy*, chs. 5, 6.

34. Gibbs, *Grand Strategy*, vol. 1, *Rearmament Policy*, p. 547.

35. Howard, *Continental Commitment*, pp. 109–110.

36. Gibbs, *Grand Strategy*, vol. 1, *Rearmament Policy*, p. 538.

37. Ibid., p. 555.

38. Pratt, *East of Malta*, p. 181.
39. Ibid., p. 173.
40. Ibid., p. 194.
41. The British might have done better at designing their military forces for punitive operations had they better understood the relationship between military means and their political ends. A credible "punitive" capability might have been mustered in the Far East at reasonable cost. Britain built a lot of submarines in the interwar period. Substantial numbers of long-range submarines might have been based at Singapore, as a threat to Japanese sea lanes; had that been coupled with the fortification of the island, and some increase in its offensive and defensive air capabilities, the Japanese might have been made to think twice about attacking British interests. Admittedly, the British were trying to outlaw submarine warfare in the interwar period. They tried to do so in 1922 and again in 1934. See Roger Dingman, *Power in the Pacific* (Chicago: University of Chicago Press, 1976), p. 212; Pelz, *Race*, p. 116. A doctrine of the kind suggested here would not have supported such an arms control proposal. However, by 1936 all hopes of naval arms control with Japan had passed. Rapid construction of submarines would not have been a difficult matter.
42. Gibbs, *Grand Strategy*, vol. 1, *Rearmament Policy*, p. 798.
43. Wolfers, *Britain and France*, pp. 229–241.
44. Gibbs, *Grand Strategy*, vol. 1, *Rearmament Policy*, p. 799.
45. Great Britain, Foreign Office, *Documents on British Foreign Policy, 1919–1939*, 2nd ser., vol. 13 (London: HMSO, 1973), p. 197.
46. Ibid., p. 506.
47. Gibbs, *Grand Strategy*, vol. 1 *Rearmament Policy*, pp. 465–483.
48. Taylor, *Munich*, p. 589.
49. Bond, *Military Policy*, p. 284.
50. Gibbs, *Grand Strategy*, vol. 1, *Rearmament Policy*, pp. 622, 667.
51. Bond, *Military Policy*, pp. 1, 7, 339.
52. Gibbs, *Grand Strategy*, vol. 1, *Rearmament Policy*, pp. 534–535.
53. Howard, *Continental Commitment*, p. 117.
54. Williamson Murray, "British and German Air Doctrine between the Wars," *Air University Review* 31:3 (March/April 1980): 41.
55. Pelz, *Race*, p. 195. Paul Kennedy argues that by 1930 the British were simply "gambling upon the hope that Japan would not be aggressive." See his *The Rise and Fall of British Naval Mastery* (London: Allen Lane, 1976), pp. 280, 283–285, 292.
56. Pelz says that the British believed the French Navy might deter Italian action (*Race*, p. 56). However, due to the absence of a formal alliance with France, the British could not be sure that the French would fight should the occasion arise. By the outbreak of the war the alliance had firmed up. However, *combined* French and British naval power was inadequate to cope with the combined axis navies, although it was more than adequate to cope with a German-Italian combination. For the naval balance in 1939, see Gibbs, *Grand Strategy*, vol. 1, *Rearmament Policy*, p. 432.
57. Pratt, *East of Malta*, p. 53.
58. Ibid., pp. 130–131.
59. Gibbs, *Grand Strategy*, vol. 1, *Rearmament Policy*, pp. 155–170.
60. Dilks, "Unnecessary War?" p. 107.
61. Gibbs, *Grand Strategy*, vol. 1, *Rearmament Policy*, p. 775; Watt, *Too Serious a Business*, p. 55.
62. Bond, *Military Policy*, p. 82; Taylor, *Munich*, p. 212.
63. Dilks, "Unnecessary War?" p. 117.
64. Ibid., p. 113.

65. Bond, *Military Policy*, pp. 41, 71.

66. Bracken, "Unintended Consequences," pp. 308–309; Howard, *Continental Commitment*, p. 112; Murray, "British and German Air Doctrine," p. 44; Watt, *Too Serious a Business*, p. 76.

67. Watt, *Too Serious a Business*, p. 77; Webster and Frankland, *Strategic Air Offensive*, p. 91.

68. Bond, *Military Policy*, pp. 321–322; Murray, "British and German Air Doctrine," p. 48; Webster and Frankland, *Strategic Air Offensive*, p. 96.

69. Murray, "British and German Air Doctrine," p. 46.

70. Ibid., p. 48.

71. Taylor, *Munich*, p. 205.

72. Kennedy, *Rise and Fall*, p. 273.

73. Ibid.

74. Pratt, *East of Malta*, p. 53.

75. Ibid., pp. 130–131.

76. Gibbs, *Grand Strategy*, vol. 1, *Rearmament Policy*, pp. 336–337, 340.

77. Bond, *Military Policy*, p. 294–295.

78. Ibid., pp. 292–293.

79. How else are we to interpret Neville Chamberlain's famous argument to the effect that Britain was not going to war to defend any particular state, but to "pull down the bully"? See Gibbs, *Grand Strategy*, vol. 1, *Rearmament Policy*, p. 695.

80. Bond, *Military Policy*, p. 308.

81. Gibbs, *Grand Strategy*, vol. 1, *Rearmament Policy*, pp. 700–701.

82. Ibid., p. 694.

83. Bond, *Military Policy*, pp. 241–294.

84. Ibid., p. 191.

85. The doctrine of the counteroffensive was the traditional RAF view. The civilians abandoned this strategy during the Munich Pact. Shortly thereafter, the RAF agreed to plan a much-restricted bombing campaign against Germany. They feared a bombing exchange since their own inflated calculations gave the Luftwaffe the ability to drop 500–600 tons on Britain, while the RAF could drop only 100 tons in response. If indeed there was any disparity in 1938 and 1939, it is unlikely to have been nearly this great. See Gibbs, *Grand Strategy*, vol. 1, *Rearmament Policy*, pp. 590, 592.

86. Bracken, "Unintended Consequences," p. 312.

87. Ibid., pp. 301–312.

88. Murray, "British and German Air Doctrine," p. 49; Powers, *Strategy*, p. 166; Webster and Frankland, *Strategic Air Offensive*, pp. 63, 67, 74, 75.

89. Gibbs, *Grand Strategy*, vol. 1, *Rearmament Policy*, pp. 656–657.

90. For instance, on British attitudes to Italy in 1937 see Taylor, *Munich*, p. 586.

91. Gibbs, *Grand Strategy*, vol. 1, *Rearmament Policy*, p. 100.

92. Ibid., pp. 106, 284, 305.

93. Bond, *Military Policy*, p. 220.

94. Derived from data in Gibbs, *Grand Strategy*, vol. 1, *Rearmament Policy*, p. 532.

95. Milward, *War*, p. 47.

96. Ibid., p. 25.

97. Dilks, "Unnecessary War?" p. 107.

98. Gibbs, *Grand Strategy*, vol. 1, *Rearmament Policy*, p. 532.

99. M. Postan, D. Hay, and J. D. Scott, *Design and Development of Weapons: Studies in Government and Industrial Organization* (London: HMSO and Longman's, Green, 1964), p. 373.

100. Ibid., p. 375.

101. Middlemas and Barnes, *Baldwin,* pp. 782–783.

102. Ibid. See also Basil Collier, *The Defense of the United Kingdom,* in *History of the Second World War,* United Kingdom Military Series (London: HMSO, 1957), p. 40.

103. A. P. Rowe, *One Story of Radar* (Cambridge: Cambridge University Press, 1948), p. 18; and Watt, *Too Serious a Business,* p. 73.

104. Murray, "British and German Air Doctrine," pp. 46–47.

105. Postan et al., *Design,* p. 379.

106. Bond, *Military Policy,* p. 250.

107. Gibbs, *Grand Strategy,* vol. 1, *Rearmament Policy,* pp. 574–589.

108. Ibid., p. 466.

109. Murray, "British and German Air Doctrine," p. 47.

110. See A. J. P. Taylor's "Introduction" to Deighton, *Fighter,* pp. 12–13; Gibbs, *Grand Strategy,* vol. 1, *Rearmament Policy,* pp. 277, 288; Watt, *Too Serious a Business,* p. 73; Webster and Frankland, *Strategic Air Offensive,* pp. 76–78.

111. Webster and Frankland, *Strategic Air Offensive,* pp. 77–78.

112. Ibid., p. 78.

113. The effect of this decision on the actual relative output of fighters and bombers is difficult to estimate precisely, although it appears to have been substantial. Scheme L for air force expansion was approved in April 1938 and projected the completion of 73 squadrons of bombers (1,352 aircraft) and 38 squadrons of fighters (608 aircraft) by March 1940. Scheme M, approved in November 1938, kept roughly the same ultimate target for bomber expansion, 82 squadrons (1,360 aircraft), but raised the ultimate fighter strength to 50 squadrons, 800 aircraft. Both of these goals were to be achieved by spring of 1941, with 70 bomber and 40 fighter squadrons as the interim goal to be achieved in spring of 1940. This was clearly amended in practice. By late 1939 Bomber Command could barely field 33 squadrons (about 500 aircraft, only one-half of which were medium or heavy machines), while Fighter Command could field 51 squadrons (over 600 aircraft). Indeed Bomber Command could still field only 500 bombers by the end of 1941. A further evidence of the emphasis on air defense is that several fighter squadrons were armed with twin-engine Blenheim medium bombers converted to the fighter role, for which they were remarkably ill-suited. The conversion consisted of installing four forward-firing .303 machine guns under the fuselage where the bomb-bay had formerly been. These figures were pieced together from Collier, *Defense,* p. 78; Ellis, *War in France and Flanders,* p. 310; Gibbs, *Grand Strategy,* vol. 1, *Rearmament Policy,* pp. 588–589; Webster and Frankland, *Strategic Air Offensive,* p. 80 and Appendices 7 and 39.

114. Webster and Frankland, *Strategic Air Offensive,* p. 76. My emphases.

115. Deighton, *Fighter,* p. 122; Collier, *Defense,* p. 37; Wright, *Dowding,* p. 56.

116. Webster and Frankland, *Strategic Air Offensive,* p. 82; Wood and Dempster, *Narrow Margin,* p. 75.

117. Webster and Frankland, *Strategic Air Offensive,* p. 82.

118. Deighton, *Fighter,* p. 13.

119. Collier, *Defense,* p. 39.

120. Wood and Dempster, *Narrow Margin,* p. 77.

121. Wright, *Dowding,* p. 71.

6. Germany

1. T. W. Mason, "Some Origins of the Second World War," *Past and Present* 29 (December 1964): 69.

2. Gordon Craig, *Germany, 1866–1945* (New York: Oxford University Press, 1978), p. 697.

3. Bond, *Military Policy*, pp. 187–188.

4. Addington, *Blitzkrieg Era*, p. 6; Matthew Cooper, *The German Army, 1933–1945: Its Political and Military Failure* (New York: Stein & Day, 1978), pp. 130–138; Herbert Rosinski, *The German Army*, ed. Gordon Craig (New York: Praeger, 1966), p. 119.

5. Gordon Craig, *The Politics of the Prussian Army, 1640–1945* (London: Oxford University Press, 1964), pp. 274–280; Cooper, *German Army*, p. 133; Walter Goerlitz, *History of the German General Staff, 1657–1945* (New York: Praeger, 1953), pp. 82, 100; Gerhard Ritter, *The Schlieffen Plan: Critique of a Myth*, foreword by B. H. Liddell-Hart, trans. Andrew Wilson and Eva Wilson (Westport, Conn.: Greenwood, 1979), p. 19.

6. Ritter, *Schlieffen Plan*, pp. 18–20. The elder Moltke, until his retirement in 1888, advocated standing on the defensive in the west and mounting *limited* offensives in the east aimed at the elimination of Russian armies threatening Germany's eastern borders. As soon as the east was secured, he would shift military assets to the west to bring the conflict with France to a successful conclusion. Schlieffen amended this plan in a manner with which we are all now familiar, concentrating the bulk of the German Army for a massive single envelopment of the French Army by way of Belgium. While the strategy employed in 1914 was considerably more reckless both politically and militarily than that of Moltke, nonetheless one can see the influence of the two-front war problem on both of them.

7. Ibid., p. 66.

8. Craig, *Politics*, pp. 275–276; Ritter, *Schlieffen Plan*, p. 19.

9. Ritter, *Schlieffen Plan*, p. 38. My emphases.

10. Cooper, *German Army*, p. 135.

11. Addington, *Blitzkrieg Era*, p. 30; Cooper, *German Army*, p. 135; Rosinski, *German Army*, p. 219.

12. Rosinski, *German Army*, p. 219.

13. Craig, *Politics*, pp. 401–405; Gaines Post, Jr., *The Civil-Military Fabric of Weimar Foreign Policy* (Princeton: Princeton University Press, 1973), p. 107 (n. 44).

14. Gibson, "Maginot and Liddell Hart," p. 370.

15. Addington, *Blitzkrieg Era*, pp. 29–30; Gibson, "Maginot and Liddell Hart," pp. 369–370.

16. Post, *Civil-Military Fabric*, p. 96.

17. Martin Kitchen, *A Military History of Germany—From the Eighteenth Century to the Present Day* (Secaucus, N.J.: Citadel Press, 1976), p. 259.

18. E. H. Carr, *International Relations between the Two World Wars, 1919–1939* (London: Macmillan, 1947), p. 30.

19. Norman Rich, *Hitler's War Aims: Ideology, the Nazi State, and the Course of Expansion* (New York: W. W. Norton, 1973), p. 121.

20. Carr, *International Relations*, pp. 37–38; Goerlitz, *History*, p. 224.

21. Fred Greene, "French Military Leadership and Security against Germany, 1919–1940" (Ph.D. diss., Yale University, 1950), p. 135.

22. J. F. C. Fuller, *The Decisive Battles of the Western World, 1792–1944*, ed. John Terraine (St. Albans, England: Granada, 1970), p. 407.

23. Harold J. Gordon, Jr., *The Reichswehr and the German Republic, 1919–1926* (Princeton: Princeton University Press, 1957), p. 255.

24. F. L. Carsten, *The Reichswehr and Politics, 1918–1933* (Oxford: Clarendon, 1966), p. 155.

25. Ibid.

26. Gordon, *Reichswehr,* p. 255.

27. Hans W. Gatzke, *Stresemann and the Rearmament of Germany* (Baltimore: Johns Hopkins University Press, 1954), pp. 12–13, 22, 111, 112; Gordon, *Reichswehr,* p. 351; Kitchen, *Military History,* p. 269.

28. Craig notes that there was "a high degree of unity and even collaboration in planning between the Foreign and Defense Ministries." See *Germany,* p. 523; also Gordon, *Reichswehr,* p. 361; Post, *Civil-Military Fabric,* pt. 2.

29. Stresemann's long-term goals were almost as extensive as those of the most nationalistic soldiers. He even looked forward to Anschluss. See Craig, *Germany,* p. 512; Martin Wight, "Germany," in *Survey of International Affairs, 1939–1946,* vol. 1, *The World in March 1939* (London: Royal Institute of International Affairs and Oxford University Press, 1952), p. 326.

30. Carsten, *Reichswehr and Politics,* p. 265; Craig, *Germany,* p. 513; Gatzke, *Stresemann,* pp. 16–17, 53; Gordon, *Reichswehr,* p. 347; Post, *Civil-Military Fabric,* pp. 161, 182.

31. Stresemann himself may have initiated some illegal military cooperation with Austria. See Gatzke, *Stresemann,* pp. 31, 53, 111–112. See also Gordon, *Reichswehr,* p. 347; Post, *Civil-Military Fabric,* pp. 72–84.

32. Rosinski, *German Army,* p. 163. Indeed, the Germans had a special word for "players" in international politics—*bundesfaehig* (capability of being an ally). Without a restoration of German military power, this status could not be regained. See Telford Taylor, *The March of Conquest: The German Victories in Western Europe, 1940* (New York: Simon & Schuster, 1958), p. 359.

33. For a slightly contrary view, see Post, *Civil-Military Fabric,* pp. 234–238.

34. Watt, *Too Serious a Business,* p. 62.

35. Cooper, *German Army,* pp. 117–121; B. H. Liddell-Hart, *The Other Side of the Hill: Germany's Generals, Their Rise and Fall, with Their Own Account of Military Events, 1939–1945,* enlarged and rev. ed. (London: Cassell, 1951), pp. 29–30.

36. Addington, *Blitzkrieg Era,* p. 29.

37. Cooper, *German Army,* p. 135.

38. Craig, *Politics,* p. 396.

39. Goerlitz, *History,* p. 223.

40. Addington, *Blitzkrieg Era,* pp. 24–26; Cooper, *German Army,* pp. 139–140; Dupuy and Dupuy, *Encyclopedia of Military History,* pp. 972, 977–979.

41. Rosinski, *German Army,* p. 217.

42. For the unconventional view that von Seeckt actually obstructed military reform, see Gordon, *Reichswehr,* pp. 259, 303.

43. Percy Ernst Schramm, *Hitler: The Man and the Military Leader,* trans. and ed. Donald Detwiler (Chicago: Quandrangle, 1971), p. 157.

44. Milward, *War, Economy, and Society,* p. 24.

45. Alan S. Milward, *The German Economy at War* (London: Athlone Press, University of London, 1965), p. 16.

46. Milward, *War, Economy, and Society,* pp. 29–30.

47. Hillmann, "Comparative Strength," p. 447.

48. Berenice A. Carroll, *Design For Total War: Arms and Economics in the Third Reich* (The Hague and Paris: Mouton, 1968), p. 138; Hillmann "Comparative Strength," pp. 445–446.

49. Burton H. Klein, *Germany's Economic Preparations for War* (Cambridge, Mass.: Harvard University Press, 1959), p. 57.

50. W. K. Hancock and M. M. Gowing, *British War Economy,* in *History of the Second*

World War, United Kingdom Civil Series (1949; London and Nendeln: HMSO and Kraus Reprint, 1975), pp. 71–72.

51. Milward, *German Economy*, pp. 4–5; Milward, *War, Economy, and Society*, p. 24.

52. Cooper, *German Army*, pp. 159–166.

53. Craig, *Politics*, p. 485.

54. Edward Homze, *Arming the Luftwaffe: The Reich Air Ministry and the German Aircraft Industry, 1919–1939* (Lincoln: University of Nebraska Press, 1976), pp. 106, 168–169; David Irving, *The Rise and Fall of the Luftwaffe: The Life of Erhard Milch* (London: Weidenfeld and Nicolson, 1973), p. 43; Suchenwirth, *Development of the German Air Force*, pp. 188–190.

55. Irving, *Rise and Fall*, p. 73.

56. Homze, *Arming*, pp. 124–125; Irving, *Rise and Fall*, p. 54; Herbert M. Mason, Jr., *The Rise of the Luftwaffe: Forging the Secret German Air Weapon, 1918–1940* (New York: Dial, 1973), p. 257.

57. Murray, "British and German Air Doctrine," p. 56.

58. William L. Shirer, *The Rise and Fall of the Third Reich: A History of Nazi Germany* (New York: Simon & Schuster, 1960), p. 323.

59. Irving, *Rise and Fall*, p. 67.

60. Ibid., p. 329.

61. *Nazi Conspiracy and Aggression*, vol. 4 (Washington, D.C.: GPO, 1948), "Excerpt from General Jodl's Diary," p. 361.

62. Ibid., "Memo from General Keitel," p. 357.

63. Ibid., "Excerpt from General Jodl's Diary," p. 361.

64. Walter Warlimont, *Inside Hitler's Headquarters, 1939–1945* (London: Weidenfeld and Nicolson, 1964), pp. 14–15.

65. *Survey of International Affairs*, vol. 2, *1938* (London: Royal Institute of International Affairs and Oxford University Press, 1951), pp. 122–139.

66. Shirer, *Rise and Fall*, p. 365.

67. Ibid., p. 366.

68. *Documents on German Foreign Policy* (henceforth *DGFP*), ser. D, vol. 2 (Washington, D.C.: GPO, 1949), p. 359.

69. Taylor, *Munich*, p. 700.

70. Shirer, *Rise and Fall*, p. 367.

71. *Documents on British Foreign Policy* (henceforth *DBFP*), 3rd ser., vol. 2 (London: HMSO, 1961), nos. 562, 563, pp. 26–27.

72. Ibid., no. 575, pp. 42–43.

73. Ibid., no. 573, p. 39.

74. Ibid., no. 577, p. 46.

75. Ibid., no. 637, pp. 104–105.

76. Irving, *Rise and Fall*, p. 62.

77. *DBFP*, 3rd ser., vol. 2, no. 721, p. 190.

78. Ibid., no. 1142, p. 574; no. 1145, p. 578.

79. *DGFP*, ser. D, vol. 2, no. 654, p. 985.

80. Telford Taylor, *Sword and Swastika* (New York: Simon & Schuster, 1952), p. 163.

81. Goerlitz, *History*, p. 320.

82. Addington, *Blitzkrieg Era*, p. 57.

83. Cooper, *German Army*, p. 165.

84. Ibid.

85. Addington, *Blitzkrieg Era*, p. 59.

86. It is worth noting that Hitler had such belief in the value of an intimidating posture that he made a horrific film of the Polish campaign which he showed in neutral capitals all over Europe. Taylor, *March*, p. 10.

87. Betts, *Soldiers, Statesmen, and Cold War Crises*, pp. 10–15; James Clay Thompson, *Rolling Thunder: Understanding Policy and Program Failure* (Chapel Hill: University of North Carolina Press, 1980), pp. 36, 38, 43, 47–48, 55–64.

88. Ansel, *Hitler Confronts England*, pp. 11–12; F. H. Hinsley, *Hitler's Strategy* (Cambridge: Cambridge University Press, 1951), pp. 6–7; Barry Leach, *German Strategy against Russia, 1939–1941* (Oxford: Clarendon Press, 1973), p. 9; Rich, *Hitler's War Aims*, p. 146.

89. Hinsley, *Hitler's Strategy*, pp. 6–7.

90. Milward, *War, Economy, and Society*, p. 29.

91. *DGFP*, ser. D, vol. 1, no. 19, p. 34.

92. Ibid., p. 36. My emphasis.

93. Ibid., no. 93, p. 164. My emphasis.

94. Ibid., no. 146, p. 263.

95. Shirer, *Rise and Fall*, p. 362.

96. Taylor, *Munich*, p. 700.

97. *DGFP*, ser. D, vol. 1, no. 19, pp. 35–36.

98. Ibid., p. 38.

99. Rich, *Hitler's War Aims*, pp. 86–87.

100. For examples of Hitler's preemptive and preventive thinking, see Rich, *Hitler's War Aims*, pp. 117, 128–129, 134–136, 147–148, 204–211.

101. The best short descriptions of the workings of Blitzkrieg are Cooper, *German Army*, 139–159; Deighton, *Blitzkrieg*, pp. 179–185; Edward N. Luttwak, "The Operational Level of War," *International Security* 5:3 (Winter 1980/1981): 67–73; and Mearsheimer, *Conventional Deterrence*. For descriptions of Blitzkrieg, Israeli-style, see Handel, *Israel's Political-Military Doctrine*; Yoav Ben-Horin and Barry Posen, *Israel's Strategic Doctrine*, R-2845-NA (Santa Monica: RAND Corp., 1981).

102. Cooper, *German Army*, pp. 141–142.

103. Ibid., p. 143.

104. Liddell-Hart, *Other Side*, p. 63.

105. Cooper, *German Army*, pp. 144–145.

106. Heinz Guderian, *Panzer Leader* (New York: Ballantine, 1957), p. 24.

107. Goerlitz, *History*, p. 252.

108. Goerlitz, *History*, p. 233.

109. Addington, *Blitzkrieg Era*, p. 34; Cooper, *German Army*, p. 145.

110. Guderian, *Panzer Leader*, p. 24.

111. Ibid., p. 26.

112. Ibid.

113. Liddell-Hart, *Other Side*, p. 122.

114. Cited in Cooper, *German Army*, p. 150, from Erwin Rommel, *Papers*, ed. B. H. Liddell-Hart (New York: Harcourt, Brace, Jovanovich, 1953), p. 517.

115. Cooper, *German Army*, p. 143; Liddell-Hart, *Other Side*, pp. 61–75.

116. Cooper, *German Army*, pp. 149–158.

117. Ibid., p. 153.

118. Ibid., pp. 115–116.

119. Deighton, *Blitzkrieg*, p. 144.

120. Guderian, *Panzer Leader*, pp. 29–30.

121. Alan Bullock, "Hitler and the Origins of the Second World War," in *European*

Diplomacy between Two Wars, 1919–1939, ed. Hanz Gatzke (Chicago: Quadrangle, 1972), pp. 228–230; Field Marshall Lord Carver, *The Apostles of Mobility: The Theory and Practice of Armoured Warfare* (New York: Holmes & Meir, 1979), p. 56; Goerlitz, *History*, p. 301. See also Leach, *German Strategy*, pp. 13, 31.

122. Craig, *Politics*, p. 485.

123. Cooper, *German Army*, p. 151.

124. Ibid., pp. 156–157.

125. Leach, *German Strategy*, p. 35; Kenneth Macksey, *Guderian, Panzer General* (London: MacDonald & Jane's, 1975), p. 74.

126. Deighton, *Blitzkrieg*, p. 147; Macksey, *Guderian*, p. 74.

127. Shirer, *Rise and Fall*, pp. 645–647.

128. See also Jacobsen, "Dunkirk 1940," pp. 33–38. This article is taken from a longer study by Jacobsen that has not been translated from German. Entitled *Fall Gelb*, it is considered by many military historians to be the definitive account of the German role in the battle for the Low Countries and France.

129. Murray, "British and German Air Doctrine," p. 55.

130. Homze, *Arming*, pp. 131–132; Murray, "British and German Air Doctrine," p. 56, and "The Luftwaffe before the Second World War: A Mission, A Strategy?" *Journal of Strategic Studies* (Winter 1981), pp. 266–267; Suchenwirth, *Development*, pp. 167–168.

131. Hanfried Schliephake, *The Birth of the Luftwaffe* (London: Ian Allen, 1971), pp. 11–30.

132. Ibid., p. 34.

133. Murray, "British and German Air Doctrine," p. 49.

134. Homze, *Arming*, p. 62; Suchenwirth, *Development*, pp. 90–91.

135. Homze, *Arming*, p. 59.

136. Macksey, *Kesselring*, pp. 50, 63. Pure security considerations also played a role. Former army officers had little difficulty understanding that Germany *had* to win the land battle. Murray, "The Luftwaffe," p. 268.

137. Murray, "British and German Air Doctrine," pp. 49–50.

138. Ibid., p. 50.

139. Schliephake, *Birth of the Luftwaffe*, p. 44.

140. Homze, *Arming*, pp. 124–125, 264.

141. Murray, "British and German Air Doctrine," p. 51.

7. Conclusions

1. Robert J. Art, "Bureaucratic Politics and American Foreign Policy: A Critique," *Policy Analysis* 4 (1973): Stephen K. Krasner, "Are Bureaucracies Important? (or Allison Wonderland)," *Foreign Policy* 7 (Summer 1972).

2. Hillman, "Comparative Strength," p. 446.

Selected Bibliography

Addington, Larry H. *The Blitzkrieg Era and the German General Staff.* New Brunswick, N.J.: Rutgers University Press, 1971.

Allison, Graham. *Essence of Decision.* Boston: Little, Brown, 1971.

Ansel, Walter. *Hitler Confronts England.* Durham, N.C.: Duke University Press, 1960.

Art, Robert J. "Bureaucratic Politics and American Foreign Policy: A Critique." *Policy Analysis* 4 (1973):467–490.

Bankwitz, Philip C. F. *Maxime Weygand and Civil-Military Relations in Modern France.* Cambridge, Mass.: Harvard University Press, 1967.

Barnard, Chester I. *The Functions of the Executive.* Cambridge, Mass.: Harvard University Press, 1968.

Betts, Richard K. *Soldiers, Statesmen, and Cold War Crises.* Cambridge, Mass.: Harvard University Press, 1977.

Blainey, Geoffrey. *The Causes of War.* New York: Free Press, 1973.

Blechman, Barry M., and Stephen S. Kaplan. *Force without War.* Washington, D.C.: Brookings Institution, 1978.

Bond, Brian. *British Military Policy between the Two World Wars.* Oxford: Clarendon Press, 1980.

——. *France and Belgium, 1939–1940.* London: Davis Poynter, 1975.

Bracken, Paul. "Unintended Consequences of Strategic Gaming." *Simulation and Games* 8:3 (September 1977): 283–318.

Brodie, Bernard. *The Absolute Weapon.* New York: Harcourt, Brace, 1946.

——. "The Development of Nuclear Strategy." *International Security* 2 (Spring 1978):65–83.

——. *Strategy in the Missile Age.* Princeton: Princeton University Press, 1959.

——. "Technological Change, Strategic Doctrine, and Political Outcomes." In *Historical Dimensions of National Security Problems*, edited by Klaus Knorr. Lawrence: University Press of Kansas, 1976. Pp. 263–306.

Brodie, Bernard, and Fawn Brodie. *From Crossbow to H-Bomb.* Bloomington: Indiana University Press, 1973.

Brown, Harold. *Department of Defense Annual Report, Fiscal Year 1981.* Washington, D.C.: GPO, January 29, 1980.

Bullock, Alan. "Hitler and the Origins of the Second World War." In *European Diplomacy between Two Wars, 1919–1939*, edited and with an Introduction by Hans Gatzke. Chicago: Quadrangle, 1972. Pp. 221–246.

[269]

Calvocoressi, Peter, and Guy Wint. *Total War: The Story of World War II.* New York: Pantheon, 1972.

Carr, E. H. *International Relations between the Two World Wars, 1919–1939.* London: Macmillan, 1947.

Carroll, Berenice A. *Design for Total War: Arms and Economics in the Third Reich.* Hague and Paris: Mouton, 1968.

Carsten, F. L. *The Reichswehr and Politics, 1918–1933.* Oxford: Clarendon, 1966.

Carver, Field Marshall Lord. *The Apostles of Mobility: The Theory and Practice of Armoured Warfare.* New York: Holmes & Meier, 1979.

Challener, Richard. *The French Theory of the Nation in Arms, 1866–1939.* New York: Russell & Russell, 1965.

Churchill, Winston. *The Gathering Storm.* Vol. 1 of *The Second World War.* New York: Bantam, 1977.

Clausewitz, Carl Von. *On War.* Translated and edited by Michael Howard and Peter Paret. Princeton: Princeton University Press, 1976.

Collier, Basil. *The Defense of the United Kingdom.* History of the Second World War. United Kingdom Military Series. London: HMSO, 1957.

Cooper, Matthew. *The German Army, 1933–1945: Its Political and Military Failure.* New York: Stein & Day, 1978.

Craig, Gordon. *Germany, 1866–1945.* New York: Oxford University Press, 1978.

————. *The Politics of the Prussian Army, 1640–1945.* London: Oxford University Press, 1964.

Crozier, Michel. *The Bureaucratic Phenomenon.* Chicago: University of Chicago Press, 1964.

Cyert, Richard, and James March. *A Behavioral Theory of the Firm.* Englewood Cliffs, N.J.: Prentice Hall, 1963.

Deighton, Len. *Blitzkrieg: From the Rise of Hitler to the Fall of Dunkirk.* London: Jonathan Cape, 1979.

————. *Fighter: The True Story of the Battle of Britain.* London: Jonathan Cape, 1977.

Deutsch, Karl W., and J. David Singer. "Multipolar Systems and International Stability." In *International Politics and Foreign Policy,* edited by James N. Rosenau. New York: Free Press, 1969. Pp. 315–324.

Dilks, David. "'The Unnecessary War?' Military Advice and Foreign Policy in Great Britain, 1931–1939." In *General Staffs and Diplomacy before the Second World War,* edited by Adrian Preston. London: Croom Helm, 1978. Pp. 98–132.

Dingman, Roger. *Power in the Pacific.* Chicago: University of Chicago Press, 1976.

Documents on German Foreign Policy. Ser. D, vols. 1–2. Washington, D.C.: GPO, 1949.

Downs, Anthony. *Inside Bureaucracy.* Boston: Little, Brown, 1967.

Dupuy, R. Ernest, and Trevor N. Dupuy. *The Encyclopedia of Military History.* New York: Harper & Row, 1977.

Earle, Edward M., ed. *Makers of Modern Strategy: Military Thought from Machiavelli to Hitler.* Princeton: Princeton University Press, 1943.

Ellis, Major L. F. *The War in France and Flanders, 1939–1940.* London: HMSO, 1953.

Ermarth, Fritz W. "Contrast in American and Soviet Strategic Thought." *International Security* 3 (Fall 1978): 138–155.

Finer, Samuel. *The Man on Horseback: The Role of the Military in Politics.* 2nd ed. London: Penguin, 1975.

Fuller, Major-General J. F. C. *The Conduct of War, 1789–1961.* London: Methuen, 1961.

————. *The Decisive Battles of the Western World, 1792–1944.* Edited by John Terraine. St. Albans, England: Granada, 1970.

_____. *A Military History of the Western World*. 3 vols. N.p.: Minerva Press, 1967.

Gatzke, Hans W. *Stresemann and the Rearmament of Germany*. Baltimore: Johns Hopkins University Press, 1954.

George, Alexander. "Case Studies and Theory Development: The Method of Structured, Focused Comparison." In *Diplomacy: New Approaches in History, Theory, and Policy*, edited by Paul Gordon Lauren. New York: Free Press, 1979. Pp. 43–68.

Gibbs, N. H. *Grand Strategy*. Vol. 1, *Rearmament Policy*. History of the Second World War. United Kingdom Military Series. London: HMSO, 1976.

Gibson, Irving (pseud.). "Maginot and Liddell Hart: The Doctrine of Defense." In *Makers of Modern Strategy*, edited by Edward M. Earle. Princeton: Princeton University Press, 1971. Pp. 365–387.

Gilbert, Felix, ed. *The Historical Essays of Otto Hintze*. New York: Oxford University Press, 1975.

Gilpin, Robert. *War and Change in World Politics*. Cambridge: Cambridge University Press, 1981.

Goerlitz, Walter. *History of the German General Staff, 1657–1945*. New York: Praeger, 1953.

Gordon, Harold J., Jr. *The Reichswehr and the German Republic, 1919–1926*. Princeton: Princeton University Press, 1957.

Goutard, Colonel A. *The Battle of France, 1940*. Translated by Captain A. R. P. Burgess. New York: Ives Washburn, 1959.

Gray, Colin. "Victory is Possible." *Foreign Policy* 39 (Summer 1980):14–27.

Great Britain. Admiralty. Naval Intelligence Division. *Economic Geography*. Vol. 3 of *France*. Cambridge: Cambridge University Press, 1942.

Great Britain. Foreign Office. *Documents on British Foreign Policy, 1919–1939*. 2nd ser., vol. 13. London: HMSO, 1973.

_____. *Documents on British Foreign Policy, 1919–1939*. 3rd ser., vol. 2. London: HMSO, 1951.

Greene, Fred. "French Military Leadership and Security against Germany, 1919–1940." Ph.D. diss., Yale University, 1950.

Guderian, Heinz. *Panzer Leader*. New York: Ballantine, 1957.

Gunsburg, Jeffrey A. *Divided and Conquered: The French High Command and the Defeat of the West, 1940*. Westport, Conn.: Greenwood Press, 1979.

Hancock, W. K., and M. M. Gowing. *British War Economy*. History of the Second World War. United Kingdom Civil Series. London and Nendeln: HMSO, 1949. Rev. ed. with amendments and confidential sources, 1975.

Handel, Michael. *Israel's Political-Military Doctrine*. Occasional Papers in International Affairs, No. 30. Cambridge, Mass.: Center for International Affairs, Harvard University, July 1973.

Harvey, Donald J. "French Concepts of Military Strategy." Ph.D. diss., Columbia University, 1953.

Hauner, Milan. "Czechoslovakia as a Military Factor in British Considerations of 1938." *Journal of Strategic Studies* 2 (September 1978):194–223.

Herz, John. *Political Realism and Political Idealism*. Chicago: University of Chicago Press, 1951.

Herzog, Chaim. *The War of Atonement*. Boston: Little, Brown, 1975.

Hillmann, H. C. "Comparative Strength of the Great Powers." in *The World in March 1939*. Vol. 1 of *Survey of International Affairs, 1939–1946*, edited by Arnold Toynbee and Frank T. Ashton-Gwatkin. London: Royal Institute of International Affairs and Oxford University Press, 1952.

Hinsley, F. H. *Hitler's Strategy*. Cambridge: Cambridge University Press, 1951.
————. *Power and the Pursuit of Peace*. Cambridge: Cambridge University Press, 1963.
Hintze, Otto. *See* Gilbert, Felix.
Hirschman, Albert O. *Exit, Voice and Loyalty*. Cambridge, Mass.: Harvard University Press, 1970.
Hoag, Malcolm W. "On Stability in Deterrent Races." In *The Use of Force*, edited by Robert J. Art and Kenneth N. Waltz. Boston: Little, Brown, 1971. Pp. 402–428.
Homze, Edward. *Arming the Luftwaffe: The Reich Air Ministry and the German Aircraft Industry, 1919–1939*. Lincoln: University of Nebraska Press, 1976.
Horelick, Arnold. "Perspectives on the Study of Comparative Military Doctrines." In *Comparative Defense Policy*, edited by Frank B. Horton. Baltimore: Johns Hopkins University Press, 1974. Pp. 192–200.
Howard, Michael. "The Armed Forces." In *Material Progress and World-Wide Problems, 1870–1898*. Vol. 11 of the *New Cambridge Modern History*, edited by F. H. Hinsley. Cambridge: Cambridge University Press, 1962. Pp. 204–242.
————. *The Continental Commitment*. London: Temple Smith, 1972.
————. *The Franco-Prussian War*. London: Granada, 1961.
————. *War in European History*. London: Oxford University Press, 1976.
Hughes, Judith. *To the Maginot Line: The Politics of French Military Preparation in the 1920's*. Cambridge, Mass.: Harvard University Press, 1971.
Huntington, Samuel. *The Soldier and the State*. Cambridge, Mass.: Belknap, 1957.
International Institute for Strategic Studies. *The Military Balance 1983–1984*. London, England: International Institute for Strategic Studies, 1983.
Irving, David. *The Rise and Fall of the Luftwaffe: The Life of Erhard Milch*. London: Weidenfeld and Nicolson, 1973.
Jacobsen, Hans Adolf. "Dunkirk 1940." In *Decisive Battles of World War II: The German View*, edited by Hans Adolf Jacobsen and Jurgen Rohwer and translated by Edward Fitzgerald. London: Andre Deutsch, 1965. Pp. 29–69.
Jervis, Robert. "Cooperation under the Security Dilemma." *World Politics* 30 (January 1978):67–214.
————. *Perception and Misperception in International Politics*. Princeton, Princeton University Press, 1976.
Kahan, Jerome. *Security in the Nuclear Age*. Washington, D.C.: Brookings Institution, 1975.
Kahn, Herman. *On Thermonuclear War*. New York: Free Press, 1960.
Keegan, John. *The Face of Battle*. New York: Viking Press, 1976.
Kennedy, Paul M. *The Rise and Fall of British Naval Mastery*. London: Allen Lane, 1976.
Kieft, David Owen. *Belgium's Return to Neutrality*. Oxford: Clarendon Press, 1972.
Kindleberger, Charles. *The World in Depression, 1929–1939*. Berkeley: University of California Press, 1973.
Kissinger, Henry. *Problems of National Strategy*. New York: Praeger, 1965.
Kitchen, Martin. *A Military History of Germany—From the Eighteenth Century to the Present Day*. Secaucus, N.J.: Citadel Press, 1976.
Klein, Burton H. *Germany's Economic Preparations for War*. Cambridge, Mass.: Harvard University Press, 1959.
Knightly, Phillip. *The First Casualty*. London: Quartet, 1978.
Krasner, Stephen K. "Are Bureaucracies Important? (or Allison Wonderland)." *Foreign Policy* 7 (Summer 1972):159–171.
Lambeth, Benjamin. "The Political Potential of Soviet Equivalence." *International Security* 4 (Fall 1979):22–39.

Landau, Martin. "On the Concept of a Self-Correcting Organization." *Public Administration Review* 33 (November/December 1973):533–542.

Leach, Barry. *German Strategy against Russia, 1939–1941.* Oxford: Clarendon Press, 1973.

Liddell-Hart, B. H. *History of the First World War.* London: Pan, 1972.

_____. *The Other Side of the Hill: Germany's Generals, Their Rise and Fall, with Their Own Account of Military Events, 1939–1945.* Enlarged and rev. ed. London: Cassell, 1951.

Lindblom, Charles, and David Braybrooke. *A Strategy of Decision.* New York: Free Press of Glencoe, 1963.

London Sunday Times Insight Team. *The Yom Kippur War.* Garden City, N.Y.: Doubleday, 1974.

Luttwak, Edward N. "The Operational Level of War." *International Security* 5 (Winter 1980/1981):61–79.

Macksey, Kenneth. *Guderian, Panzer General.* London: MacDonald & Jane's, 1975.

_____. *Kesselring: The Making of the Luftwaffe.* London: B. T. Batsford, 1978.

Mandelbaum, Michael. *The Nuclear Question: The United States and Nuclear Weapons, 1946–1976.* Cambridge: Cambridge University Press, 1979.

March, James, and Herbert Simon. *Organizations.* New York: John Wiley & Sons, 1958.

Mason, Herbert M. Jr. *The Rise of the Luftwaffe: Forging the Secret German Air Weapon, 1918–1940.* New York: Dial, 1973.

Mason, T. W. "Some Origins of the Second World War." *Past and Present* 29 (December 1964):67–87.

McDougall, Walter. *France's Rhineland Diplomacy, 1914–1924.* Princeton: Princeton University Press, 1978.

McElwee, William. *The Art of War: Waterloo to Mons.* Bloomington: Indiana University Press, 1974.

Michel, Henri. *The Second World War.* Vol. 1. Translated by Douglas Parmee. New York: Praeger, 1975.

Middlemas, Keith. *Diplomacy of Illusion.* London: Weidenfeld and Nicolson, 1972.

Middlemas, Keith, and John Barnes. *Baldwin: A Biography.* London: Weidenfeld and Nicolson, 1972.

Milward, Alan S. *The German Economy at War.* London: Athlone Press, University of London, 1965.

_____. *War, Economy, and Society, 1939–1945.* Berkeley: University of California Press, 1977.

Montross, Lynn. *War through the Ages.* New York: Harper & Brothers, 1960.

Morgenthau, Hans. *Politics among Nations: The Struggle for Power and Peace.* New York: Alfred Knopf, 1978.

Murray, Williamson. "British and German Air Doctrine between the Wars." *Air University Review* 31 (March/April 1980):39–58.

Nazi Conspiracy and Aggression. Vol. 4. "Excerpt from General Jodl's Diary." Washington, D.C.: GPO, 1946–1948.

Oman, C. W. C. *The Art of War in the Middle Ages.* Ithaca, N.Y.: Cornell University Press, 1953.

O'Neill, Robert J. *The German Army and the Nazi Party, 1933–39.* New York: James Heineman, 1966.

Osgood, Robert E., and Robert W. Tucker. *Force, Order and Justice.* Baltimore: Johns Hopkins University Press, 1967.

Park, Robert E. "The Social Function of War." In *War,* edited by Leon Bramson and George Goethals. New York: Basic Books, 1964. Pp. 229–244.

Parkinson, Roger. *Dawn on Our Darkness: The Summer of 1940.* London: Granada, 1977.

Pelz, Stephen. *Race to Pearl Harbor.* Cambridge, Mass.: Harvard University Press, 1974.

Post, Gaines, Jr. *The Civil-Military Fabric of Weimar Foreign Policy.* Princeton: Princeton University Press, 1973.

Postan, M., D. Hay, and J. D. Scott. *Design and Development of Weapons: Studies in Government and Industrial Organization.* London: HMSO and Longman's, Green, 1964.

Powers, Barry D. *Strategy without Slide Rule: British Air Strategy, 1914–1939.* London: Croom Helm, 1976.

Pratt, Lawrence R. *East of Malta, West of Suez: Britain's Mediterranean Crisis, 1936–1939.* Cambridge: Cambridge University Press, 1975.

Quester, George. *Offense and Defense in the International System.* New York: John Wiley, 1977.

Reiners, Ludwig. *The Lamps Went Out in Europe.* Translated by Richard and Clara Winston. New York: Pantheon, 1955.

Rich, Norman. *Hitler's War Aims: Ideology, the Nazi State, and the Course of Expansion.* New York: W. W. Norton, 1973.

Ritter, Gerhard. *The Schlieffen Plan: Critique of a Myth.* With a foreword by B. H. Liddell-Hart. Translated by Andrew Wilson and Eva Wilson. Westport, Conn.: Greenwood, 1979.

———. *The Prussian Tradition, 1740–1890.* Vol. 1 of *The Sword and the Scepter.* Translated by Heinz Norden. Coral Gables, Fla.: University of Miami Press, 1969.

Rommel, Erwin. *Papers.* Edited by B. H. Liddell-Hart. New York: Harcourt, Brace, Jovanovich, 1953.

Rosecrance, Richard N. "Biopolarity, Multipolarity, and the Future." In *International Politics and Foreign Policy,* edited by James N. Rosenau. New York: Free Press, 1969. Pp. 325–335.

Rowe, A. P. *One Story of Radar.* Cambridge: Cambridge University Press, 1948.

Safran, Nadav. *Israel: The Embattled Ally.* Cambridge, Mass.: Belknap Press, 1978.

Schelling, Thomas. *Arms and Influence.* New Haven: Yale University Press, 1966.

———. *The Strategy of Conflict.* New York: Oxford University Press. 1963.

Schramm, Percy Ernst. *Hitler: The Man and the Military Leader.* Translated and edited by Donald Detwiler. Chicago: Quadrangle, 1971.

Selznick, Philip. *Leadership in Administration.* Evanston, Ill.: Row, Peterson, 1957.

Shanahan, William O. *Prussia's Military Reforms, 1786–1813.* New York: Columbia University Press, 1945.

Sherwig, John M. *Guineas and Gunpowder.* Cambridge, Mass.: Harvard University Press, 1969.

Shirer, William L. *The Rise and Fall of the Third Reich: A History of Nazi Germany.* New York: Simon & Schuster, 1960.

Shlaim, Avi. "Failure in National Intelligence Estimates: The Case of the Yom Kippur War." *World Politics* 28:3 (April 1976):348–380.

Sienkiewicz, Stanley. "SALT and Soviet Nuclear Doctrine." *International Security* 2 (Spring 1978): 84–100.

Simon, Herbert. *Administrative Behavior.* New York: Free Press, 1957.

———. "Rationality and Administrative Decision Making." In *Models of Man, Social and Rational,* by Herbert Simon. New York: John Wiley, 1957. Pp. 196–206.

Smoke, Richard. "National Security Affairs." In *Handbook of Political Science,* vol. 8, edited by Fred Greenstein and Nelson Polsby. Reading, Mass.: Addison-Wesley, 1975. Pp. 247–362.

Snyder, Glenn. *Deterrence and Defense: Toward a Theory of National Security.* Princeton: Princeton University Press, 1961.

Sokolovsky, Marshall, V. D. *Military Strategy: Soviet Doctrine and Concepts*. London: Pall Mall Press, 1963.

Spykman, Nicholas. *America's Strategy in World Politics: The United States and the Balance of Power*. New York: Harcourt, Brace, & World, 1942.

Steinbruner, John. *The Cybernetic Theory of Decision*. Princeton: Princeton University Press, 1974.

Stinchcombe, Arthur L. *Constructing Social Theories*. New York: Harcourt, Brace, & World, 1968.

Stolfi, R. H. S. "Equipment for Victory in France." *History* 52 (February 1970):1–20.

Suchenwirth, Richard. *The Development of the German Air Force, 1919–1939*. Edited by Harry R. Fletcher. USAF Historical Studies, No. 160. Maxwell A.F.B.: Air University, USAF Historical Division, Aerospace Studies Institute, June 1968.

Sumner, William Graham. "War." In *War*, edited by Leon Bramson and George W. Goethals. New York: Basic Books, 1964. Pp. 205–228.

Taylor, A. J. P. *The Struggle for Mastery in Europe, 1848–1918*. Oxford: Oxford University Press, 1971.

Taylor, Telford. *The March of Conquest: The German Victories in Western Europe, 1940*. New York: Simon & Schuster, 1958.

———. *Munich: The Price of Peace*. Garden City, N.Y.: Doubleday, 1979.

———. *Sword and Swastika*. New York: Simon & Schuster, 1952.

"The Colloquium: Exploring Ideas." *Tech Talk* (News Office, Massachusetts Institute of Technology) 24:37 (May 1980):6–7.

Thompson, James Clay. *Rolling Thunder: Understanding Policy and Program Failure*. Chapel Hill: University of North Carolina Press, 1980.

Thompson, James D. *Organizations in Action*. New York: McGraw-Hill, 1967.

Thompson, V. A. "Bureaucracy and Innovative Action." In *Bureaucracy and the Modern World*, by V. A. Thompson. Morristown, N.J.: General Learning Press, 1976.

Thucydides. *History of the Peloponnesian War*. Translated with an Introduction by Rex Warner. 1954; Harmondsworth, England: Penguin, 1972.

Tilly, Charles, ed. *The Formation of National States in Western Europe*. Princeton: Princeton University Press, 1975.

Turner, L. C. F. *Origins of the First World War*. London: Edward Arnold, 1970.

United States. Congress. Senate. Committee on Foreign Relations. *Military Implications of the Treaty on the Limitation of Strategic Offensive Arms and Protocol Thereto (SALT II Treaty)*. 96th Cong., 1st Sess., pt. 1, 1979.

Vagts, Alfred. *Defense and Diplomacy: The Soldier and the Conduct of Foreign Relations*. New York: King's Crown Press, 1950.

———. *A History of Militarism, Civilian and Military*. New York: Free Press, 1959.

Waltz, Kenneth. *Man, the State and War*. New York: Columbia University Press, 1959.

———. *Theory of International Politics*. Reading, Mass.: Addison-Wesley, 1979.

Warlimont, Walter. *Inside Hitler's Headquarters, 1939–1945*. London: Weidenfeld and Nicolson, 1964.

Watt, D. C. *Too Serious a Business: European Armed Forces and the Approach to the Second World War*. Berkeley: University of California Press, 1975.

Weber, Max. *From Max Weber: Essays in Sociology*. Translated, edited, and introduced by H. H. Gerth and C. Wright Mills. New York: Oxford University Press, 1946.

Webster, Sir Charles, and Noble Frankland. *The Strategic Air Offensive against Germany, 1939–1945*. Vol. 1, *Preparation*, pts. 1, 2, and 3. *History of the Second World War*. United Kingdom Military Series. London: HMSO, 1961.

Weigley, Russell F. "Military Strategy and Civilian Leadership." In *Historical Dimen-*

sions of National Security Problems, edited by Klaus Knorr. Lawrence: University Press of Kansas, 1976. Pp. 38–77.

Wheeler-Bennett, J. W. *Munich: Prologue to Tragedy.* London: MacMillan, 1948.

White, Lynn. *Medieval Technology and Social Change.* London: Oxford University Press, 1962.

Wight, Martin. "Germany." In *The World in March 1939.* Vol. 1 of Survey of International Affairs, 1939–1946. London: Royal Institute of International Affairs and Oxford University Press, 1952. Pp. 293–365.

Wildavsky, Aaron. "The Self-Evaluating Organization." *Public Administration Review* 32 (September/October 1972):509–520.

Wilson, James Q. "Innovation in Organization: Notes toward a Theory." In *Approaches to Organization Design,* edited by James D. Thompson. Pittsburgh: University of Pittsburgh Press, 1966. Pp. 193–218.

Winterbotham, F. W. *The Ultra Secret.* New York: Dell, 1974.

Wolfers, Arnold. *Britain and France between Two Wars: Conflicting Strategies of Peace since Versailles.* New York: Harcourt, Brace, 1940.

Wood, Derek, and Derek Dempster. *The Narrow Margin: The Battle of Britain and the Rise of Air Power, 1930–1940.* London: Hutchinson, 1961.

Wright, Robert. *Dowding and the Battle of Britain.* London: MacDonald, 1969.

Young, Robert J. *In Command of France: French Foreign Policy and Military Planning, 1933–1940.* Cambridge, Mass.: Harvard University Press, 1978.

———. "The Strategic Dream: French Air Doctrine in the Interwar Period." *Journal of Contemporary History* 9 (October 1974):57–76.

Index

Weygand, General Maxime, 128, 132, 257n48
Wolfers, Arnold, 150
World War I:
Britain in, 144, 145
France in, 21–24, 107, 116
Germany in, 21–24
military doctrines in, 22, 32–33
World War II:
Britain in, 23–24, 95, 97–99. *See also*

Britain, Battle of; Britain, in Battle of France
defensive doctrines in, 23–24
France in, 23–24, 81–94, 161, 181, 252n7, 252–253n8
Germany in, 23–24, 81–102, 95, 97, 181

Yom Kippur War, 25, 28–29, 31–32, 48
Young, Robert, 134
Y-service, 98

Library of Congress Cataloging in Publication Data

Posen, Barry.
    The sources of military doctrine.

    (Cornell studies in security affairs)
    Bibliography: p.
    Includes index.
    1. Strategy—History—20th century.   2. Military art and science—France—
History—20th century.   3. Military art and science—Germany—History—20th
century.   4. Military art and science—Great Britain—History—20th century.
I. Title.   II. Series.
U162.P66   1984   355'.02   84-7610
ISBN 0-8014-1633-7 (alk. paper) (cloth)
ISBN 0-8014-9427-3 (pbk.)